W9-BKO-217

NEXT STOP,
RELOVILLE

NEXT STOP,
RELOVILLE

LIFE INSIDE AMERICA'S NEW
ROOTLESS PROFESSIONAL CLASS

PETER T. KILBORN

DISCARDED

Times Books · Henry Holt and Company · New York

Times Books
Henry Holt and Company, LLC
Publishers since 1866
175 Fifth Avenue
New York, New York 10010
Henry Holt® is a registered trademark of Henry Holt and Company, LLC.

Library of Congress Cataloging-in-Publication Data

Kilborn, Peter T.
    Next stop, Reloville : life inside America's new rootless professional class / Peter T. Kilborn.—1st ed.
        p. cm.
    Includes bibliographical references and index.
    ISBN-13: 978-0-8050-8308-8 (alk. paper)
    ISBN-10: 0-8050-8308-1 (alk. paper)
    1. Professional employees—Relocation.   2. Professional employees—Relocation—United States.   3. Moving, Household—United States.   4. Relocation (Housing)—United States.   5. Home—United States.   I. Title.
    HD8038.A1K55 2009
    305.5′530973—dc22   2008055350

Henry Holt books are available for special promotions and premiums.
For details contact: Director, Special Markets.

First Edition 2009

Designed by Meryl Sussman Levavi
Chapter opening and title page illustration by Alex Eben Meyer

Printed in the United States of America

10   9   8   7   6   5   4   3   2   1

To Susan, my favorite American

Contents

NEXT STOP,
RELOVILLE

America's Top Twenty-five Relovilles

Alpharetta, Georgia

Huntersville, North Carolina

Apex, North Carolina

Parker, Colorado

Castle Rock, Colorado

Flower Mound, Texas

Frisco, Texas

Cary, North Carolina

McKinney, Texas

Roswell, Georgia

Fishers, Indiana

Carrollton, Texas

Franconia, Virginia

The Woodlands, Texas

Sandy Springs, Georgia

Leesburg, Virginia

Centreville, Virginia

Dublin, Ohio

Allen, Texas

Highlands Ranch, Colorado

Woodbury, Minnesota

Overland Park, Kansas

Gaithersburg, Maryland

Round Rock, Texas

Plano, Texas

Introduction

In the United States a man builds a house to spend his latter years in it, and he sells it before the roof is on; he builds a garden, and lets it, just as the trees are coming into bearing; he brings a field into tillage and leaves other men to gather the crops; he embraces a profession and gives it up; he settles in a place, which he soon afterwards leaves, to carry his changeable longings elsewhere. . . . The recollection of the shortness of life is a constant spur to him. Besides the good things that he possesses, he every instant fancies a thousand others that death will prevent him from trying if he does not try them soon. This thought fills him with anxiety, fear, and regret and keeps his mind in ceaseless trepidation, which leads him perpetually to change his plans and his abode.

—Alexis de Tocqueville, *Democracy in America*

Katharine Link (née Kessler) grew up in Highland Park, a self-governing, old-money oasis inside the city limits of Dallas, Texas, four miles north of downtown. The daughter of a homemaker mother who worked off and on as an accountant and an airline pilot father, Kathy ran track and played basketball, softball, and volleyball. She played the violin, too, but dropped it. "It wasn't cool," she said. She dreamed of driving a sleek Mercedes coupe and of seeing the world. "I wanted to be a flight attendant, in the old days when they would get on a plane and go somewhere far. I interviewed, but I didn't get it. I wanted to be a writer, a famous fiction writer. And I wanted to be a mommy."

Valentine James Link Jr.—Jim—grew up in the Houston subdivision of Bellaire, in a three-bedroom ranch house that his parents bought in 1972. His mother retired from Rice University, where she was a librarian. His father is a jewelry maker, sculptor, and art professor at the University of Houston. Jim played basketball but felt he was too short, at five foot eleven, to excel. He played Little League baseball and had the second-highest batting average on his high school varsity team. He took up golf and worked his handicap down to a respectable thirteen. He wanted to be a coach, or run upscale restaurants.

On his twenty-first birthday, Jim was a passenger in a car that was hit broadside. He was thrown through a closed window, severed an artery, and the nerves in his left shoulder were permanently damaged. His face was still mending when Kathy, lightly freckled and finely hewn, composed but unsure of herself, ventured alone into a student pub in College Station, Texas, site of Texas A&M University, where both were students.

Jim was paying his way through A&M tending bar. Darker than Kathy and two inches taller, he was serving drinks on the patio. She was struck by his self-assurance and how unselfconsciously he wore his wounds. He made her laugh. She thought him a goofball, as she put it, and younger than she was, though he was seven months older. He thought her distant, and dazzling. "She had nice legs," he said. "She was particular. She ordered a White Russian. That's made from cream, but we made it from powder. She was aggravated about that. We had a long conversation."

They married three years later, in 1988. Kathy became a technical editor for a company that made aircraft and aerospace flight simulators. Jim went to work as a headwaiter for Pappas Restaurants, an upscale chain, and applied to become a manager. But Kathy objected to the late hours and talked him out of it. He went to the Prudential Insurance Company to sell insurance, annuities, and mutual funds.

The Links bought their first home in the master-planned community of Clear Lake City, now a part of Houston. Kathy juggled career and family after their daughters Kelsey and Kristina were born. But in 1994, when T. Rowe Price, the mutual fund company, hired Jim and sent him to its headquarters in Baltimore to manage sales of 401(k) retirement plans to businesses, she was expecting their third child, and she stopped working. It made sense, with Jim's transfer.

The Links had become Relos.

I had never heard the word *Relo* (pronounced REE-low) until a visit to Alpharetta, Georgia, in early 2004, a decade after Jim and Kathy Link left Houston, to do research for the *New York Times*. Then I heard it on every lawn. I came upon a Memorial Day fair in Medlock Bridge, a subdivision of 636 homes with an Alpharetta mailing address in an unincorporated northeastern corner of Atlanta's Fulton County. I met Jim, still the affable bartender, manning the beer cooler. In the past ten years the Links had already moved from Houston to Baltimore to Rochester, New York, and, in 2000, to Alpharetta. In twenty-five years, Alpharetta had grown from three thousand people dispersed over pastures and cotton fields to a checkerboard of fresh asphalt and tidy subdivisions with forty thousand people.

Young and middle-aged families at the fair, all with kids, all into sports, all with spacious late-model houses and late-model vans and SUVs, were calling themselves Relos. "Relo" was a noun, a verb, an adjective. Relos were Relo-ed by a Relo company, which employers would hire to help Relos pack up, line up a van, and find suitable neighborhoods and schools in the next Reloville. Relos found homes through the "Relo Man" or "Relo Woman," a special breed of real estate agent who catered to them. Relos got Relo mortgages, geared to buyers who expected to sell in just a few years. Strictly speaking, some real estate firms and moving companies called anyone whose company covered the cost of moving a Relo, but no Relo would call herself one until she has been moved two or three times.

This book is about Relos, a disproportionately influential strain of the vast middle class. With its mix of family traditions, education, incomes, and attitudes, the middle class eludes crisp definition. But at its core is a faith in open horizons and a willingness to risk losing ground to gain ground, the trait most characteristic of Relos. They are an affluent, hard-striving class. They inflate the American Dream and put it on wheels. Following the money as they migrate through the suburbs of Atlanta, Denver, and Dallas and the expatriate villages of Beijing and Mumboi, they create an insular, portable, and parallel culture with little-recognized but real implications for American society at large.

Relos, too, got caught in the tsunami of 2008 and 2009 that struck the spectrum of world industry. Normally circumspect prophets promised seismic sea changes in the old order, crushing a half-century-old American Dream that sprang from union-won wages and foolhardy lending for everything from groceries to housing. The worst recession in two generations tripped up hardy icons of capitalism like Warren Buffett, General Electric, Google, Toyota, Merrill Lynch, Sony, and Microsoft, to say nothing of graybeards like General Motors, Chrysler, and Citigroup. It stripped the cover from Countrywide Financial's reckless mortgage lending for one in five American homes and from Bernard Madoff's $50 billion financial scam, the biggest and brassiest investor rip-off ever known. As U.S. layoffs surged to tens of thousands a week, to nearly one in ten unemployed workers by the spring of 2009, even recession-safe civil servants, accountants, and lawyers (except for those specializing in bankruptcy) lost jobs.

Relos, however, held on tighter than most. While some in world financial centers were left stranded, Relos remained the shock troops of national and world commerce, the conscripts who stalk and collect markets. To all but businesses knocked off in the recession, Relos were too essential to employers bent on holding their hard-won turf, lest China and India swoop in and take it. To cut expenses as their revenues slid, they were keeping their new college recruits close to home and putting off moving many veteran Relos. And one emblem of the Relo economy and Relo-packed towns like Alpharetta—the big splashy house—would change. The house would shrink, and it might be a decade before Relos could again buy low, sell high, and collect 20 percent annual gains to fatten their nest eggs. But once the twenty-first-century global economy resumes growing, companies will see to it that their Relo ranks do, too.

Relos aren't the onetime movers who fled the Rust Belt or the inner cities for the suburbs or who forge twenty-first-century stucco frontiers in places like Las Vegas, and Gilbert, Mesa, and Chandler, Arizona, and then settle down. Unlike the many other uprooted Americans who make the United States one of the world's most mobile countries, Relos hold jobs that move them again and again. Some companies and government agencies make periodic relocation a condition of employment or of promotion. A record of periodic relocation—climbing the ranks of one company or bounding from company to company—can grease the way to chief executive. About a third of recently appointed CEOs of Fortune 1000 companies worked in three or more locations, at their current companies or others, before moving to headquarters.

Like most Americans, Relos value their health, homes, jobs, weekends, and immediate neighbors—at least, that is, while they are among them. They get Christmas cards from the last subdivision, but after a couple of years the cards stop. Relos don't have accents. Wherever they go, they don't belong. Their kids don't know where they are from. Relos don't know where their funerals will be or who might come. They might value close family ties and deep friendships and keep parents' and siblings' pictures on their computers and refrigerators, but they see them only for the ritual week at the beach or the year-end holidays. Relos tend to know mostly other Relos, from their offices, subdivisions, PTAs, and kids' soccer and baseball teams. At Reloville megachurches, which rival Las Vegas for pyrotechnic stagecraft and showmanship, none of the parishioners acknowledged me. Then I noticed that no one acknowledged anyone.

I grew up in the 1940s and 1950s in Providence, Rhode Island, in a detached single-family home with a yard just big enough to play catch in. Of my neighbors—the Knowleses, the Huntoons, the Durfees, the Humphreys, the Simonses, Mrs. Haffenreffer, the Graveses, the Lowneses, Mrs. Fales, and reclusive Old Lady Merchant who wouldn't let us ride our sleds down her lawn—only the Graveses moved on and then only next door to Connecticut. Some of the children, my school friends, left but came back, or they drilled roots in new places and stayed.

But after working at the *Providence Journal* for two years, I wanted to go somewhere faraway and exotic. All the songs were about Paris, so I took an overnight TWA flight from New York to Le Bourget airport. For two beguiling August days, I walked. I climbed the interminable medieval steps to Montmartre. I toured the multi-domed, alabaster-white Sacré-Coeur basilica overlooking the city's mosaic of chestnut trees, white limestone facades, and red chimney pots. I went back down toward the Seine and happened upon the Place Vendôme, surely the most majestic urban square in the world.

I noticed buildings there bearing discreet logos—of IBM, Morgan & Cie. (the French branch of the American bank), the stock brokerage Smith Barney. How, I wondered, did they get into a place so emphatically French? I went up the Champs-Elysées, past the First National City Bank of New York, past signs flogging Coca-Cola and Marlboro and Kodak film and kiosks displaying *Time* magazine and the *Herald Tribune.* I went on, to the Tour Eiffel, and passed parked French Simcas bearing the five-pointed star of the Chrysler Corporation.

The third day I enrolled at the Alliance Française, where foreigners learn French. I found a room near the Sorbonne and bought a student meal ticket. I met Susan Woodward, a Francophile from Virginia who had started in Paris as an *au pair* girl. A year later, after hounding English-language news organizations for work, I became a correspondent in the Paris bureau of *Business Week,* and Susan and I got married.

We stayed in Paris for three years, and then the relocating began: to Stanford University in Palo Alto for a year, back to *Business Week* for two years in New York, two in Los Angeles, and another in New York, then to the *New York Times* for a year in New York and three in London. With two children, nine and three, I went to *Newsweek,* which brought us back to New York, and a year later I returned to the *Times.* After four years, we were sent to the paper's Washington bureau. Except for stints without family in Miami, Rio de Janeiro, and Riyadh, that would be our last stop.

In all these places, a few serial movers I met worked for the government. Those with the armed forces and the State Department—still the biggest employer of civilian Relos—moved inside a government cocoon of schools, doctors, housing, transportation services, and post exchanges. But I also met people from Boeing, Lockheed, General Electric, and ITT, then an insatiable conglomerate that was buying up household names among European companies and sending over its own managers and bookkeepers.

Like me, these corporate Relos fended for themselves finding schools, housing, stores, and doctors, tackling new cultures and languages. Often Relo wives complained of traumas over furniture that broke in the vans, thefts, packing and unpacking, of discarding friends, of missing family funerals, weddings, and holidays, and of traveling husbands leaving them stranded in unfamiliar places much of the week.

In 1976, the *New York Times* bureau chief in Belgrade, Malcolm Browne, took a comprehensive poll of the thirty *Times* foreign correspondents. Ten of the seventeen who responded had been abroad more than five years. Five of the ten—50 percent—had been divorced. But moving is often unavoidable, too. It is ambitious breadwinners' best career option, often their only real option, upon finishing college. They can choose to swim with the tide of the global economy, or sink in the quicksand of the hometown that the tide leaves behind.

Relos have been around for a while. In the 1600s, Britain's Hudson's Bay Company and East India Company began dispatching their traders and accountants across the Americas and Asia. In *A Nation of Strangers* (1972), the social critic Vance Packard spotted Relo pioneers encamped in the New York suburb of Darien, Connecticut. A "transfer town," he called it, and a "fine prototype of the town for company gypsies."

But the number of Relos was small then, no more than a few hundred thousand. Aspiring managers starting out at companies like United States Steel or General Motors could rise through the hierarchy without ever leaving the mother ship in Pittsburgh or Detroit. Today, a young accounts payable clerk at United Parcel Service in Atlanta would never be anything else without leaving town. Stalling only during the economy's relapse in 2008 and 2009, companies' need for Relos has ballooned with the expanding American economy and a mind-boggling surge in foreign trade—the goods and services that Americans buy from abroad and sell abroad.

American foreign trade leaped from $374 billion in 1970 to $3.3 trillion in 2007. *Someone* knocked on doors to buy and sell all those goods and services, negotiate contracts, run marketing and advertising campaigns, and balance companies' books. Many of those knocking were Relos.

Never staying long in any place and often leapfrogging through a succession of employers, Relos are characters in the West's transformation from an economy built on a bedrock of durable institutions and relationships to a postindustrial economy built on airplanes, ships, the Internet, and short-term arrangements. "Marriage vows, the homestead, corporate stability, and job security—all have suffered in the ever-evolving world" of international commerce and the Internet, writes Ellen Dunham-Jones, head of the architecture program at Georgia Tech. Homes, subdivisions, factories, malls, office parks, and employees, too, become "disposable assets" covered by "temporary contracts."

"Temporary contracts—of all kinds—are based on consuming rather than sustaining relationships," Dunham-Jones says. "The more one's life, property, and landscape consist of temporary contracts, the more one operates as a lone nomad, a sole proprietor within the overwhelming structure of global capital. The lack of constraining relationships affords tremendous individual freedom—but at a cost. A world of temporary contracts inhibits sustained belonging of any kind, inhibits bonding to either people or place." She adds, "The exchange of long-term relationships for short-term transactions has left us a crowd of perpetual strangers who often fail to recognize the value of shared needs and aspirations."

The numbers of Relos among all movers—one in seven, or 40 million Americans each year—are hard to pin down because they get lost in demographic statistics. The Census Bureau doesn't differentiate serial corporate movers—the real Relos—from those who are moved just once. Relos also elude census takers when abroad and beyond the bureau's purview, and when moving more than once during the five-year intervals that the bureau uses to measure mobility. The numbers also fluctuate as employers cut back on relocations, and employees, when the economy shrinks and brings them on as it rebounds.

But in general the Census Bureau has found that employers transfer or recruit and move about 4 million Americans, including children and spouses, each year from another county, state, or country. The Worldwide

Employee Relocation Council, a trade association that represents many companies that employ Relos, calculated that in 2007 employers transferred 800,000 households, mostly families, within the United States. That and reports of moving van operators and companies that manage relocations for employers suggest that active Relos—people who were moved in the last year or two and will be moved again soon—come to around 10 million, or 3 percent of the U.S. population.

Whatever their numbers, Relos' sway over the economy dwarfs them. Because Relos concentrate in affluent, fast-growing communities where their companies have increasingly built headquarters and branch offices over the past two decades, they exert disproportionate influence over the look and character of towns that become models for much of suburbia. "The short-term people don't give a damn," said Fred Adam, a sixty-four-year-old lawyer and a regular at the B&B Café's luncheon roundtable in Castle Rock, Colorado. "They don't plant trees, and they don't plant bushes." A home buyer typically holds back 10 percent from the builder until construction is complete, but some Relos, leaving town soon or not, won't pay until Adam goes after them. "They aren't going to sit there and bargain. They'll jump in and buy something. They have driven property values up. Corporations take care of them."

And life in Reloville was wearing on Jim and Kathy Link. Home from the Memorial Day fair, Jim said what made Medlock Bridge so neighborly and comfortable also left it flavorless. He was living among clones of himself. "You play tennis with them," he said. "You have them over to dinner. You go to the same parties. We're never challenged to learn much about other economic groups.

"When you talk about tennis, guess what? Everybody you play against looks and acts and generally feels like you. It doesn't give you much of a perspective."

1. Mobile Homeless

The psychology of place is essentially about belonging. Because it is a fundamental part of human psychological makeup, we know that all people need to belong. Each and every human being needs a place to call home.

—Mindy Thompson Fullilove,
The House of Joshua: Meditations on Family and Place

When I met Kathy Link in August 2004, she was forty-one, still a runner and straight as a spear. She was in the blond-streaked pigtails, red sun visor, and tennis whites she wore leading a fitness class at the Forum Gym near her home in Medlock Bridge and winning a doubles match afterward.

Kathy runs her household with the attention to detail of her former work editing for an aerospace company, a career that was already five years in the past. Tucked next to the seat of her white, eight-seat 2003 GMC Denali SUV was the week's color-coded itinerary. Kaleigh, eight, is red. She is the most excitable of the girls. Deep-dimpled and gallant, she runs to open doors for adults. At soccer she is fast and ferociously focused and shimmers with sweat.

Kelsey, the oldest at thirteen, is yellow. Tall, strong, and unflinching, she plays stopper, or center fullback. She can pound the ball half the length of the field. She got a concussion in a collision with an opponent weeks before. To keep playing she must wear a thick-cushioned headband for six months.

Kristina, eleven, is dark green. She can be distant and inscrutable. Left-footed, playing both right and left forward, her mission in life is outperforming and outgrowing Kelsey. She made a cheerleading squad. Pleased with herself, she said, "Kelsey tried out twice and didn't make it." But Kelsey has figured her out. In a charity road race, she sensed Kristina coming up behind, let her get close, and took off.

With school over that afternoon, Kathy (blue for work, light green for family and volunteering) had already dropped Kaleigh at her practice field blocks from home. She had to take Katrina to her practice four miles north and Kelsey to hers fourteen miles south. Her husband, Jim (orange), couldn't help much. Two to five days a week, every week, he's on the road seeing clients. For Monday and Tuesday, the itinerary said, "Jim in meetings, Charlotte." For Wednesday, it said, "Jim in meetings, Philadelphia."

Kathy surveyed the clotted intersection at the mouth of her 636-house subdivision. After moving to Medlock Bridge four years ago and choking on traffic, she made a rule: "Wherever I'm going has to be within one mile of the house." But she breaks the rule two or three times a day, all days but Sunday, with ten- and fifteen-mile trips. She does most of her mothering not at home but from the sidelines of soccer games and from her roost in the big Denali. She passes out snacks, water, Kleenex, Band-Aids, and medication, takes soundings of the girls' spirits and school day, and talks through homework assignments.

Impatiently, she squeezed the wheel. "Go, people," she pleaded. Her knuckles went white. Twice she tapped the horn. A timid driver in a gray van three cars ahead tiptoed into the Atlanta-bound avalanche along Medlock Bridge Road. Kathy pulled abreast, saying, "I have to see who she is." A rookie Relo, she decided, someone new to north Fulton County's chronically clogged traffic.

Kathy herself is a veteran Relo. She had already moved three times in the past ten years to help keep Jim's career selling pension and employee-benefit management services on track.

As Relos, the Links are corporate relocatees, or career transferees. Employers like Microsoft, Intel, and Apple; Procter & Gamble and General Electric; PepsiCo and Coca-Cola; UPS and FedEx; and Citigroup and JPMorgan Chase move them every few years to fly the corporate flag and work in far-flung factories and offices in the United States and abroad.

Americans working for American companies and Americans and foreigners working for one another's companies, Relos are twenty-first-century heirs of William S. Whyte's *Organization Man*, who exchanged the promise of job security and a pension for his loyalty and toil. Relos exchange not so much their loyalty and toil as their friends, their family ties, and the comforts of a hometown for bigger money and a bigger job—or to hold on to a job. Like Sloan Wilson's Tom Rath of *The Man in the Gray Flannel Suit*, they run on a corporate leash and sell out, too, but to the road.

Relos tend to be economically homogenous, with mid-career incomes of $100,000 to $200,000 a year. They differentiate themselves by their kids' activities and by the disposable tokens of their success—the leased car and the home *du jour*. Most go to state universities, disproportionately to schools of the Great Plains and the Midwest, where good jobs can be scarce, and many go on to graduate school. They vote two-to-one Republican (although in the 2008 presidential election, their votes for Barack Obama narrowed the gap). Most are Presbyterian, Methodist, Lutheran, or nondenominational Protestant. The vast majority of Relo breadwinners are white men aged thirty to fifty. In many Relovilles, unlike the nation as a whole, Asians tend to outnumber African Americans and Hispanics.

Some Relos find their salaries, toys, and perks compensating—the schools with top SAT scores, tennis and golf clubs, parks for youth sports, and upscale shopping strips. But they often complain of stress and anomie. They trade a home in one place for a job that could be anyplace. Perched in their Relovilles, they have little in the way of community ties or big, older city amenities like mass transit, museums, zoos, professional sports stadiums, and live theater.

Outside the gates of their subdivisions, in the towns beyond, Relos are ghosts. They support their own subdivisions' causes like runs to cure breast cancer or lupus, or fund drives to buy computers for their kids' schools and gear for their teams. But with the father on the road most weekdays and another move always looming, Relos have neither the time nor the need to sit on town boards or run in local elections, or join the church vestry or the Rotary Club.

Mayors and chambers of commerce complain that Relos shun campaigns to build a museum, a theater, a stadium, or a homeless shelter. They know they will be gone before the cement is poured. A Relo breadwinner's community is the company and his professional associations. Relos build networks of contacts and colleagues across the Internet and see them at conferences and conventions, when they find a few hours for a round of golf. They can tell you the way to the airport but not to City Hall.

On the face of it, Relo families seem no more or less striving or stressed or self-satisfied or absorbed in their kids, kitchens, and lawns than many middle-class Americans. They patronize the same ubiquitous chain stores, restaurants, and fitness centers. But on a drive through Alpharetta's subdivisions, Bradd Shore, an anthropologist at Emory University in Atlanta, made a novel observation: "The American family lasts only a generation and a half." He said families tend to keep up their rituals and sentimental connections after the children move out and begin having children. But when the second generation of children starts leaving, the original family disintegrates unless it makes great efforts to preserve itself. The disintegration, Shore said, is most pronounced among families who abandon their generational moorings—that is, Relos.

Yet in another way, Relos are cultural echoes of the 1950s' Andersons of *Father Knows Best* and the *Ozzie & Harriet* Nelsons. Relo spouses, more than 70 percent of them wives, drop promising careers to advance their spouses' careers and settle for temporary jobs, volunteer work, and stay-at-home mothering. Without grandparents and cousins and old friends nearby and bounding off like tumbleweed from town to town, Relos have also resurrected a relic of the American frontier—the tight nuclear nest of mother, father, and kids.

Relo children, growing up rootless, have little choice but to hit the job market running themselves. Gone from their parents, they beget an elderly variation of Relos. To reweave generational ties, they invite parents to come along on their moves. North Atlanta's latest trend in suburban housing is the stair-free, low-maintenance, "active adult" subdivision, which is cropping up near the developments oriented to young families. For these "collateral" Relos, the moves can be a mixed blessing. When their children are moved again, they can leave their parents, by then too old to move, stranded in a town where they only had ties to their children.

In 1994, when the Links moved from Houston to Baltimore for Jim's job at T. Rowe Price, they rented a house in Severna Park, Maryland, an established riverside suburb where, by happenstance, Kathy's parents had moved from Dallas so her pilot father could take a new job. Jim and Kathy found the town haughty and indifferent to newcomers with small children. They had Kaleigh there, and Kelsey started school. In three years, in 1997, a headhunter recruited Jim to a financial services company in Rochester, New York.

They bought a house in Pittsford, an affluent, apple-pie town with a congenial mix of transient and long-settled families. Kathy dug in to stay. "Up there each town has its own little village and one main street where you can walk and ride your bike and get someplace safely," she said. She became a certified personal trainer and began volunteering. She joined the Junior League. Kristina started school, and she and Kelsey started soccer.

But after three years, Jim was discouraged with his job and faced a dilemma common among Relos. For a well-paid, skilled, and specialized financial services sales manager, there was no other similar work in Rochester. He would have to start over in another business or relocate. In 2000, the First Union Corporation of Charlotte, a bank, took him on and sent him to its office in Atlanta. A year later First Union and Wachovia Corporation, another big bank in Charlotte, merged, and Jim stayed on.

Inching along, Kathy passed strip malls. She went by the gym, chiropractors, nail shops, colonnaded stucco banks, hair salons, sixteen-pump gas stations, self-storage lots filled with the possessions of coming-and-going Relos, Waffle Houses, a tanning place, and a salon that tattoos on lipstick and eyeliner so they will not fade in the pool. She dodged the orange barrels of road-widening crews spreading asphalt to try to keep up with a north Fulton County population that in the 1990s swelled from 170,000 to 273,000. Sidewalks started and stopped. Only a fool walked a dog or rode a bicycle there.

She passed new subdivisions with signs in wedding invitation script trumpeting price points, or ranges, which developers use to stratify neighborhoods. The signs read *Longlake, $200's; Wolf Creek, $300's to $500's; Inverness, $600's to $800's.* They tell families where they fit. She passed four alert cement lions, prone on their paws, guarding a semicircular driveway. "Lions, Mommy?" Kelsey asked. "Why do they have lions?"

She passed a development called Ellard with closely packed houses mimicking the bluestocking quarters of Savannah and Charleston. "A Turn-of-the-Century Community," the sign at Ellard's gate said, "Est. 1998." She crossed over Georgia 400, the sclerotic artery from Appalachia to Atlanta that pumps hundreds of thousands of commuters into Alpharetta's glass and brushed-metal office parks.

After dropping off Kelsey and Kristina, Kathy would double back and pick up Kaleigh and take her to golf. She would wait for Kelsey to finish soccer before picking up Kristina and taking her to cheerleading practice. Another mother would retrieve Kristina so that Kathy could be home when Kaleigh's math tutor came.

When the Links began house hunting around Atlanta in 2000, the girls were ten, eight, and five. "School was number one," Jim said. Without connections in their new towns—to the doctor who might steer a friend's child to medical school, the union steward who could sign her up for a job in the factory, the café owner who could take her on for the summer—Relos can't give their kids much of a boost into college and careers. They rely on the schools.

Once settled on the top school districts, the Links looked for homes within subdivision price points. At their $300,000 range, they wanted four bedrooms, two and a half baths, a basement, and a backyard. Easy drives from Jim's office in Atlanta they found only small 1970s ranch houses that they could afford. But twenty-five miles north of the city, they came upon Alpharetta. In the Medlock Bridge subdivision, they found a five-bedroom, four-bath home with a secluded backyard for $313,000.

Alpharetta was a departure from the Rochester suburb of Pittsford and Severna Park, outside Baltimore. The trees were sticks, the yards coiffured. Beyond Kaleigh's Medlock Bridge Elementary School, a Montessori school, and the Medlock Bridge community center, with its clubhouse, tennis courts, soccer fields, and pool, nothing, no stores or churches or parks, was within a safe walking distance. But at least everyone seemed from somewhere else and predisposed to mix—a good thing, the Links thought, compared with Severna Park. Of the thirty thousand people living in their Medlock Bridge–Alpharetta Census tract, 75 percent were born outside Georgia.

In other ways, too, the tract had the complexion of Relovilles. Less than 3 percent of the people were over sixty-five, compared with a national average of 12 percent. Less than 2 percent were poor or unemployed. Two-thirds of the adults had four or more years of college, two and a half times the national average. Families earned just over $100,000 a year, twice the average. The typical home was worth $400,000, also twice the national average, and with nine or more rooms was twice as big. Steve Beecham, the leading local home mortgage broker, explained, "Everybody here is in the top ten percent of what they do, or they desire to be in the top ten percent."

Pit Stop

On a sunny October school day in 2004, a white stretch Hummer with black windows and chrome wheel spinners was winding past Coles Hill Court where the Links had lived for four years. Under purple and yellow disco lights throbbing on a black velvet ceiling, twenty joyriding four- to seven-year-olds dined on fruit juice and peanut-butter-and-jelly sandwiches. "Welcome to every day in Alpharetta," Julianne Hahn, the parent-chaperone, said. The ride was the children's reward for leading their classes in selling $44,000 of gift-wrapping paper for Medlock Bridge Elementary School's fund-raising drive.

The Links' house, in the center of the cul-de-sac at the end of Coles

Hill Court, was thirteen years old when they bought it. It has 3,900 square feet on the first and second floors and 1,100 more in a basement, where a wall of tall windows face the backyard. It stands on a slight rise with tall young oaks raining acorns over a small front yard and a curtain of cedar and pine bordering the back. It is sheathed in beige stucco and wide fieldstone panels flank a varnished oak front door with leaded glass.

Inside on the first floor are a two-story family room hung with folk art, with a fireplace and a ficus tree; a bedroom for guests and the girls' upright piano; a small, little-used dining room; and a large airy kitchen with wide glass doors to the deck and the grill. Upstairs were a bedroom for Kelsey, another for Kristina and Kaleigh, and a master suite. The parents' bathroom had wide white his-and-her vanities on each side of the door and a Jacuzzi enclosed in pale pink marble tiles. The basement had a bedroom and bath, a fully equipped bar, and room for entertaining. Jim said, "The basement is approximately the same size as my parents' entire house."

The Links were pleased with so much house and their three-block walk to the community center. Within a couple of months of moving in, everyone knew Jim and Kathy, both extroverts. Jim had run for the board of the homeowners association and won. The board then made him president and, in effect, the mayor. Kathy, calling upon her pre-Relo editing skills, took on the subdivision's newsletter.

She also set up an e-mail chain that reached 350 Medlock Bridge homes to rally neighbors behind causes like stopping a Fulton County school redistricting plan. She spent two hours on Tuesday mornings at a Bible study meeting and joined a neighborhood group to play bunko, a social dice game favored by suburban women who tend to view it as an excuse to get together and have some wine. They met at one another's homes one Friday night a month, when the men were home to watch the kids.

She bored into the schools. She became a vice president of the elementary school PTA and edited its newsletter, too. She was a room parent and organized science projects for Kaleigh's third-grade class. At her kitchen computer command post, she tracked the girls' reports and test scores on school Web pages. Kelsey's usual monthly report showed a 97 average, but then she got a 78 on a Spanish test. Within a week, she had a tutor.

Kathy also made time for the gym. She had had a scare in Houston, pain so acute that her lungs burned and it hurt to climb stairs. Thirty then, she was diagnosed with spondylolisthesis, a form of arthritis. "You may be in a wheelchair in the not too distant future," her doctor told her, "and you may never get out of it." He told her to try to fight the prognosis with exercise. Prescription painkillers like Vioxx helped. After the public health warnings, she dropped Vioxx but took an Advil before playing tennis. Except for a flare-up in Rochester, the condition had greatly subsided. But she couldn't get a full night's sleep. Rocking a hand up and down, she said her wrists hurt. It was hard to lift an iron skillet.

Apart from his work for the homeowners association, Jim was out of town too often to help much during school days. Away from home, he led the life of a loner, sometimes meeting a colleague or a client for dinner. Otherwise he would work out in the hotel fitness center and hole up in his room, cramming for the next day's appointments and calling home. For most trips he drove to the Atlanta airport, parked there, and flew to Philadelphia, San Diego, New Orleans, or Phoenix. But every couple of weeks he had to make a 220-mile, three-hour-twenty-minute drive to meetings at Wachovia's headquarters in Charlotte.

He had fit out his Ford Taurus with a Bluetooth device so he could speak without holding his BlackBerry, and he brought along his golf bag in the trunk. But he could go from September to December without a four-hour break to play. His handicap, once down to 8, was back to 13.

Heading north from Georgia on I-85, through South Carolina to Charlotte, he would pass some Americana: bumper stickers ("If it ain't King James, It ain't the Bible"), state troopers in unmarked black SUVs, a megachurch, the billboards of the (three) "World's Largest" fireworks dealers, Martha's Fabrics, Russell Stover Candies, and Abbott Farms, which, in season and out, hustled peaches and more fireworks. For a snack and gas, he could choose among Flying J, Pilot, and TA truck stops. He listened to sports radio. He would lose the station in South Carolina, switch to National Public Radio, and pick up sports radio again a half hour from Charlotte.

With him gone so much, Kelsey, at fourteen, has figured out the Relo family pecking order. "The women are like the rulers," she said on a drive with Jim to a weekend soccer tournament in Columbus, Georgia. "They have the big cars. The dads have the little cars and just go to work." She thought Jim could be more assertive. He slows down and stops at orange lights. "Kathy becomes impatient with me when I'm going seventy in a sixty-five-mile zone," he explained. "No, Daddy," Kelsey said, pulling on her soccer shoes, "it's when you're going sixty."

Jim and Kathy agree on most things. Both voted for George W. Bush in 2000 and 2004 and supported John McCain in 2008. They are committed to the girls' sports. "Every area you move into," Kathy said, "you buy into the lifestyle. For instance, Alpharetta is very big on tennis and soccer. We have chosen to participate in that."

"It's the whole lemming effect," Jim said. "In Rochester it was festivals."

Kathy also hopes sports will be a key to building her girls' self-esteem. As a child, she says, she didn't have much.

But they do have differences. "Kathy's goal for the girls' college is like her mother's was for her—that they not have to work," Jim said.

Jim's parents drilled frugality into him. They felt working his way through college built character and prepared him for life. Kathy's parents wanted her to concentrate on academics. But she had to work anyway. Soon after she started College at A&M, her father's airline, Braniff International Airways, shut down, and it was months before he went to Piedmont Airlines in Maryland, later a part of US Air, and moved to Severna Park. Kathy took student loans and, briefly, part-time jobs.

Over other issues that matter to Jim, like coming straight home after school or soccer, or speaking respectfully, Kathy and the girls allow him the last word. But with those exceptions, they take him in stride. He will rebuke the girls for littering his vanity upstairs with crumpled wet towels, their hair dryers, and the electric irons they use to straighten their wavy brown hair. They do it anyway.

On a Saturday morning that autumn, Jim looked fresh and alert, though he had not come home until 10 p.m. Friday. In his weekend khaki shorts and blue polo shirt, he was folding laundry while watching a Texas A&M–Kansas State football game in the family room. His plan for the day: taking Kelsey to a soccer game fourteen miles away and bringing Kaleigh along for her game later. Kathy would shuttle Kristina thirty miles into Cherokee County, where she would be cheerleading, and then they would all meet at Kaleigh's game.

Some weekends during breaks in the girls' sports schedules, Jim joins friends in football pools. As a guest of a contractor for the Atlanta Falcons, he stole the weekend of his forty-second birthday to watch the team play the Chiefs in Kansas City.

Like Kathy, he works out at the Forum Gym. He joined the posh St. Ives Country Club across Medlock Bridge Road, paying a deeply discounted $15,000 initiation fee during a membership drive.

Neither parent has much interest in fashion and labels, a trait that tests their suitability for the Relo culture. In Alpharetta, old cars parked at subdivision curbs were thought to pollute property values. "You become very aware of your car and how old it is," Kathy said. "We moved here with a 1994 Ford Taurus, and people gave us a hard time about it, just razzed us a little." When the old Taurus wore out, Jim bought his used four-year-old Taurus. He found it at CarMax for $10,000 and paid for it with cash.

On an income of roughly $200,000 a year—it fluctuates with commissions and bonuses—the Links splurge on sports, tutoring, and piano lessons. A five-day summer soccer camp for Kelsey and Kristina cost $700 each. Tennis lessons cost more than $2,000 a year. Over Christmas, 2004, they would take their first winter vacation, to Steamboat Springs, Colorado, so the girls could learn to ski.

But they were feeling a squeeze. Some stucco near the dining room windows had to be replaced, and a leak in the basement wall had to be fixed. The wallpaper they inherited in the kitchen, depicting bouquets of red roses against a white sky, had to go. With $10,000, they started a college tuition fund earlier in 2004, and with Kelsey entering high school next year, they had to build it up.

To monitor their credit card spending, the Links installed a Quicken program on their computers. With all her driving and gasoline prices starting to rise, it showed Kathy spending $70 to fill the Denali's tank every three or four days. The beauty salon called Kathy a low-maintenance woman because she spent less than a hundred dollars for tinting and clipping. But for a treat now and then, she and the girls would go in for $25 pedicures. "Jimmy cringes when he sees the charges," she said.

For all the adjustments they made over four years in Alpharetta, the Links did not seem to have found a way to make their life work. The traffic and demands on Kathy were only getting worse. They had not counted on how far everything was, on the stresses of Jim's absences, and on how much was asked of volunteers. They had nowhere to turn for comfort, no old friends or parents to visit or sit for their children so they could get away for a weekend alone.

The demands of the life were testing the marriage. "The single biggest thing to change is, Kathy has to be more judicious about how she volunteers," Jim said. "She would never give up Bible study. But she's now playing in three or four tennis leagues."

She agrees. "I volunteer way too much," she said.

"It doesn't mean you shouldn't be involved," he told her, "but it doesn't mean you have to be the leader."

Making dinner one night, Kathy said, "It's like I'm on a hamster wheel." She spoke of Highland Park, with her Presbyterian church and easy access to Dallas. She spoke of the settled, less transient towns of Pittsford and Rochester. "In Rochester," she said, "everything fell into place."

In Alpharetta, what weighs on her most is the daily grind. She can't find a rheumatologist to check her arthritis without giving up half a day in Atlanta. "We haven't found a church," she said. "We went church shopping. We found one, but it's a half-hour drive away. We don't have that kind of time. It's all here, but it's an hour drive away. It's like, 'Get the heck out of my way.' It's like go, go, go. We're just going, going, going. I call it drowning. It's when you can't see the top of the water."

She wants a friend, a real confidante. "We have a lot of friends," she said, "but no one person I can call up. I called up one girl, and I scared her. Jimmy's my best friend. I don't have a girl best friend here in Alpharetta. That really bothers me." In Rochester, she said, "I had two really good friends.

"Jimmy has been saying, 'This travel is killing me.'" Flying, with the crowds, interminable security lines, and longer and longer delays, is wearing him down. So were the drives to the Wachovia meetings in Charlotte that consumed seven hours each round-trip.

Early in their marriage, Kathy said she told Jim, "'Wherever you choose to work, we will make a life.' Jimmy's the one making the money. I want him to be happy and successful." But she had not considered the challenge of making a life in Alpharetta, or how long she would have to work at it. "I'm shocked we're still here," she said. "Every home we went to, I asked the realtor, 'Could you sell this house?' I did not think we would be here four years."

Yet for all the travails of life in Alpharetta, it dawned on the Links that they might be locked in there. The summer before, in 2003, Jim and Wachovia officers discussed job changes that could have led to a move, but nothing came of that. Jim would have to keep driving to Charlotte, but the bank did relieve him of his one-hour commute to the Atlanta office on the days when he wasn't traveling. It shipped him furniture and computer and communications gear so he could set up an office at home.

There were other reasons to stay. As yet, the girls weren't complaining. They were all playing soccer, all playing piano, all well established in school. As long as they kept getting good grades, they could go to state universities in Georgia tuition-free.

Jim and Kathy thought that if they remained for nine more years, all three girls will finish high school in one place. Then, as they were turning fifty, they could bail out of Alpharetta and maybe scout around for jobs in Austin, their favorite city in their home state of Texas, and maybe retire there.

Yet Medlock Bridge was comforting as well. Asked one day what she feared most, Kristina said, "Walking home from the bus because the squirrels are throwing acorns off the trees at you." She knew it was the squirrels, she said, because the acorns kept coming even when the wind stopped shaking the trees.

Compared with the wider world, the Links rarely thought about crime, though there had been episodes of neighborhood vandalism. Once in a while, a car would get keyed, golf clubs stolen, and mail boxes dinged. Past midnight once in June 2002, joyriding kids drove a stolen minivan into the old clubhouse, hit a gas line, and the building burned down. Never caught, they left behind a twelve-pack of beer. The girls would ask about drugs.

Then, in November 2004, Wachovia promoted Jim. It made him a national sales manager in the institutional trust division and assigned him a broader range of the bank's money management services to sell. His boss at headquarters in Charlotte told him he could go on working from home in Alpharetta and just show up for meetings in Charlotte every week or two. But he suggested that moving to Charlotte and getting to know the top officers might lead to more promotions.

Jim stalled. He had to weigh the costs of moving and the toll on the girls against his ambitions and a chance to live in a more settled, less harried place. In the end, he said, "I told my boss, 'If you're willing to fund a full relocation package, I'm willing to do it.' " And if they did relocate, he told the bank, they could not move again for nine years.

Jim and Kathy didn't tell the girls or friends about the discussions. They had seen that once word got around a Reloville that a family might move, friends, coaches, and teachers might write them off. Soccer coaches, looking ahead to building the next year's teams, would favor other kids with prized starting positions.

Kelsey, however, sensed a change looming. Kathy said that during the ski trip to Steamboat Springs in December, "She asked, 'Are we moving?' Jimmy couldn't lie. He said, 'It looks like it,' " and told her to keep mum. He didn't tell her where but in the car with him later, she mused, "We've only lived in states where the capital begins with an *A*. Austin, Annapolis, Albany, Atlanta." She paused. "Augusta, Maine?"

"Pretty remote for a sales manager of a national bank," Jim said.

"So Raleigh. The second letter is A."

"Harrisburg?" he said. "Tallahassee?" But Kelsey knew it had to be Raleigh.

The Links worried most about Kristina. She had been slow to take to Alpharetta. She was diagnosed with ADHD and dyslexia. She was too thin and was finicky about eating. With medication and counseling, she bloomed. In her special-education reading class, she got 100s and was moved to a regular class. She won her soccer team's Golden Boot award for scoring the most goals.

In March 2005, when Jim got home after three days in Phoenix, he found a long e-mail message from Wachovia. "We got our paperwork," he said—the relocation package. The bank would cover costs like the moving van, real estate fees, temporary housing, and meals until they moved into another home in Charlotte.

They told the girls after school. Kelsey took it easily, sad only that she would not be going to Northview High School with her friends. Kaleigh beamed, then frowned about losing friends and teachers. Kristina was in the kitchen with Kathy when Jim came in.

"Your dad's got something to tell you," Kathy said.

"We're moving to Charlotte," he said.

Kristina grimaced. She would be leaving Rebecca, a friend of five years.

"I hate you," she said. "When?"

"In June," he said.

"What about soccer?"

She would keep playing in Alpharetta through May, they told her, and then join a team in Charlotte.

Kathy was ready to go. "I like everyone here," she said. "But I'm done with the new subdivision thing." They would make what Jim called a "this-is-it" move and correct the mistakes of the last.

That Was It

In June 2005, Jim and Kathy Link bought a brick one-and-a-half-story Cape Cod in Myers Park, an eighty-year-old, onetime streetcar neighborhood close to downtown Charlotte that had the ageless patina of Kathy's Highland Park. No two houses looked alike. With a high pitched roof and only the first floor's three black-shuttered windows and door visible from the road, the one at 2718 Picardy Place looked well groomed and unembarrassed, at 2,800 square feet, to be smaller than most of its neighbors.

Among features that the Links missed in Alpharetta, Picardy Place had sidewalks, on both sides of the road, and along them century-old oaks with the girth of an oil barrel. The house was fifty-eight years old and last renovated in 1970, so it would need a new kitchen and the floors refinished and perhaps an addition.

But it was ideally situated, with stores and the girls' three public schools less than a mile away. Close by was the Myers Park Presbyterian Church. Straight up busy Providence Road, the Links could see the Wachovia Center tower, a mere twelve-minute, four-mile commute in Jim's old Taurus.

Life was simpler on Picardy Place. Rarely having to venture onto Charlotte's interstates, Kathy could go three and four weeks before refilling the Denali's tank. For some errands, she rode her bike. Jim was traveling less and getting home most nights for dinner.

It was odd that as they were moving in, Jim's boss, who brought them to Charlotte, inexplicably left the bank. Rumors began flying about changes in Jim's corporate trust and custody group. But after having just promoted Jim and making a costly commitment in moving him, they thought he was safe.

In October, their pictures hung and boxes unpacked, Jim and Kathy went off without the girls to Cancún, Mexico, for a family wedding and a week at a new five-star, beach-front hotel. After three days in the sun, they were upended by Hurricane Wilma and then by word that Wachovia might be selling Jim's group. The hotel ordered the guests out of their rooms and corralled them for two days in the two ballrooms. A gust-propelled window sliced Jim's scalp, requiring four stitches. With the airport in turmoil, it would be another week before he and Kathy could get a flight out.

Once back in Charlotte, Jim learned that U.S. Bank, in Minneapolis, would be buying his group for $720 million. He knew it would bring some of its own people into management jobs like his. To protect the severance pay he would get if he were let go, he decided to stay. He was notified in January 2006 that his job would end in March.

As in Rochester, he could find nothing that worked in Charlotte, no openings for a seasoned sales manager of financial management services. Calling around, he remembered a former colleague at Wachovia who was married to an officer of the 400-employee PFM Group, a firm in Philadelphia originally called Public Financial Management, that managed more than $30 billion of financial assets, primarily for state and local governments.

His call to her led to meals and interviews. In May 2006 he went to work at PFM with the title of senior managing consultant and charged with selling the firm's asset-management services to governments. Jim, gun-shy after his travails at Wachovia, asked the firm to commit to keeping him for two years. It agreed, and also assured him a shot at becoming one of fifty managing directors, the equivalent of partner in a law firm, with a stake in the ownership.

Kathy stayed behind so the girls could finish their one year in Charlotte schools. In May she put the house up for sale, for $668,000, about $40,000 more than they had paid for it—$280,000 more than they got for the house in Alpharetta. But by then the market was stagnating, and the house on Picardy Place wouldn't budge.

To buy time, the Links wanted to rent a home where they hoped to buy one, in the affluent Radnor Township community of Wayne, on the Philadelphia Main Line, that met their criteria for good schools. They found nothing suitable, so Jim used most of his Wachovia severance to make a down payment on a small, $425,000 town house a few steps from downtown Wayne.

Moving in August, they needed three self-storage units, two the size of a two-car garage, for the things the town house couldn't hold. The girls started their third schools in three years—Kelsey as a sophomore at Radnor High School, Katrina in the last year of middle school, and Kaleigh in the last year of elementary school.

About fifteen miles from Philadelphia and a few blocks from downtown Wayne is Greystone Woods Circle. It seems, improbably, a satellite of an Alpharetta townhouse development. It is about fifteen years old and is a compact arrangement of two-and-three-story, beige houses, some with garages and with little street parking.

The houses look well kept but transient and heartless. As if to repel the jumble of city life just beyond, along Lancaster Pike's random spectrum of commerce—luxury car dealers, a Courtyard by Marriott, an Eckerd pharmacy, a garden supply store, a McDonald's, and other restaurants and merchants occupying old buildings with indeterminate legacies—Greystone's front doors are tucked behind individual stalls of stockade fencing that mask them from view.

No. 31 made no boasts of homeowner pride. On a chilly, gray day in February 2007, an umbrella, a spent tennis racket, and a running shoe rested against the frame of the door. Just to the right was a small, dark, weed-ravaged patio, also fenced, that had room for two or three chairs. The Links set the gas grill from Medlock Bridge there, but since their arrival they had not turned it on.

Inside, the house was a deep, inviting cavern of angles, high ceilings, and open space, except for the kitchen where Kathy Link was unloading a trunkload of staples from Costco. By Relo standards, the kitchen was small and tight, with short and shallow counters. It had a table too small for the family of five, but convenient for parking the shopping.

The short hallway from the kitchen led to a portrait-lined stairway to the second floor with Jim and Kathy's room and a bedroom for Kaleigh, now ten, and then up to a loft that Kelsey, sixteen, and Katrina, fourteen, shared. Beyond the stairs was a formal dining area that Kathy arranged like those of her last houses. Down one step was a living room with a wide fireplace and Jim's prodigious new Samsung plasma TV filling one corner. In another corner was the shrine, a table of framed family photographs. French doors at the back of the room opened on a second, larger patio.

An albino blond standard poodle and golden retriever mix, Aggie, had moved in. Jim and Kathy bought her to placate the girls after the traumas of moving and the loss of their long-haired black and white cat, Gabby, run over by a truck in Charlotte.

One headache was over for the Links. After nine months on the market Picardy Place sold, miraculously for the $668,000 asking price, and Kathy was scouting Wayne neighborhoods for a permanent home.

But she was at loose ends. She didn't feel welcome in town. They weren't invited to Christmas parties. She was an oddball again, a Relo in a place where most people were not. Perhaps because she was southern and Texan, or was a parent with kids too old for neighborhood playgrounds where newcomers met, she could claim only one friend—the woman who was her real estate agent.

She thought about friends and friendships in her old Reloville of Alpharetta. She knew just about everyone in the Medlock Bridge subdivision, but needed something more. "Medlock Bridge was like a sorority, a club," she said. "After a while, it felt incestuous. A subdivision offers you an instant social life. Everybody lived in the same place. It's the same people over and over again. I used to think they were on a different page from me, maybe a different chapter."

Wayne, alas, was a whole new and bewildering book. It is a much older town, with fewer newcomers. "People don't know who I am," she said. "People will talk to you really nicely, for five minutes, and then, 'Oh, okay, got to go.' People are very blunt up here. People speak faster. You ask them to repeat themselves, and they get offended. You don't know where they're coming from."

Their values, whether about politics or the economy or the war in Iraq or about dating and coed sleepover parties for teenagers, were all over the board. She said she had met people who had lived there for two years before they stopped hating it. At Kaleigh's school she said a mother told her, "'We're nice, but that's as far as we go. We don't include you.'"

Still, Kathy was digging in again. "When you move, you're trying to find people like you," she said. "You've got to put yourself out there." She began volunteering at the schools and helped out at a book fair. "They say I'm so competent," she said. On Halloween, she led the girls around the neighborhood knocking on unfamiliar doors. "That was fun," she said. "We met people."

Backpacks drop. The girls have come home from school. "Not *home*," Kristina said. "I feel like it's a house I come home to. When we're coming home from a long trip, I think Charlotte."

For Kelsey, nearly a grown woman now at sixteen with convictions and a firm sense of herself, Wayne has proved tough. "The first day she walked into high school she was frozen with fear," Kathy said. Starting as a sophomore among 1,200 students at Radnor High, she found that as freshmen, girls had already formed their cliques and boys and girls their after-school packs. "My homeroom teacher assigned me a girl," Kelsey said. "I made friends with her and her group of friends, but I didn't really click with them."

One Saturday, Kelsey steeled herself and went off to a school football game alone. She began running cross-country and track and made headway with classmates. But she had to keep alert. "Drugs," she said. "I saw a transaction. She was handing him money. I went to a girl's sweet sixteen party. They were drinking. Girls brought in water bottles with vodka and drank it in the bathroom. They had to call an ambulance because one girl got alcohol poisoning. They have Gatorade with alcohol."

She had lost some momentum leaving the high-achiever, international baccalaureate program at Myers Park High School only to have to plunge into the scramble of getting into college at Radnor High. "They've freaked us out," she said. "They talk about transcripts, advance placement." They were urging students to apply to at least ten colleges to be sure of getting into one. Kathy said, "Parents are hiring tutors for SATs and college applications. A teacher said there's so much pressure to go to the top twenty-five, kids feel they have to get in to be worthy."

In Charlotte, Kaleigh, then nine, settled in quickly. Her teachers voted her the most responsible in her class. But breaking into Wayne was hard for her, too. Still excitable, she was acting up more. "She's so boisterous," Kathy said. "She's so out there she can be offensive." She's a challenge for teachers. "She looks busy," Kathy said. "But when it comes down to it she's not doing anything. The teachers say, 'She's very, very bright. We have to get that knowledge out of her brain and put it down on paper.'"

Kristina, for all her anger about leaving Alpharetta, had transformed herself upon settling in Wayne. Once wary and shy, she talked a blue streak. She took seats in the front of her classes. "In my first-period English class," she said, "there were no assigned seats. Two girls said, 'You can sit with us.'" She played tennis at school and sang and acted in a school

The Latest Home: *The Link family (from left, Kathy, Kelsey, Katrina, Kaleigh; in back, Jim) settle into life in their new home—their seventh in just over a decade—in the Philadelphia suburb of Wayne, Pennsylvania. For Relo families, serial moving, especially to Relovilles that cater to similar vagabond families, can foster a sense of insularity.* [PHOTO BY LAUREN SHAY LAVIN]

production of *Home Room*. Boys like her. "Boys in Charlotte," she said, "they were like friends. Now it's more, 'I like boys.'"

Jim gets home at 7:30. He is traveling a lot again, two or three days a week, sometimes over weekends, to state capitals. But he loves his job. "People hire us because they value our counsel," he said. "This is 179 degrees from Wachovia in terms of the way that things get done. Wachovia was very slow and hierarchical." Would he make managing director—be made one of fifty partners and be granted a piece of PFM's profits? "I damn well better be," he said.

Incentives

By May 2007, the Links felt they had crossed their last threshold, at least until the girls were off to college. Their town house had sold quickly and they bought a doctor's small and unassuming sixty-year-old, beige-painted clapboard and stone split-level on Rose Glen Drive in Wayne. Shrouded by rugged old trees, it is barely visible, set back on three-quarters of an acre off a cul-de-sac, and an orphan among its neighboring Main Line colonial dowagers and theatrical new McMansions. Half the size of the house in Alpharetta, it is a tight fit for the family of five. The Links paid $579,000 to buy it from the doctor's estate, or nearly $90,000 less than the sale price for Picardy Place and $200,000 below Wayne real estate agents' estimate before the 2008 plunge in home prices. The Links had lucked out, after the cost of carrying two homes—Picardy Place and Greystone Woods Circle—consumed so much of their savings.

Philadelphia was winning them over. Though still outsiders, they were finding a rhythm that worked. They had been to the Liberty Bell, up and down Market Street, around Rittenhouse Square. They were taking ninety-minute Amtrak trips to New York City. For the first time in years, Kathy's parents were close, still in Severna Park, less than two hours away. From Rose Glen Drive, Jim could walk to the train station to get to work.

Kristina, starting high school, was in honors classes and was a high jumper for the track team and was playing for two soccer teams. She liked herself. At five-foot-nine, she had outgrown Kelsey. She weighed running for class president but backed off. She wondered what lay ahead. She wanted to be a chef, or an athlete. At school she took a career-guidance test with puzzling results. It said no to practicing law but yes to becoming a judge. It also proposed modeling.

Kaleigh was simmering down. She'd made some friends and was playing soccer with the passion of her games in Alpharetta and started playing lacrosse. At eleven, she had won a middle school lottery to join an ungraded program that integrated art, social studies, and English. She was writing short stories, though with a disconcerting motif: in all of them, somebody dies.

But in early June 2007, as they were moving into the new house, the question of relocation once again intruded. In his year on the job, Jim had impressed some managing directors. One pulled him aside. "Hey," he said, "you're a Texan. You know your way around down there. What about reorganizing the office in Austin?"

"Jimmy and I had always talked about moving to Austin," Kathy said. They like college towns. To many a Texan, Austin is the cream of the crop, with the flagship campus of the University of Texas. As state residents, the girls would pay about $8,000 for tuition a year, about $4,000 less than they would pay as Pennsylvania residents enrolling at Penn State's University Park campus. What if PFM sweetened a move with the coveted promotion to managing director? "It's traumatic," Kathy said. "I feel bad for Jimmy."

It wasn't just that the girls would revolt. Jim and Kathy named their dog for their Texas A&M Aggies, Jim still tuned in to the games, and Kathy still talked Texan. But they were Texans no more, if not yet and perhaps not ever Philadelphians. Approaching their fifties, they were career-long Relos making the best of their home of the moment. Because of her deference to Jim and his career, Kathy didn't press him to stay in Wayne. But he knew how she felt. For the duration of the girls' schooling at least, she was committed to Wayne.

She was talking about punching out a wall to expand the kitchen. Though still working on friendships, she could get to her parents. Most places she went were less than a mile away. She was riding a bike again. Freed from her time-eating grinds around Alpharetta, she could enjoy volunteering again. She took on the middle school's Web site as well as the newsletter. She joined the PTA boards of both the middle school and Radnor High. She joined a tennis league.

Life was simpler for Jim, too. To commute, he left the driving to Amtrak. The moves from Pittsford to Alpharetta to Charlotte to Wayne were occupational hazards, but things seem to have stabilized. Kelsey would intern at Jim's office that summer—her first serious job. She would be entering her junior year and was taking honors classes again. Soon she would be driving. She had made a couple of friends. "I'm never moving again," Kelsey told her parents, and she was adult enough that they doubted they could bring her around. Jim, however, still couldn't be sure of his prospects at PFM. About nine months remained of his two-year trial before he would be considered for managing director. But he felt secure in his job, and if he lost it, Philadelphia seemed a big enough financial services arena to accommodate him. He knew it was an impossible time to move.

Late in June, Jim called Kathy from the office. He had talked to his boss's boss. Kathy said the boss had told him, " 'I'm not happy with your going to Texas. I would appreciate your staying here.' We were going to stay anyway."

In December 2007, five months before his job trial was up, PFM asked Jim to fill out a questionnaire reviewing his qualifications to become a managing director. In January, he was approved. Soon Kelsey would be taking the Taurus when Jim was away and sharing the big Denali. Kathy hardly needed it. In Wayne, she could ride her bike.

2. First City

The whole assemblage of buildings is commonly called Manchester, and contains about four hundred thousand inhabitants, rather more than less. The town itself is peculiarly built, so that a person may live in it for years, and go in and out daily without coming into contact with a working-people's quarter or even with workers, that is, so long as he confines himself to his business or to pleasure walks.

—Friedrich Engels, *Condition of the Working Class in England*

From the Hartsfield-Jackson Atlanta International Airport, Georgia 400, the highway that opened the pastures and cotton fields of north Fulton County to the sprawl engulfing Sandy Springs, Dunwoody, Norcross, and Roswell, makes four stops in Alpharetta. The fourth, at Windward Parkway, passes interchangeable blocks of metal and glass office buildings of AT&T, Automatic Data Processing, Choice Point, Siemens, McKesson Corporation, Nortel Networks, Hewlett-Packard, Verizon, IBM, and the Bank of America.

Scattered beyond the office parks are winding subdivision roads with names like Plantation Trace, Courageous Wake, Marquess Moor, and Oxford Close. Builders call their architecture—a mélange of Georgian, Victorian, Loire Valley châteaux, and Disney World—"American Traditional." Bermuda grass lawns as trim as a diamond salesman's fingernail, with tidy boxwoods and azaleas propped on sculpted pillows of pine straw mulch, surround stiff haughty houses aligned like formations of Prussian troops.

These houses, the subdivisions and office parks, suit some master schemer's ideal of propriety and orderliness. Homeowners association regulations and local government ordinances prohibit exterior displays of spontaneity, domestic discord, whimsy, charm—anything humanizing that might differentiate them. An unconventional mailbox, a jungle gym, a swing on a tree, a car left overnight in the driveway, a hose left uncoiled, even patches of weeds in the mulch—all are taboo.

The subdivisions are segmented, stratified, and separated by income, lifestyle, age, house size, and price points. A subdivision of $250,000 homes suits $75,000- to $100,000-a-year couples with young children. It will have a private neighborhood pool, tennis court, and playground. Another subdivision of $375,000 to $400,000 homes caters to empty nesters with incomes of $150,000. It will have a community center for card games and parties. To discourage sales to families with boisterous children, it won't have sidewalks or pools. The subdivisions climb the scales of income, price, and amenities, topping out in gated ghettos of 7,000- to 8,000-square-foot homes and more counterfeit castles and golf clubs that cost $100,000 to join.

Straying beyond Windward Parkway on a still Saturday morning in April, before the spring's surge of mosquitoes and wet Georgia heat, I stopped at a garage sale at 8450 High Hampton Chase in the mid-scale subdivision of Hampton Hall. Having coffee on folding aluminum frame chairs among old clothes and toys of their seven- and four-year-old girls were Paul and Audra Feirstein. They had lived here for nineteen months.

They were moving, they said, yet again, this time to Hellertown, Pennsylvania. Not yet forty, Paul was leaving Johnson & Johnson for Schering-Plough to be a vice president. He grew up in Matawan, New Jersey, went to the University of Pittsburgh, and had begun work in Connecticut when he and Audra got married. Then, recruited company by company in the pharmaceutical industry, the Feirsteins moved from Connecticut to Delaware to Chicago to Alpharetta.

"As long as you're willing to be open to relocation and have a modicum of talent," Paul said, "you have an opportunity to travel the world." When moving, he had four priorities. "One, it's a community we can be comfortable in and meet folks with common interests. Two, there are kids of similar ages to ours. Three, the school system. I'm a firm believer in public schools. Four, she's got to be happy."

Meeting priorities one, two, and three meant Paul would drive sixty-eight miles to his new office in New Jersey. Audra, a pharmacist before she had children, was happy enough for now. But by the time the girls start middle school, she said, "I hope we'll find a place and just stay."

City Hall, the Chamber of Commerce, and real estate agents' Web sites contend that "Alpharetta" means "first city," formed from *alpha,* the first letter of the Greek alphabet, and *retta,* which they say is Greek for "city." But that's as much myth as the brand-new "Historic Downtown Alpharetta" the city is planning to build from scratch. More likely the name is a variation of Alfarata, an Indian maiden in a ballad—*The Indian Girl* or *Bright Alfarata*—composed in 1860. It was popular among Yankee and Confederate troops during the Civil War, who left themselves and the area unscathed because it had nothing to fight over or burn.

Alpharetta is, however, the first city of something else—of twenty-first-century Relovilles. Among communities with more than 25,000 people (and excluding those with churning populations of retirees and college students), Alpharetta has the highest concentration of Relos in America. The 2000 census found that 52 percent of Alpharetta's men, women, and children over five had come from another county or state or from abroad since 1995. Most were employee transferees. When a company moves a family to a Reloville, it is likely to move it again, and again—or a competitor swoops in to recruit and move them.

Beyond the Edge

Relovilles are the bedroom communities and headquarters, plants and branch offices, of a global diaspora of corporations that compete across continents and invest in one another's economies. Their antecedents were the suburbs that bloomed after World War II as industrial behemoths like General Electric, IBM, General Dynamics, Lockheed, and RCA began to dominate the economy. In moving beyond the Rust Belt and central cities, the companies spurred the development of mixed commercial and bedroom "urban villages," a phenomenon identified two decades ago by writers Christopher B. Leinberger and Charles B. Lockwood in the *Atlantic Monthly.*

Relos alight in scores of communities that have captured a disproportionate share of the growth in world commerce. By 1991, these urban villages—once-rural places like Plano, Texas; Naperville, Illinois; White Plains, New York; Rockville, Maryland; and Sunnyvale, California—had matured into what another social commentator, Joel Garreau of the *Washington Post,* called "edge cities." To meet Garreau's standard for an edge city, a town needed to host shopping areas, at least 5 million square feet of office space, and more jobs than residents. It needed to be perceived, by insiders and outsiders, as a self-contained city.

Relovilles, many younger than the edge cities, meet those criteria and then some. They cling to interstate exits and have a major airport nearby. By East and West Coast standards, their land is cheap—a big attraction to families and expanding employers—and at least 20 percent of their residents have moved in from outside their counties within the previous five years. Alpharetta is a distended edge city, offering 10 million square feet of office space and more than two jobs for every bed. Thirty-eight percent of its residents come from outside Atlanta's Fulton County.

Many more Relovilles have sprung up in the South and Southwest, beyond the peripheries of Dallas, Houston, Austin, Atlanta, Raleigh, and Charlotte, and also outside Denver, Chicago, Washington, Minneapolis, Indianapolis, and Columbus, Ohio. Relovilles have corralled new regional outposts for hardy graybeards like GE, IBM, Intel, and Lockheed for stars of the digital age like Microsoft, Google, Cisco Systems, and Apple, and for foreign contenders for world markets like Siemens of Germany, Nokia of Finland, Nielsen of the Netherlands, Lenovo of China, and Hyundai of South Korea.

These global companies and their migrating workers stoke most of suburbia's growth. Of the nation's one hundred fastest-growing counties from 2000 to 2005, five of the top ten—Loudoun County in Virginia, west of Washington, D.C.; Forsyth in Georgia, abutting the north Fulton County city of Alpharetta; Douglas County, south of Denver; Delaware County, north of Columbus; and Plano's Collin County, north of Dallas—also had the country's highest proportions of newcomers from out of town, many of them Relos.

They were affluent, too. Among the one hundred counties, Loudoun, Douglas, Forsyth, Delaware, and Collin ranked first, second, fourth, eighth, and tenth in median family income. They ranked in the top ten for residents who had bachelor's and graduate degrees and held management and professional jobs. These five counties—and a dozen more among the fastest-growing, including Denton (north of Dallas), Cherokee (north of Atlanta), and Scott (near Minneapolis)—have become young-money heirs of old-money Fairfield County, Connecticut; Westchester County, New York; Lake County, Illinois; the Philadelphia Main Line; and the North Shore of Boston.

For a population that the census has yet to classify, it seems a stretch to attribute the homogenization of these suburbs' homes and neighborhoods to Relos. Yet in the choices they make, Relos shape and define the communities as much as developers and politicians. They exert what economists call a multiplier effect on their local economies. By buying and selling homes every three or four years, re-landscaping, redecorating, and refurnishing them along the way, Relos generate many times more business than people who move to a town to stay.

In selecting their neighborhoods and homes, Relos seek sanctuaries of the familiar—another boon to builders who, like any savvy businessman, welcome the economies of scale, or lower production costs, that come with replicating a product en masse. By using the same floor plans, hardware, appliances, and materials, subdivision to subdivision, builders offer houses as predictable as a Big Mac and sell them for significantly less than custom houses.

Inside these Relo-defined homes, there will be a two-story foyer with a small office on the right, a small dining room on the left, and, farther back, a large open kitchen–family room. Upstairs, on one side of the entry to the bath in the parents' master suite, the mom has a big walk-in closet and the dad has a smaller closet across from hers. The kids' bedrooms, down the hall from the parents', are connected by a "Jack 'n' Jill" bathroom. Pricier homes have large and airy variations on a family room—called a keeping room or a great room—and in the back of the foyer a bowlegged pair of stairs to the second floor. In all but entry-level homes, the kitchen counters will be granite and the appliances stainless steel. Downstairs, there will be a "men's room" for a bar and a foosball table.

By buying new homes similar to those they leave, Relos concoct illusions of stability that allay the traumas of moving. In a study of mobile families, Raymond A. Noe at the University of Minnesota and Alison E. Barber at Michigan State University write, "Employees will be less willing to move to communities substantially different from their present community than they are to accept moves to communities substantially similar to their present community." James and Jane Lee, a couple in their forties, started out in small towns in Arkansas and had moved eight times, most recently to Roswell, Georgia, Alpharetta's southern-abutting neighbor. With each move, they have painted their living rooms a deep beige that is called, they swear, "saucy taco." "We've always taken a little bit of home everywhere we went," James said.

Common-denominator houses also suit Relo pocketbooks. Conventional houses sell faster than unconventional houses. Relos want houses they can sell fast so they can buy another one fast and hit the ground running in their next town, especially in towns where most buyers are other risk-averse Relos who want something they can settle into fast and sell fast when they, too, are called to move.

More than for well-anchored Americans, a home's value, as well as its prospects for quick sale, is critical to Relos' finances. In their thirties and forties, Relos haven't amassed savings enough for retirement and children's college funds. But with help from the economy, their houses become sizable nest eggs. Except during stretches of housing market turbulence like that of 2007 to 2009, Relos can count on their homes' value to rise. They can take their gains from a sale to make the down payment on a bigger and better house in the next town. When the kids go to college, they can take a bigger loan on the appreciated value of the house for tuitions or buy a smaller house and use the accumulated gains for tuitions.

Employers collaborate. To speed an employee's relocation, many companies, or the relocation companies they hire to manage their Relos' moves, buy their houses when they have trouble selling. When the time comes, they ask realtors to appraise the house and propose a price. If the Relo can't sell within sixty or ninety days for as much as the company proposes, the company or the relocation firm buys it and covers the Relo's loss.

Employers also influence the design of homes. They steer employees from homes with synthetic stucco, for example, because they're susceptible to water damage, and from homes with wet basements or unlicensed additions. In Alpharetta, one result has been a freeze on construction of homes with stucco siding and wider use of brick and cement-based clapboard.

Often, too, employers, discourage their Relos from buying homes more than ten or fifteen years old. In that way, they speed older neighborhoods' decline. Alpha Park, Alpharetta's oldest subdivision, built in the 1970s, has skidded from middle class to working class in a decade because of Relo flight. Alpha Park's houses, even though they're on large one-third-acre lots with three bedrooms, were selling for an average of $120,000 in 2007, less than half the $270,000 average in Alpharetta.

The importance of home values might explain why many Relovilles, more than towns with older and stable populations, zone out blue-collar subdivisions, apartment buildings, and mobile homes. One town's denser housing—say, fifty living units on an acre instead of another town's three or four single-family homes—requires higher property tax revenue to support additional police, fire, sewer, road maintenance, and other public services. Among other effects, more services can mean raising everyone's taxes, which can depress home prices.

Underlying homeowners' opposition is what William A. Fischel, an economist at Dartmouth College, calls his "homevoter hypothesis."

In *Homevoter Hypothesis: How Home Values Influence Local Government,* Fischel contends that homeowners will fight anything that might depress home values, such as a factory nearby, a landfill, or apartment houses. "They balance the benefits of local policies against the costs when the policies affect the value of their home," Fischel writes, "and they will tend to choose those policies that preserve or increase the value of their homes."

As these practices spread across like-minded and abutting Relovilles—like Alpharetta, Roswell, Silver Spring, and Duluth, north of Atlanta, or Plano, Frisco, Allen, and McKinney, north of Dallas—Paul A. Jargowsky, a professor of public policy at the University of Texas in Dallas, says they push the poor and the working class to other communities. The city of Alpharetta is typical. Of its 365 full-time employees in 2005, less than a third—112—lived in the city. Of its 74 police officers, only the chief and two others lived in town.

Driving north from his office, Jargowsky, who writes widely about geographic concentrations of wealth and poverty, enters Richardson, Texas, an early and faded Reloville of mostly thirty- and forty-year-old ranch houses. He turns north into Plano, a thriving Reloville on the west side of town, to the aging east side, similar to part of Richardson, and north toward upscale Frisco, Allen, and McKinney and their swirls of office parks and new subdivisions.

"These geographic patterns that have developed over time have consequences," Jargowsky said. "The more we separate ourselves out into small atomistic units, where nobody wants to take responsibility for the overall picture, the more we'll end up with endemic poverty." If he were an office worker in Reloville with a median U.S. family income of $50,000, who wanted a good school system and a safe place to live nearby, "I want to be able to buy a smaller house there. Or, if I don't have kids and don't care about education, I might want to buy a bigger house in a place with a really rotten school system. But actually I don't have that choice because they don't have the smaller houses in the places with the good school systems.

"There are lots of builders who see the need for small and energy-efficient and high-quality homes in suburbs. They try to build them, and city councils in suburbs often try to block them. I am serving as an expert witness on behalf of developers who want to build these units

and know they could sell them. We're not talking about guys who want
to put up shacks. These are guys who get awards for their designs and
energy efficiency and they use quality materials. They get blocked from
building these units and they get sued."

The isolation of rich communities from the less affluent has costs.
One is the commuting cost of workers—teachers, firemen, maids,
landscapers—that the rich communities rely on for services. "To have
a functioning community you do have to have people on a wide variety of income levels," Jargowsky said. "The presumption of people
who want to have their own little towns and exclude everybody below
$75,000 of household income is that they don't depend on those peo-
ple. But they do."

Donald Rolader, a fifth-generation Atlantan and a prominent zoning
lawyer, recalled that in 2000, the Herman Miller office furniture company
shut its plant in Roswell and moved to rural Cherokee County. "They said,
'None of our employees can afford to live here.' This place is elitist. We
have become so homogenous and multinational. 'Apartment' is an ugly
word here now. It's getting to where townhome is an ugly word. Our own
children can't afford to live in north Fulton County."

The isolation puts the poor out of sight—and out of mind. The city
of Roswell wanted to sell a prominently situated former post office to a
charity that serves the working poor, including many blacks and Hispanics. But the charity backed off when residents complained of seeing,
as one told a city council meeting, "some things that would not be pleas-
ant to look at."

Household Name

On a thirty-five-degree Saturday morning in January 2007, John
Wieland's office was a black Buick Rendezvous SUV, his in-box the
shelf of his dashboard, scattered with thirty or forty printouts of e-mails.
He dictated his responses to a Sony tape recorder, which his secretary
would later transcribe. As he handled each reply, he folded the letter in
half, so he would know he had seen it, and dispatched it to his out-box,
the floor of the passenger's side.

Wieland pulled out of the lot at the Olde Ivy at Vinings subdivision and away from the big sign at the side of the lot listing "John Wieland," "John Wieland Homes and Neighborhoods," "New Home Center," "JW Designs," "Wieland Financial Services," "CabinetCraft," "Wieland Realty Associates," and "Remodeling Specialists." Still working at seventy, Wieland is metropolitan Atlanta's biggest developer of housing for Relos. Once he sold the last of the Olde Ivy's 268 apartments and town houses, priced from $200,000 to $450,000, he would move the Wieland namesakes to the next development and make room for the leased offices and retail shops that will serve this compact, gated, clubhouse community just north of downtown.

Wieland is tall, straight, and patrician, a double for the Duke of Edinburgh, with a thin thatch of hair that used to be blond. He speaks with the unguarded assurance of a man who owns his universe and retains the flat *A* of his youth in the upper-crust suburbs of Shaker Heights, Ohio, near Cleveland, and Kenilworth, outside Chicago. Since 1979, he and his wife, Susan, have lived in the antithesis of his manicured subdivisions. Their sixty-eight-year-old home, which with a tax-appraised value of about $1 million is below that of some of the houses he builds, is just north of downtown Atlanta. It is wide, low, and big, stretching over 6,000 square feet, and is set off among 2.6 forested acres with a creek running by.

Though numbed by the devastation in real estate in the late 2000s, which bankrupted thousands of builders across the nation—the worst rout, he says, "since ever"—Wieland has done well building houses, more than thirty thousand of them around Atlanta and across the Southeast. Through the daily torrent of his real estate advertising and his and Sue's volunteer work, the Wieland name is as prominent around town as Hank Aaron and Coca-Cola. The *Chronicle of Philanthropy* ranked the Wielands forty-ninth among the nation's individual philanthropists in 2003. They gave away $16.5 million that year, including $12 million for additions to Atlanta's High Museum of Art. They have also given the city an eleven-unit shelter for homeless mothers.

In some quarters, Wieland is not so admired for the stamp he has put on the landscape of metropolitan Atlanta. He commands the bull-dozers that scrape away woodlands, fields, and farms to spread the lava of asphalt and rooftops fifty miles to the north of the city—halfway to Chattanooga. He and Atlanta's hundreds of other builders and developers have so choked the roads with traffic spilling in and out of their subdivisions that Atlanta has displaced all cities but San Francisco for long and grueling commutes.

For Wieland, such growth is a natural outcome of the economy's growth. His father was an advertising man for oil companies and for the Leo Burnett agency in Chicago, and he grew up among Relo pioneers. "We only moved once," he said, "but for the kids I grew up with, Shaker Heights and Kenilworth were just Alpharetta forty years earlier. I felt I had an affinity for their circumstances and what they were looking for. We're much more diversified now, but these are my customers. These are people that are affluent and want something better." He attended Amherst College in Massachusetts, then, after a year at Procter & Gamble in Cincinnati, Harvard Business School. Newly married to Sue, a teacher, he left a job at General Foods and moved to Carrollton, Georgia, west of Atlanta, where he went into the building supply business with a Harvard roommate whose family owned feed and seed stores. In 1970, after five years, he started a business of his own. "I talked to a lot of people, which is what you do when you're making a decision, and they told me Atlanta was ready to get going," he said. "I believed them and became a self-taught homebuilder."

Wieland and another Atlanta builder-developer, Jim Cowart, spotted the nascent Relo market when they were starting out in the early 1970s. Cowart was building ranch houses then. "A lady came in my office and said she had seven kids and needed a lot of space," he said. "Her husband worked for 3M, which was moving them here. They could spend $28,800. That wouldn't pay for a ranch on a big enough lot for seven kids.

"So I said, 'I could give you more space with a two-story house. I could put a box on top of a box.'" A new neighborhood model was born. "That was the beginning of what we referred to as a Five, Four, and a Door—five windows above and four below with a door in the center—that was Atlanta subdivisions' cookie-cutter standard well into the 1980s.

Wieland was just starting out in 1973 when Atlanta-born historian

Daniel J. Boorstin warned of communities becoming "a commodity, a product to be sold at a profit." "It was the paternalism of the market place," Boorstin wrote, "the suburban developer, unlike the small-town booster, seldom intended to live in the community he was building." Wieland went on to become a master of commodified segmentation. In 2007 he was completing a gated, neo-Georgian subdivision of $450,000 to $550,000 two- and three-story town houses close to downtown Alpharetta, called Academy Park. "Who would buy these houses?" I asked the real estate agent there. "Retirees," she said. But they had a lot of stairs, a disincentive for old buyers. "Yes, but these are for early retirees—fifty-five, sixty."

Compared with tract and starter-home builders, Wieland and Cowart specialized in semi-custom, highly detailed, move-up homes evoking the Georgian and Federal styles of the colonies. As a semi-custom builder, Wieland uses standardized floor plans. Alongside one another, the houses don't look cloned because he alternates the plans from house to house and adds decorative and architectural touches like dormers and columns. His prices range from $200,000 for condos and smaller town houses to over $1 million. In the wavering market of 2007 and 2008, with the Atlanta area stuck with twice the usual inventory of unsold new homes, Wieland's higher-priced homes were still moving.

Still, Wieland and generic developers get more than their share of criticism for the look of suburbia. Local planners and politicians, not developers, write the restrictive zoning codes favoring detached single-family homes and discouraging denser, multi-family housing. Fulton County's and the State of Georgia's chronically slow road building and mass transit authorities don't help, either. Wieland favors a wider and denser mix of housing. Indeed, he makes more money building twenty homes on an acre instead of one. "But it's impossible politically," he said. "If you talk to the city staff, or if you talk to the mayor, he'll tell you he's concerned. And then you go to get property zoned, and they're not concerned. Because they're really concerned about getting reelected, and the way they get reelected is by not offending people." Echoing William Fischel, he added, "The way to avoid offending people is by making sure that nothing damages property values. And one way you do that is to make sure you don't allow any affordable housing."

Class distinctions are an obstacle, too. "If we really had affordable homes for the firefighters," he said, "neighbors think, 'They're going to bring their kids, and they're probably going to have more kids per household than we've got, and they may not look like our kids, and then our kids are going to have to go to school with their kids.' It's an insidious kind of thing."

Of course, by building for Relos, Wieland also found he could generate more business than he could with people who expected to stay in one house for thirty or forty years. "These transferees want instant neighborhoods, friends, activities," he said. "That's great for the new home business because they gravitate to a new house as opposed to buying a resale house in an established neighborhood.

"I think if I were to move, I'd want to buy a new house in a new neighborhood," he said. "Presumably the guy that's going to buy the house next door is going to have two kids, too. We're going to have a lot in common. It's just an easier way to make friends than to move into an established neighborhood, where everybody has their patterns. It goes to the schools; it goes to the churches that everything's new. It's just easier."

He began including clubhouses and recreational facilities in his subdivisions. "We were in the early part of that trend and in many ways created the trend, along with people like Cowart. We created these places that seem special and safe," he said, "and where your transferees knew they were going to meet other people who kind of looked like them and where they would be comfortable."

Without old-boy status of long, local connections, Relos look for prestige in their houses, he said. "If you have a big new bathroom, you feel better about yourself because you wake up in the morning with an affirming experience of your success. You don't think about it consciously, but you know in the back of your mind that not everybody has a bathroom that looks like this bathroom. It's almost like there's a checklist—items you can do to your house that prove your affluence.

"One of my theories is, you move to Atlanta and you want to impress your relatives. When your relatives from Chicago come visit you,

you want to show them 'grand.' You want to show them this big expan-
sive house that flows from room to room while they're living cooped up
in Winnetka. They've got a very nice home in Winnetka, but you know
it doesn't have granite and it doesn't flow from room to room." In Winnetka, he said, "you don't have a keeping room," the Reloville adapta-
tion of a nineteenth-century farmhouse's room off the kitchen, where a
family would eat and sleep when other rooms got too cold.

Relos differ from most home buyers in another way. "They know
they're going to be moving again," Wieland said. "So they're really focused on property they know they can sell. One of the interesting phe-
nomena about them is they're building substantial personal equity over
the years as they move.

"One of the attractions of these new neighborhoods, and especially
of buying in them early, is the economic upside." In new subdivisions,
he said, home values rise most sharply until the point when the subdivision's construction is nearly complete. "If you're an early purchaser," he
said, "you're a little bit of a pioneer."

To keep prices down, Wieland resorts to illusions of permanence,
like bricks that are thinner than standard bricks and would let rain soak
through without sufficient waterproofing. "What's happened in housing," he said, "is a little bit of fakey-fakey."

Well into the recession, Relo-rimmed cities with high concentrations of global companies—Atlanta, Dallas, Houston, Denver, Charlotte, Raleigh—were suffering far less from unemployment, plunging
home prices, and foreclosures than fast-growing areas around cities like
Miami, Tampa, Phoenix, and Las Vegas with few global employers.
"Expansion plans have been shelved," said H. Cris Collie, who for decades, until the start of 2009, was executive director of the Worldwide
Employee Relocation Council, the association of companies that employ
Relos and those that move them. To protect markets that employers spent
decades building, he said, "You don't bail out. You just put your expansion
plans on hold."

But Reloville was slammed in other ways. In the decelerating market of 2007 and 2008, Wieland, like builders everywhere, choked on
unsold homes. Nationwide, in the year since I had visited him at Olde

Ivy, 76 percent fewer homes were built nationwide than in the peak year of 2005, and Wieland was stuck with more than four hundred completed and half-finished homes. He parked his bulldozers, laid off fifty-nine workers, and stopped work on the unfinished homes until buyers committed to taking them.

He abandoned some loftier dreams, too. He had cleared and graded land across from the High Museum of Art in resurgent midtown Atlanta for a spectacular $350 million, twenty-story building of ninety-six condos, starting at $2 million each and designed by modernist British architect David Chipperfield. The Wielands, pushing into their seventies and itching for a place where they could walk to restaurants, were to take a showplace apartment for themselves. But in the collapse of the credit market, the project lost its financing, so Wieland suspended construction for at least eighteen months. He also suspended a $5 million gift for a new ethics center at Emory University's Candler School of Theology that was to have immortalized him with his name on the frieze. In January 2009, he said, "The end of last year was the most miserable of my life."

Wieland has witnessed a lot of recessions, but nothing as brutal—or sea changing—as this one. "When we pull out," he said, "we'll have an entirely different housing industry." The recession and its concomitant jolts—$100 to fill the tank of an SUV, $1,000 month to heat and air-condition a Reloville house—had eclipsed his four decades–old vision for housing Atlanta's global employees. Those exurban palaces, many on lots of an acre or more, their soaring, two-story atriums and family rooms, their great rooms, keeping rooms, media rooms, fitness rooms, their three- and four-car garages: "They're gone," he said, for at least a decade and maybe for good. Newcomer Relos were shunning departing Relos' big houses in far out Relovilles, and their subdivision homeowners associations were shuttering their stately gatehouses. Sumptuous new golf courses, he predicted, would revert to wildflowers and scrub. "They'll get the sheep out there," he said.

As demand and prices for homes retreated, Relo family math, founded on the early 2000s' annual home price increases of 20 percent, could no longer make piggy banks of houses. "We're in the process of seeing a total sea change in how people are looking at housing," Wieland said. "There's no assurance you're going to be able to put that house on the market and make money. People have gone there and done that. They don't need as much gaudy. It's no longer 'get the biggest house you can get.' It's 'get what you need.'"

Historic Downtown

Long before John Wieland began carving up Alpharetta and the Relos arrived, there was a lethargic old downtown Alpharetta. On five or six blocks are City Hall, a Methodist, a Baptist, and a Presbyterian church, an undertaker, a gas station, four restaurants, a flower shop, two beauty salons, a bridal shop, a decorator, a fitness center, a photographer's studio, a furniture store, and a variety store. The downtown has lost traffic to a mall and large retail chains out by the subdivisions. Most of it is being scraped away and replaced by a new yet "historic" downtown derived not from Alpharetta's extinct cotton culture but from the hardier precedents of colonial Boston and Charleston.

Among the few old-timers downtown who witnessed Alpharetta's transformation into a Reloville were two genteel Georgian ladies—Frances Byers, seventy-five, who owned the Cotton House furniture store near the corner of Milton and Main, and Dimp Phillips, then eighty-six, owner of Phillips Variety Store, half a block down Milton from Main—and old boy Bob Burgess, owner of the Alpharetta Bargain Store on Main, just south of the center. They had done their own psychoanalysis of the Relos moving through town.

Byers, who died in a fall at her home months after I saw her in 2005, was rumored to be Alpharetta's richest woman. I found her hobbled by diabetes and a broken ankle far in the back of her store, in a purely functional office with a 1950s Formica-topped desk, an electric typewriter, and beige metal file cabinets. "I grew up in a little community halfway between Norcross and Doraville," she said. "I got married to a boy from here. We started in the furniture business in 1953 with a little store in Roswell and then another on Highway 9.

"In 1972, here in Alpharetta, I saw that Mr. Wills had placed a For Sale sign on this building. I agreed to buy it. A few days later I stopped in to see Mr. Wills, who was sitting with a group of men. 'These men have offered me $20,000 more than I told you that you could have the building for,'" she said Wills told her. He explained that he would give her $20,000 to drop their agreement. "I said, 'No, I'll just go and buy it.' He said, 'Fine.' He was a perfect gentleman."

Then she bought other buildings downtown, including the one housing the Masonic Lodge. "I assembled little pieces of real estate and I started renting off this and that," she said. However long she had been there, she was unsentimental about the downtown and was cheered by the city's plan to plow it over and build anew. "You can't follow in somebody else's footsteps all the time because their footsteps get too deep," she said. "You have to make some new steps. Old towns die, like old people and old trees. There's not much bad about cutting down an old tree. Sometimes that's the right thing to do."

But Relos baffled her. In her store, she sold reproduction antiques, most of solid cherry and mahogany. "I don't want a lot of flaky boards," she said. Relos seemed to have money enough, but not much respect for a durable table or chair. "Here's what you have in the furniture world," she said. "There are the people who know, the people who don't know, and the people who don't care. People who know, some come in here. People who don't know, they hire decorators. Decorators have all their sources for furniture, so they don't need my furniture store. Those who don't know and don't care buy imported. The don't-care people don't care if it's good or not. It's temporary. I see these big trucks in front of these big houses, and you wouldn't even dream of having that kind of furniture in that house. They don't know any better."

Down the street, the front window of Phillips Variety displayed a half dozen dusters—thin cotton smocks for women to wear when they clean house. "They're an old-timey thing," said Ermine "Dimp" Phillips, the mother by marital proxy of Georgia 400, the highway from Atlanta to Alpharetta and points north that her husband, an engineer, laid out. She had owned her store for more than fifty years. On the counter she had an old Burroughs cash register and an electric calculator the size of a shoe box. Mrs. Phillips gift wrapped and made keys. Across the store, in wide, shallow, tabletop bins, she stocked sewing materials, glassware, lace handkerchiefs, baby supplies, socks, slippers, work gloves, stationery, candles, artificial flowers, some hardware like hammers and pliers, and teddy bears and small toys. No one entered the store during the midday hour that I was there.

"I carry a lot of little bitty things," she said. "Kids come here and get little things. But parents want big things." She said Wal-Mart and the stores near the subdivisions where Relos shop had drained most of the business from downtown. "I don't have no business now," she said. "I'm just sitting here for something to do."

"The new people in town are from up North," Phillips said. "That's about all that's here. A lot of them, I've been told, you go in their houses, and there's no furniture. I say to them, 'You don't think you'd like to go back north?' 'No, no, we like it here.'"

A "Going Out of Business" sign had been stretched above the door of the fifty-year-old Alpharetta Bargain Store, which Burgess, a longtime banker and prominent property owner, inherited from his father. The store had one saleswoman and no customers. It was cavernous, with a floor of worn, all-weather gray carpet and barely navigable with racks of clothes displayed under rows of fluorescent lights running the length of the ceiling.

In Alpharetta, Burgess said, "bargain" in the store's name once meant new clothes for a low price. But to Alpharetta's new population, he said, it meant "used"—items of little interest to affluent Relos. "I think everybody likes to show off a little bit," he said. "What you drive, where you live might be important for a business reason. Companies strive to be perfect. They're not human. People strive to achieve the perfection the company wants."

The Planner

Steve Beecham is a Georgia-born ole boy who grew up in Roswell and prospered as a "connector," he says. Whatever anyone needed—a plumber, a lawyer, a job, a real estate agent—they called Steve Beecham. He would offer phone numbers and run interference by calling ahead. Sometime later, the plumber or the lawyer or the real estate agent would repay the favor by referring someone who needed a mortgage to Beecham.

Bald, tanned, lightly bearded, in his mid-forties, Beecham hotdogs up his long, rutted, and tree-shrouded drive in his blinding yellow Hummer, the name of his firm, Home Town Mortgage, painted in black on the sides. He brings a Heineken to the patio by the pool of his new, custom-built, mock Mount Vernon. Asked who runs Alpharetta, he unfolds his cell phone and starts calling off his programmed numbers—someone in City Hall, a developer, a zoning lawyer. "Diana Wheeler," he says. "For some reason, nobody crosses her."

Wheeler's official title is director of community development, but she wields an influence over the shape and life of Alpharetta that matches, if on an infinitely smaller canvas, that of Robert Moses over New York City. Her own role model is George Edgar Merrick, who in the 1920s developed Coral Gables, Florida, the gated, affluent Miami suburb of 44,000 that calls itself "City Beautiful" but is caricatured for restrictive covenants like banning pet snakes and prohibiting parking of residents' trucks— even spotless, new $50,000 pickups—unless they're tucked in a garage with the door down. As it happens, Wheeler served as planner of Coral Gables before coming to Alpharetta.

At city council meetings, Wheeler is the decorous, mid-forties blonde in a beige suit sitting a couple of rows back in the audience facing the mayor, Arthur Letchas, the six council members, the city attorney, and the city manager. The council and Mayor Letchas, a retired high school teacher and coach, are low-tax, high-property-value conservatives, officially nonpartisan, who nearly always vote unanimously. They usually run unopposed after their first elections, rarely with more than 10 percent of eligible residents turning out to vote. They get knocked out of their seats only for personal transgressions, such as the member who in 2007 lost re-election after police charged her with driving under the influence.

The council argues at length about the police and park budgets, roads and development. But it is Wheeler who defines Alpharetta. When she faces the council, she is unflappable and unassailably informed. When builders confront her over their appeals for variances, the council might modify her recommendations but rarely rejects them. She gores local oxen—old boys like Beecham—but they put up with her because they all come out winners. During most of her tenure, their property values have climbed.

Wheeler is not sure what to make of Alpharetta. "This is really like a world city molded into a small town trying to be what a whole bunch of diverse people want it to be, and I'm trying to figure out what that is." She is surer about what she hopes it will be. She grew up in Boston, sipping sodas on porches, and went to Columbia University, where she studied urban planning and architecture. In planning, she envisions the timeless hometowns that she caught as a late–baby boom child in the waning days of *Ozzie and Harriet* and *Leave It to Beaver*. These Hollywood fantasies, she says, have become frozen in myth and the model for people without roots, in places without roots like Alpharetta. "We all watched 1950s television," Wheeler said. "It's all part of my memory. It's part of your memory. And neither one of us lived there. We were all brainwashed to believe that's what the idyllic town was like. Even if you don't believe it's true, you recognize it when you see it, and when you see it, it conjures up a good feeling."

Relos reinforce Americans' shared myths with their preferences for homogenous towns, with the same housing, the same chain stores and restaurants, the same activities for kids, the same diversions. As houses become prosaic commodities, Wheeler said, "we don't have any sense of loyalty to the house or the community.

"You can take the pieces of the puzzle and rearrange them, but they're the same pieces. That's what lets them move around without having a jarring experience and know that their children are not going through a trauma because they've been totally uprooted. 'Look, we've come here. We've never been to Georgia, but here's the mall, here's the park, here's the school, here's the house. Your bedroom is right down the hall from your sister's bedroom and the kitchen is right over here.' There's a lot of comfort to it."

Once Relos reach a critical mass of a town's population, they thwart its tendencies to differentiate itself, stir some pride, and give residents reason to stay. "To have a real long-term community," Wheeler said, "you have to short-circuit the trend of transience. People have a need to have connections. If they find it, they stay. If there's no compelling reason to stay, they go."

Wheeler faces a special challenge in distinguishing Alpharetta because it lacks precedents to build upon. The whole terrain, in the northern reaches of Atlanta's Fulton County, was little more than pasture and cotton fields until the 1970s. For historical reference, the Alpharetta branch of the county library had only a couple of large yellow envelopes of newspaper clips and a single book about the town, a small collection of a former weekly newspaper writer's columns.

The city's downtown forms the hub of roads radiating to towns and hamlets like Roswell, Crabapple, Birmingham, and Canton, but not a single edifice or landmark dates to the city's incorporation in 1857 or for another half century. Near the downtown, the Alpharetta Historical Society occupies a handsome, white-clapboard Victorian home that is itself a Relo. It was built in Roswell and brought to Alpharetta on a truck. Old homes near the principal intersection in town are routinely scraped away to make room for stores, roads, and parking lots.

So it is Wheeler's mission to invent a history. Her plan envisions a brand-new, neo-Georgian, "historic" downtown that would become Alpharetta's "premier destination." The intent, says the plan, "is to make a Historic Downtown Alpharetta attractive for shopping, living, working, recreation and entertainment by developing a mix of uses in a pedestrian-friendly environment."

But there's reason to wonder whether the new downtown will appeal to Alpharetta's churning population of Relos any more than the sleepy existing downtown. Adjacent to new subdivisions for miles around the downtown, developers continue to install upscale shopping strips with many of the dining, shopping, and entertainment features that Wheeler would put downtown. Alpharetta must also compete with a proliferation of New Urbanist developments—suburban communities with downtowns and mixed housing that, like downtown Alpharetta, evoke the same myths and historical illusion that Wheeler admires.

A half hour drive from downtown Alpharetta, in Cumming, was the new, eventually 600-home community of Vickery with a retail area, nostalgia-infused townhomes crowding the sidewalks, and more detached homes beyond them. "It dilutes what we have," Wheeler said. "We don't want subdivisions becoming mini-cities."

Alpha Park

Alpha Park is a seven-block subdivision of small ranch and split-level houses. Some houses are as prim and buttoned down as those of most Alpharetta subdivisions and some are not. Downwind from an adjoining parking lot for 130 Fulton County school buses, Alpha Park is boxed in by four busy roads, two too precarious for Roger Scott to cross in his motorized wheelchair. It is just beyond the southeastern corner of downtown.

Alpha Park's days are surely numbered. Built in the 1970s, it is limping through the last stage of its life cycle, a phase characteristic of older Reloville subdivisions. In 1993, when Roger and Barbara Scott moved in, the last Relo owners were leaving, and most of the houses were becoming rentals. When I last saw the Scotts, in April 2008, Barbara was seventy-one and looking no older than Roger, who was sixty-two.

Barbara wears her black and gray hair like a helmet, short and pressed close to her skull. She and Roger have seven children from previous marriages, including a daughter who lives in another Atlanta suburb. Barbara never had to work, but with the collapse of Roger's health and the toll of his medical bills, she was supplementing their Social Security income with a part-time job as a supermarket cashier.

Roger has the lush white beard and gregarious affect of Santa Claus. He makes light of his ailments, which include diabetes, end-stage kidney failure, and a bad pancreas. He goes in for dialysis every Tuesday, Thursday, and Saturday. "If I'm on fire," he said, "I can walk thirty-five feet. If I'm not on fire I can walk twelve."

Until he stopped driving, Scott was a fixture at Alpharetta City Council meetings, inveighing against official waste and neglect. "If you're going to take my tax money," he would say, "give me something in return." To the city, he said, "I'm a barbed-wire enema," which perhaps exaggerates the council's general view of him as a pain and a windbag.

Life Cycle: *In 1993, Roger Scott and his wife moved to Alpha Park, a subdivision built in the 1970s in Alpharetta, one of Georgia's first Relovilles. The emphasis on newer homes leaves older subdivisions like Alpha Park in the lurch. Most Relos want the bigger homes farther north in Fulton County, so most houses in Alpha Park are now rentals.*

Like the former residents of Alpha Park, the Scotts were Relos. Roger left Oklahoma City after high school and went into computer system and software installation. For twenty years starting in St. Petersburg, Florida, he and Barbara moved sixteen times—to Raleigh, Chattanooga, Little Rock, and Columbus, South Carolina, among other cities and towns, and sometimes without the comforts and perks afforded most Relos. "In Columbus, we had seven children in a two-room apartment," Barbara said. "We did what we had to do for his job."

Most of that time Scott worked for Wang Laboratories, which made big mainframe computers that were later displaced by small desktop computers. He installed central computer systems for the states of Tennessee, Arkansas, North Carolina, South Carolina, and New Jersey and for the Tennessee Valley Authority. Wang sent him to Atlanta in 1993 to take on a contract with the federal government, and the Scotts bought their house on Jon Scott Drive. But Wang's heyday was over, and the company would later disappear. The Scotts decided to stay in town. Roger found work in the parts department of a Radio Shack, but left with his declining health.

Soon after moving in, Scott became president of Alpha Park's homeowners association, but with Relo owners going and renters moving in it soon folded. He tried to organize a residents' association that would appeal to both renters and owners, and that failed, too. But then, freed of community covenants and regimentation, Alpha Park unwound. It humanized. Homes became a cacophony of self-expression, with the most exuberant being the Scotts'.

Up the gravel driveway on the right, parked in front of the garage, is a vintage Jeep. On the hood of the Jeep is a power lawn mower. Barbara put the lawn mower there so Roger could work on it without stooping. The house, with earth-toned wood siding and a roof pitched high over the living room, sits about one hundred feet back from the road, up a slight incline and in the shadow of a thick ceiling of trees.

The Scotts have planted the front yard with perennials and ivy. Scattered about are a wishing well, a windmill, and a sitting area with a fireplace—all features a controlled Relo subdivision would prohibit. "Everything you see in a pot was started by my wife," Scott said. "She started three peach trees from seeds we ate."

He did not invite me into the house. "I've got egg-laying birds in there," he said. The living room is an aviary for parrots. "I have seven sun conures, two yellow-crested cockatoos, five cockatiels, one budgie, one red-tailed African gray. Whenever they get upset, they won't sit on the eggs." He makes a little money selling the eggs.

Alpha Park can't go on much longer with people like the Scotts doing any old thing with their American Dream. Developers are hovering. Scott said one went door-to-door offering owners $250,000 for their houses. He wanted to take the $250,000 and run, but others balked. Just across Devore Road, one of the four roads bordering Alpha Park, a builder has begun a cluster of fifty-six town houses, an inviting setting for newlywed Relos and Relos whose kids have moved on.

3. The Company

Thank you, and good evening, everyone. It's great to be back in San Francisco—one of my favorite places in the world. I had the good fortune of living here during the 1980s and vowed I would never leave. Of course, plans change, and I've actually moved to four different cities since. My daughter is with me today . . . and she would tell you that every time her dad came home from work and said, "Kids, we have something to talk about" . . . it always meant another move.
—Michael L. Eskew, chairman and chief executive officer,
United Parcel Service, 2006

United Parcel Service of America, Inc., was the country's second-largest private employer in 2007 after Wal-Mart, having surpassed McDonald's and General Motors, and among the largest employers of Relos after the federal government. Its workers drove one hundred thousand vans, trucks, and motorcycles enameled with UPS's trademarked dung brown and nearly six hundred brown-tailed planes to circumnavigate the globe bringing 15 million packages and envelopes five days a week to 193 countries and territories.

Off a lushly groomed road winding through the Glenlake Office Park in Sandy Springs just north of Atlanta, I could barely make out the drive into the dimly lighted commuter garage of UPS's world headquarters. Beyond the garage, spanning a deep ravine beneath a canopy of hickories and poplars, a low-slung office building of unpainted concrete slabs formed sandwiches of glass and the cubicles of 3,000 employees, mostly executives and managers, of UPS's workforce of 428,000, including 67,000 outside the United States.

At noon on a casual Friday, waves of employees, none with beards or mustaches or visible tattoos or piercings other than one in the lobe of each ear, all in tightly tucked blouses and shirts (suits and ties for men—no sports coats—the other days) spilled from elevators and stairways into a sunny 650-seat cafeteria with counters and carousels of varied and good-enough food to discourage treks to the restaurants outside. High-level managers, who share secretaries and answer their own phones, got no special treatment at lunch, no executive dining room or attendants. No one called anyone "Mister" or "Miz."

Few of the managers streaming through the cafeteria started out in Atlanta, and few would stay for very long. In normal times, before the economy's upheavals starting in 2007 had put relocations on hold, the company moves twelve hundred to thirteen hundred of its thirty thousand managers a year, usually for promotions. Thus one in five works at their current location for less than five years, and most make at least three or four moves over twenty or twenty-five years. As they reach their mid-forties and early fifties, the executive pyramid thins, and promotion to vice president and to the top-stratum, twelve-member Management Committee of the chief executive and senior vice presidents becomes a game of musical chairs. Those left standing might be relocated again, but in lateral moves to the sidelines. Or they retire or quit.

At UPS employees are a team—"UPSers"—who play for "Big Brown," or, in the view of detractors among the 240,000 loaders, sorters, package handlers, mechanics, and drivers represented by the International Brotherhood of Teamsters, for "Nanny UPS" and as anonymous cogs of a "Big Brown Machine." Every step that workers take, every package they label, sort, and deliver is digitized, weighed, and recorded. Drivers are drilled on how to lift and stack packages, how to get quickly in and out of a truck, how to walk (briskly, without slipping), how to carry the ignition key to save time restarting the truck. They must meet the Driver Appearance Standards, leaving, for example, only the collar button of their brown shirts unfastened.

Probably no major company uses more data from time-and-motion analysis to promote worker safety, on the one hand, and to maximize worker performance, on the other. Apart from the weather and traffic congestion, UPS leaves nothing to chance. Drivers, paid an average of $75,000 a year, carry a proprietary, state-of-the-art electronic clipboard—a brown, GPS-equipped Delivery Information Acquisition Device. In plotting routes to customers, the DIAD avoids time-wasting left turns and steers drivers to gas stations on the right of the road. It knows the location of packages and pinpoints where to deliver them—to what entrance of an office building, to what floor. When the customer taking delivery signs the screen, the device matches the signature with one it has stored. Collected from hub to hub, district to district, the DIAD's data help UPS set goals for workers and award stock and cash bonuses to the supervisors. They also help UPS spot managers who are ready to move up.

Relocation, like time-and-motion analysis and the egalitarian uniforms and cafeteria lines, is a pillar of a corporate culture built on promotion from within. Seventy-eight percent of the vice presidents and nine of the twelve members of the Management Committee started out in nonmanagement positions—as drivers or as college students working nights part-time sorting and loading packages. They master UPS's "340 Methods" of job performance and move up by moving out, to supervisor at one location, and to local manager, district manager, regional director at others.

Another cultural pillar is employee—primarily management—control of the company that insulates it from Wall Street raiders and meddlers. Like a few other prominent companies, including Warren Buffett's Berkshire Hathaway, Google, the *New York Times,* and the *Washington Post,* UPS issues two classes of common stock: two-thirds of its stock is Class B, which is traded on the New York Stock Exchange. Investors in the Class B stock get one vote per share. The remaining third is Class A stock, which has the same value as Class B but is owned by UPS employees and traded within the company. It confers ten votes per share, easily enough to rebuff investors who would challenge management prerogatives and executive succession.

John F. Saunders, vice president for human resources and a veteran Relo, was having soup and a salad in the cafeteria. He started out as a driver in Manhattan. "To get to the next level, you had to relocate," he said. "We were sent to Raleigh. We had an eighteen-month-old and a brand-new baby." He was moved again in two years to Coral Springs, Florida. There he was promoted to another job but one close enough to let him stay in the same house for seven years. He was sent on to Rockland County, New York, for a year and a half and then to Atlanta where with another promotion he could become a senior vice president and member of the Management Committee.

Gesturing at the lunching workers, he said, "We have a discussion. 'Are you ready to relocate?' He says yes or no. If he says he can't, I'm not going to put him on our Ready to Promote list." Discussions about moves abroad are more probing. Managers and their partners, most often wives, are invited to a "spousal interview" with a human resources officer. If the spouse is reluctant to move, promotions don't stop, but they can be slowed. Norman Black, the head of public relations, explained, "Relocation is just a tool of our culture. The company is committed to exposing you to a lot of different jobs." Thus top executives in Atlanta can be expected to know the world's airports, bridges, and roads. They can marshal resources fast to route packages through a tsunami.

UPS is itself a Relo. At nineteen in 1907, James E. Casey started delivering messages by bicycle around Seattle. He added packages and bought small Model T Ford vans, "package cars" he called them, that he painted brown. He expanded down the West Coast into California, and at the dawn of the Great Depression, in 1930, he moved the company to New York City, then the headquarters of corporate America. In 1975, UPS joined companies like IBM, PepsiCo, American Airlines, and JC Penney that were fleeing New York's congestion and high costs, and settled in Greenwich, Connecticut.

Within a decade, however, New York's corporate exiles had driven home prices in Greenwich's Fairfield County so high that UPS managers were resisting promotions to move there or putting up with hour-long, stop-and-start commutes to lower-rent Danbury. So in 1991, UPS bailed out of Greenwich and began building the current home in Sandy Springs. More than six hundred of eight hundred managers and staff accepted the company's offer to relocate them there and to swallow the costs of their move.

For UPS management, the rationale for the move was incontestable. It would position the company at a crossroads of the global economy. Atlanta, the capital of the booming New South, had abundant cheap land for expansion, easy access to three intersecting interstate highways and to an airport that would become the world's busiest. Employees found housing that cost half as much as in Fairfield County. They could take the proceeds from homes they sold there to trade up for something fancier—what they called "wow houses." Even the more frugal among them, who might otherwise have bought cheaper houses and saved the gains from Connecticut, joined in. If they didn't pour their gains into the new homes, the Internal Revenue Service would sock them with the capital gains tax. Middle-level UPSers became Atlanta's new landed gentry.

Later, in 1997, Congress changed the law. It exempted couples who had owned a house for at least two years from taxes on up to $500,000 in gains and up to $250,000 for single sellers. UPSers were subject to taxes on gains above those ceilings, but they could spend the limited gains, tax-free, on whatever they liked—another house, tuitions, retirement, boats, or SUVs for their three-car garages. Congress added yet another break of special interest to Relos. It exempted sellers whose employers moved them from the two-year ownership provision. As long as employers kept moving Relos, however often, and home prices kept rising—as they did into 2007—Relos collected windfall upon windfall.

Two years later, in 1999, UPS employees reaped another bonanza. The company was privately owned then by employees and retirees. It wanted to buy businesses that would help it expand in the global economy. To pay for the acquisitions, management needed a publicly traded stock.

On November 10, a 72-degree Indian summer day on Wall Street, UPS launched the New York Stock Exchange's biggest initial public offering ever of its Class B stock. It collected $5.5 billion from selling 109 million shares—10 percent of the company—for $50 a share. By the end of the day, investors had driven the stock to $68. It has drifted since, rarely exceeding $80. But veteran UPS loaders, sorters, drivers, and managers— their retirement accounts loaded with once-untradable UPS stock— suddenly had six- and seven-figure jackpots to save or spend.

Atlanta shared in the spoils from the UPS invasion of flush Yankees. In coming to town, the company helped reverse the regional damage from the 1990–91 recession. General Motors abandoned an assembly plant, the military contractor Lockheed in Marietta laid off thousands of highly paid workers, and Eastern Airlines, based in Atlanta, shut down. Area home sales plunged to half their peak in 1989.

Rich UPSers came along and colonized new gated subdivisions in Alpharetta, Roswell, and Duluth, sweeping up showplaces with media rooms, patio kitchens, and master bedroom suites bigger than a floor of bedrooms in Fairfield County. They bought seventy-five homes in the opulent St. Ives subdivision, rescuing it from probable receivership, and twenty others in even swankier Country Club of the South, home of chief executives, players for the Falcons and Braves, and various celebrities like Whitney Houston and her then-husband, Bobby Brown.

UPSers became celebrities. One local Croesus, Ronald G. Wallace, started as a delivery-truck driver in Idaho. He became a Relo and amassed a fortune in UPS stock as he rose to head of international operations and member of the Management Committee. Wallace bought a twenty-acre property on the rural fringe of Alpharetta. He retired at fifty-eight after thirty-seven years and built a 28,000-square-foot fantasy house with a central courtyard and two large wings. One wing housed Wallace's recreation of the O.K. Corral in Tombstone, Arizona, scene of Wyatt Earp's gunfight in 1881. The other housed his collection of cars. One was a police cruiser. Wallace bought it to use in his second career as an Alpharetta police officer. He won an award for nabbing drunk drivers.

Relocation has moved beyond that golden age when Alpharetta bloomed with its first Tara. It has become routine. Serial relocation is baked into the culture of global titans like UPS, Coca-Cola, Procter & Gamble, General Electric, ExxonMobil, and IBM. It is essential to the growth of the newer generation like Intel, Microsoft, and Apple. But the corporate model for relocation is shifting. With the real estate bust of 2007–9, Relos could no longer count on building their nest eggs with each move. But many employers do at least protect them from losses: UPS wants them working in their new posts, not waiting around to sell a house. So the company turns to relocation management firms, part of a new industry that specializes in facilitating Relos' moves. If the Relo can't sell within a month or two for as much as he paid, the Relo firm buys the house and bets that, in time, it will at least break even.

But robbed of the real estate incentive to move, some once-willing Relos try to stay put. They have aging parents nearby. The children have adjusted well to school. The spouse would have to abandon her own career. Their doubts weigh on UPS. "We are hearing more noise than ever before from employees who are reluctant to relocate," John Saunders of UPS said. "Both the husband and wife have careers. Even if there are not two careers, they want to be close to their families for social support."

To keep their Relo pipelines flowing, employers dig deeper into their ranks for candidates and seduce those going abroad with perks like luxury cars, a housekeeper, a nanny, first-class travel, and subsidies for housing and tuitions. UPS also goes to some lengths to avoid the costs and disruption of moving a manager who then quits or asks to be moved back. "We might have a guy we want to move from Washington State to Singapore," Saunders said. "We'll send his wife and him to look at houses and schools in Singapore. They can come back and say no." UPS also sets him up with third-party interviewers to test his adaptability. "They will give us a risk assessment of how this looks," Saunders said.

Company Man

In early 2008, Ray and Kathy Howard, both forty-six, were living in Canton, Georgia, twenty miles north and a forty-five-minute drive from UPS headquarters, in a house that they bought new in 2004 for about

$400,000. It is high-gabled and brick, on a large sloping lot much like others in builder John Wieland's Woodmont subdivision. The Howards have made the house their own with touches like the cedars Ray planted in the yard that have climbed from three feet to seven. They shelter a pond and waterfall he also built. Inside, the house is spacious and lightly furnished, and with few rugs, it echoes. Parked prominently on a counter between the kitchen and the breakfast nook is a UPS party favor, a model of a brown UPS van about the size of a toaster.

The Howards could be out of the house in a day without leaving a trace, not a nail hole or smudge on the walls, and for a year they thought they would be. Ray, who has been training a Relo in Philadelphia to succeed him, thinks his own next promotion will be his last, the one to let him retire in comfort after thirty years soldiering from outpost to outpost, from Missouri to Iowa, to Illinois, to New Jersey, to Georgia. He doesn't know where he might be moved next, or when. He heard it might be Philadelphia, then Manhattan, then Chicago or Dallas. But with most moves put on hold in the flagging economy of 2008, the Howards were sitting tight. "They don't say, 'Yes, it's going to happen,'" Kathy said. "It just happens, right then. That's how it always is with UPS. One day they'll offer him the job and want him to start the next day."

For almost thirty years, and throughout his adulthood, Ray has been a loyal, line-toeing, hard-toiling UPS careerist. He has been richly rewarded with promotions, cash, and UPS stock, but he has begun to wonder whether he might have achieved as much with fewer moves. For the family, most were traumatic. Ray and Kathy missed being present for their older daughter Courtney's senior year in high school. "The youngest, Amber, went to three different high schools," Kathy said. "We went through some hard things with her."

Ray and Kathy grew up in Kansas City, Missouri, and went to North Kansas City High School. Ray was the eighth of ten children of a General Motors accountant. Kathy and two brothers were children of the maintenance manager of the Lee Jeans factory and then of a nursing home after Lee moved production to Mexico. Kathy and Ray were baptized at the Victory Freewill Baptist Church in Kansas City, she as a child, he in his teens, and were married there at nineteen after Ray finished a year at

Kansas University. They remain attached to the city, where Ray's widowed mother and most of their siblings still live, and to the church. Courtney was married there; Amber, two years younger, would be married there, too, with Kathy's pastor brother presiding. All family members have contracts with a single cell phone service—Sprint—so they can make unlimited calls.

Upon their own marriage, Ray's local options for the kind of job opportunities that big employers can offer, like his father's with General Motors and Kathy's father's with Lee Jeans for most of his career, were evaporating, so he threw in his lot with UPS. He started working part-time loading and unloading trucks. With tuition help from the company, he enrolled at Park College, which is geared to working adults. He became a full-time driver and spent eight years attending classes on weekends. Kathy worked as a bookkeeper and a waitress, but stopped to raise the children. Ray got an MBA at Baker University in Baldwin City, Kansas. Proficient by then in accounting and finance, he was moved into management, and he and Kathy bought a house in suburban Shawnee, Kansas.

When Courtney was entering ninth grade and Amber the seventh, Ray made his first big move, two hundred miles north, to Des Moines, Iowa, to set up and manage UPS billing systems there. "It started off as an 'adventure,'" Kathy said, curling her fingers to make quotation marks. "It was exciting for me in the beginning." The job was exhilarating, but moving was hard on the family. Courtney and Amber had to leave their Shawnee schools. Ray's father died just before the move, and Amber took it hard. "She would scar her wrists with her fingernails and wear long sleeves to cover it up," Kathy said. She was diagnosed with panic anxiety disorder, a condition she inherited from Ray and his father. "She fears she's going to faint or pass out," Kathy said.

The Howards bought a home in a subdivision of Urbandale, a suburb of 29,000 close to Des Moines that was once a coal-mining town and had become an affluent bedroom community. Kathy hoped to find neighbors like her—eager to make friends, play cards, and make up book groups and foursomes for golf. But of 12,000 people who moved there in the late 1990s, only 20 percent came from outside Des Moines County, compared with about 50 percent for true Relovilles like Alpharetta and Canton.

"There were a lot of sandbox kids"—kids who started out together in Urbandale—Amber said. Kathy couldn't connect. "The neighbors didn't need any more friends. You'd wave at people in our subdivision, and they'd look at you like you were strange. There was not one neighbor I felt I had to say good-bye to when we left."

In principle, she was more than ready to go three years later when Ray was promoted to district controller in Decatur, Illinois. But Courtney was starting her senior year in Urbandale. "Bloom where you're planted," Kathy had admonished the girls, and both had. Courtney was working on the school paper, singing in the choir, and dating the schoolmate she would later marry. Decatur was a six-hour drive east of Des Moines, too far for Ray to try commuting on weekends so the family could stay in Urbandale another year, and he thought better of asking UPS to defer the move. "When you got to management," he said, "you had to be willing to relocate. If you said no, you were off the promotion list and they would find you a job you didn't like." The Howards could take Courtney along and put her in a new school in Decatur for senior year, or they could let her stay behind with friends. They let her stay.

If they had had a choice, the Howards wouldn't have chosen Decatur, an old industrial and grain-milling town. But five miles from the city they came upon the village of Forsyth, a folksy, prosperous community of only 2,400 people and many big new houses. Forsyth unleashed Kathy Howard. She discovered an informal UPS wives' club. She volunteered at a center to help young women grapple with pregnancy and joined the women's bowling league. She started a group to play bunco, the dice game popular among Relo wives everywhere.

Amber, entering the tenth grade in a school of 250 students compared to the one in Urbandale with 2,100, discovered a virtue in making new starts. "I got to keep parts of me that I liked and throw away parts I didn't like," she said. "I'd been the shy girl in Iowa, the outgoing girl in Decatur. Then I didn't care what people thought." She was getting straight A's when a friendship with a boy had turned tumultuous. Her anxiety attacks flared up.

The Howards were in Forsyth barely two years. Over the next three, Ray marched up the corporate ladder. UPS made him district controller in Secaucus, New Jersey, a lateral move but to a much bigger district, and then to Manhattan as northeast region controller coordinator. They settled in Asbury Park, New Jersey. Amber began senior year in her third high school. She graduated and enrolled at North Carolina State University in Raleigh. Courtney was a third-year student at Western Washington University in Bellingham. But Ray had a dreadful commute. He was traveling seventy miles by car to work in Secaucus, and then seventy by car and train to New York. "I asked to be moved because the commute was killing me," he said. UPS brought him to the corporate office in Atlanta and made him southeast region controller coordinator.

Except for their respite in Forsyth, the Howards enjoyed few of the pleasures and benefits of many Relos, like seeing exotic places, venturing into big cities, and building solid if brief friendships. The moves also led to marital disputes. When they packed, Ray took charge. Early on, he ruled that they get rid of anything that was packed for one move and not unpacked by the next. "What did you get rid of that I don't know about?" Kathy would ask him. To cope, she devised her own strategy. Coming to Canton, she said, "we unpacked everything."

In their early forties then, with both children grown, the Howards bloomed in Canton, a town of 20,000 and as pure a Reloville as any around Atlanta. Ray's commute could take forty-five minutes, but Secaucus had been worse. He joined the Woodmont Golf Club, which had a Robert Trent Jones Jr.–designed course, and began knocking digits off his 12 handicap. One day he shot a 76, just four strokes over par. Relos Doug and Heidi Herbert, living across from the Howards and originally from California, became good friends. Four days a week, Kathy began meeting a neighbor from down the street for lunch and three- or four-mile walks. She befriended a younger neighbor, Janelle, who stopped by nearly every day with her four small children.

At work, Ray was promoted—without having to move—to controller coordinator for the domestic corporate controller, a senior financial job. UPS also made him one of three trustees for the workers' pension fund that the company had set up with the Teamsters. In late 2007, he was taken aside. What would he think about going international, most likely to Singapore? Close to one hundred UPS Relos, high among the elite, work abroad. From Singapore, he would help lead UPS's expansion across China and enjoy travel and perks unlike any at home. After five years, he would be called back to Atlanta and, at age fifty-one, would be closer to promotion to the Management Committee.

But he couldn't visit family in Kansas City very often, and it would be hard to keep in touch by phone. He and Kathy wanted to keep an eye on Amber. She had been living with them since finishing college and enrolling at Georgia State for a master's degree. She would get the degree in a subject she knew something about—adolescent psychology—and become a therapist. Finishing school and planning for her wedding in August 2008 brought on flashes of her anxiety disorder, but with finer tuning of her medication, she was managing it. Her fiancé was looking for work as a financial analyst. That could put them anywhere, and Amber could live with that for a while. "I got used to moving," she said. But once she has children, she said, "I don't want to move anymore."

If Ray had known what Amber knows now, he might have resisted most moves, and for the first time he refused one. "He told them, 'Absolutely not'" to Singapore, Kathy said. He would be willing to move within the United States. But she said he told UPS, "'I'm not leaving my kids for five years.'" Ray also questions the utility of many moves. "Moving didn't really make a difference in my career," he said. "In Kansas City I think I could have moved once and got to where I am now."

UPS's views have been changing, too. "If you say 'no' now, there are no bad consequences," Kathy said. "You always have a choice now," Ray said. "You have to verbally say, 'I'm willing to relocate. If you say up front, 'I won't move,' it's okay." You might drop from John Saunders's Ready to Promote list for a while, but you won't be punished—knocked down a notch or sent to the tundra.

By the end of the year, the Howards were still waiting out the sour economy and word from UPS to pack up one more time. But they had begun planning beyond that. In eight years, at fifty-five, Ray will be eligible to retire. Their Woodmont subdivision was displacing Kansas City as the place to call home. Amber and her new husband had settled nearby in Alpharetta. By chance, Courtney and her husband had been relocated from northern Virginia to Atlanta. The Howards thought they would sell their house in Canton upon their next move. But to stay near the girls, they would build a retirement home right in the same neighborhood.

Cube N423B

Deep into Reagan-Bush country, at a community fair in Alpharetta in the spring of 2004, I noticed a silver Chrysler minivan with a license plate spelling PASION8. Across the rear window were a Vietnam-era peace symbol and other stickers that said "Keep Tahoe Green" and "Be the Hope of Humanity." The driver was a gregarious blonde, deep-dimpled and forty-three, who was handing out flyers for her five-year-old daughter Charlotte's pre-school. Patti Silva and her husband, Kevin Silva, forty-five, then a UPS Relo, call her Carly, for the melancholic pop star. Carly's three-year-old sister, Roxanne, is Roxy, like the movie theater on Sunset Boulevard.

Patti might not have been up to fulfilling the hopes of the species, but she would soon become passionate about grafting to the heart of Dixie an agenda that she brought from the coffeehouses of the Pacific Coast. By 2008, her causes, most of them at least partially successful, included restraining suburban sprawl into her neighboring farmland and getting an unabashedly liberal man elected to her local governing council. She formed committees on the arts and historical preservation. She became president of Roxy's pre-school PTA and a volunteer stable hand at a horse farm so the girls could learn to ride.

Kevin, who is graying and tends toward stocky, collects wine, speaks excitedly about the Sunnis and Shiites, Somalia and the Sudan, and soaks up bestsellers on current affairs. He is attuned to Patti's worldview but shares none of her new nesting instincts. Traveling most of the workweek and busy with the girls' activities on weekends, Kevin knows the roads to the office, the airport, and the girls' playgrounds and schools, but little more. He has no friends in Alpharetta, nor has he sought any.

Kevin views relocation, work, and bonds to employers differently from longtime UPSers like Ray and Kathy Howard. Like some other managers, he came to the company through the acquisition of another company. He arrived too late in his career for the rites of passage that might have locked him into the company, like the stint in Big Brown's loading-dock incubator or years building a pension with privately held UPS stock. Instead, he joined the newer class of opportunistic Relos, who move from company to company across the global economy. Offer him a better job elsewhere, and he's off.

Kevin spent most of his youth near San Francisco, in the Silicon Valley community of Menlo Park. From the ages of four to ten, he lived in Pakistan, where his father was an engineer for an international construction company that built airports, dams, and hydroelectric power plants. After graduating from California State University, Chico, he went to work with an oil exploration crew in the Australian Outback. In six months he had made enough money to backpack for three years—to Italy, France, Spain, Scandinavia, the South Pacific, New Zealand, Hong Kong, and China. "I went to over a hundred countries," he said. "I grew up with happy feet."

Back in San Francisco, he looked for work to keep him traveling. He went to Consolidated Freightways, an interstate shipping company that would soon go out of business, and other shipping companies. He went to iShip.com, which two former UPS managers formed to provide Internet shipping services.

Patti Parker has been around, too. She was raised by her divorced mother in a condo in Miami Beach and later in a house in Los Angeles. She attended Beverly Hills High School with children of Hollywood celebrities and the University of California, Los Angeles. She left college after three years, moved to San Francisco, found work with a developer, and met Kevin. She and Kevin were married on the Presidio. After Carly was born, iShip moved them to Seattle. They settled in Issaquah, a liberal-leaning Reloville seventeen miles east of Seattle and the site of Costco's headquarters and big offices of Boeing, Siemens, and Microsoft. Not long after Roxy was born, iShip sold out to UPS, and after three years in Issaquah, the Silvas were sent to Georgia. "Issaquah and Alpharetta are both transient corporate towns," Kevin said. "But it's as radical a move as you can make in America—from Seattle to Alpharetta, Georgia."

It was radical in one unexpected way. Home prices in north Fulton County are a third to half those of equivalent houses in the West, and the

Silvas built a sizable nest egg from buying and selling homes there. Ten minutes from the office, adjacent to Alpharetta in an unincorporated corner of the county, the Silvas came upon Wood Valley, a ten-year-old subdivision of $400,000 to $900,000 houses on one- and two-acre lots. For close to $500,000, they bought a large white clapboard house with a wide front porch and two acres of grounds thick with trees and untamed shrubbery. Inside, the house felt inviting and informal, yet big and exuberant, with soaring ceilings, columns, two crystal chandeliers, and trendy kitchen gear. It felt Californian.

The Silvas were also relieved to find in Wood Valley a rare upscale subdivision without a meddlesome homeowners association to dictate the look and maintenance of the neighborhood. The Silvas could mow or not mow, mulch or not mulch, or paint the house pink. They could leave cars overnight in the driveway, though they did press their luck. In winter, their leaf-denuded trees exposed the Jayco Escapade motor home they took on vacations. "People hinted," Patti said. "They'd say something like, 'Oh, do you have somebody staying with you?' " So they rented a space in an RV storage lot.

Adapting to a southern Reloville culture was trickier for the Silvas. Patti is shamelessly unconventional. "I'm Jewish!" she proclaimed in explaining herself to a universe thick with megachurches. "Some of the women wear panty hose with their shorts," she said, amazed. People were friendly enough but seemed to hold something back. "People don't show their true colors here—whatever they're thinking," she said. "We're misfits. Carly said one of her friends said, 'I think your mom is weird.'

"We didn't realize how competitive it is here. I have to go to the Y at five a.m. to sign the girls up for swim lessons before they run out of places." At Carly's ballet class in Issaquah, she said, "you'd have parents sitting in the studio with cameras and Birkenstocks. Here I put a four-year-old in a ballet class and I got reprimanded because I wanted to open the door and take a picture. They're very serious, and these are four-year-olds. They think parents disrupt the class."

At work, Kevin was assigned a cubicle—Cube N423B—at UPS's Supply Chain Solutions, the hub of the company's expansion beyond

The Motor Home: *Patti and Kevin Silva (pictured with their daughters Roxanne and Charlotte) were relieved to find a Reloville subdivision that was free of a meddling homeowners association that would dictate the look of the neighborhood, down to the color of the paint on the house. But neighbors commented on the Jayco Escapade motor home they parked discreetly behind the house, so the Silvas rented a space in an RV storage lot.*

package delivery into managing corporate clients' warehouses, inventories, and shipping and receiving activities. UPS moves everything from letters and parcels to truckloads of chemicals and auto parts. Kevin became a link in the chain, first selling the services to clients and later working as a project manager in the technology group.

He knew that any day UPS would ask him to move again, perhaps to another inland community far from the lights of big cities. "UPS requires you to move, and in most cases they don't ask you," he said. "Even in my division it was not uncommon at all for somebody to be called in by their boss—I saw this happen—and he said, 'We need you in Laredo, Texas, on Monday, and you're going to be there for six months, maybe a year. On Monday. So you decide if you're going to move your family or not.' "

Home from his cube one day, he said, "I believe, like any big organization, UPS is highly, highly political. And depending on who you work for and how well they like you, how you get along, as well as how you perform, will determine your assignment. Obviously the better assignments and the better locations go to the people who are not only doing well but are well connected. If you piss somebody off they send you to Erie, Pennsylvania, or Laredo.

"If you are going to move your family, they do have a great Relo package. They take care of everything, coming and going. In our case, when we went to Atlanta to look for houses, they flew Patti's mother from Los Angeles to Seattle to babysit for the children. They take care of that. They take care of the complete Relo. They have to do that. But you don't have an option."

In late 2005, Kevin's boss at UPS jumped ship, and Kevin followed. They went to Schenker AG, a global supply chain service company based in Essen, Germany, that is much like UPS but more specialized in handling bulk freight. Kevin was made vice president of global sales for two industrial sectors—semiconductors and electronic manufacturing services.

The address on Kevin's business card is Freeport, New York, Schenker's U.S. headquarters. But he could live anywhere. He plumbed real estate sites on the Internet for details about Charlottesville, Virginia, and Asheville and Durham, North Carolina—all lively and diverse university towns. He drove the family up to Charlottesville for a look.

But Patti balked. In December 2006, the Silvas' corner of Fulton County became a city called Milton. Watching the planning, she set out to help define Milton and to salt the southern conservative culture with some of the values of Berkeley. She came up with a slogan for the town: "Pastures are greener in Milton." She set up a blog, Miltonville.com, to circulate lush photographs of Milton's idyllic setting and to publish the oral histories of old-timers she interviewed. She became a community activist and vociferous foe of building sewers that would let developers layer the pastures with houses and clog local roads. Her picture appeared on the front page of the weekly *Milton Herald*. Moving to the South as a Relo spouse, Patti had become Reloville's anti-Relo. "I didn't leave my heart in San Francisco," she told a local blog. "It came here with me and never wants to leave."

Kevin and Patti tried to thrash out their differences as they stood at the kitchen's island counter over a take-out sushi dinner. Kevin was entreating her to move.

"It's hard to find like-minded people around here," he said.

"That's your problem," Patti said.

"That's my problem," he said, slapping a palm on the counter. "That's it. There's nobody here that I've met that I'm interested in."

"Wait a minute," Patti said. "We haven't given it a big chance. We've only made friends with our neighbors—Dee Dee, Tim. Think about it. You have a job, the people that you work with. We haven't spent time looking, like spending time in Midtown Atlanta."

"We won't," Kevin said. "Because we have children and I'm traveling all the time. The reality is, although there are people that are interesting and nice and more like . . ."

"Right," she said.

". . . more like me and more like us. You can find them in pockets of Atlanta, but they're not here."

"We do have some issues with friendships," she agreed. "We're really different. We don't belong to a church or a temple."

"I was actually talking to my boss about this," Kevin said. "I was saying, 'You know maybe I could commute out of Asheville, North Carolina.' It's a very cool town. And the kind of people I like, they actually come from all over the country to live there. There's great music and art. There's Bend, Oregon; Charlottesville, Virginia. There are pockets of these cool little towns, and that's where we belong."

He paused, reflecting, and simmered down. The towns he liked most were two- or three-hour drives from big airports. "I got the packet from the Bend City Hall or whatever, you know the packet if you're moving to Bend, and it's a cool town. But for what I do, it would kill me. People do it, the commuting. On Tuesday I'm flying to Budapest, and I'll be there Wednesday morning, nine o'clock. If I had come from Bend, I'd be there Friday. It doesn't work for what I do. It's more of a pipe dream than anything else."

"That's good," Patti said. "I want this to be a place I'm proud of. I feel it's not my time to leave."

Two years later, approaching fifty, Kevin had corralled his happy feet, for at least the duration of the global economy's funk and maybe for much longer. He had made friends around town and took up riding a bike along rural county roads he didn't know were there. In the backyard, Patti ventured into farming—raising chickens. A friend, a longtime Relo, left her house in the pricey subdivision of White Columns for the backwoods and an unimposing house on nine acres. "She has a pig," Patti said.

4. Workers of the World

In Globalization 1.0, countries had to think globally to thrive, or at least survive. In Globalization 2.0, companies had to think globally to thrive, or at least survive. In Globalization 3.0, individuals have to think globally to thrive, or at least survive.
—Thomas L. Friedman, *The World Is Flat*

"**M**y name is Colleen," Colleen Dunn wrote, introducing herself in May 2007 to Moveable Families, a Yahoo! group for Relos. "My husband, Joe, and I have a two-year-old son. My husband's company recently offered him an expat assignment (our first?) to Kolkata, India. In two weeks, our family plans an apartment-hunting trip where we will also get acquainted with living in the city. My husband has traveled to India about twenty times in the last two years, and most of those trips were to Kolkata, so he is very familiar with the city. This will be my son's and my first trip to India. We are U.S. citizens currently living in Pennsylvania."

Two months later, on a Thursday morning in July, a truck was lifting a dumpster-like storage container—a POD—from Colleen and Joe Dunn's driveway at 369 Buckingham Drive in Bethlehem, Pennsylvania.

It is a wide quiet street of sturdy, fifty-year-old, $300,000 ranch houses with thick trees and deep obedient lawns. Once a neighborhood where Pennsylvania Dutch families and gray-suited organization men from the old Bethlehem Steel Company dug generation-deep roots, it felt comatose. Its young commuters, like the Dunns, spend summers out of sight, on backyard decks they build as large as their living rooms.

Colleen's mother, Mary Ann Klosterman, fifty-nine, had driven three hours from Reston, Virginia, to help pack and clean. She was wearing a red St. Louis Cardinals sweatshirt and drawing in the kitchen with Sean, the two-year-old. In the family room, Joe and Colleen were unwrapping McDonald's sandwiches. They would be leaving behind the beige leather couch and matching easy chair for the U.S. Marine officer's family that would be renting the house.

The day before, Colleen sold their 2000 Saturn to CarMax for $2,500; Joe's parents in Towanda, Pennsylvania, would be taking their 2004 Subaru SUV. A woman they found on Craigslist bought Sean's crib for fifty dollars, and through Freecycle.com, they found others to take things for free. Finally, the 1-800-JUNK-USA guys would haul off the rest so they could sweep up and check into the Residence Inn for the night.

Monday, July 9, 2007, was Joe's last day at the Murray Hill, New Jersey, offices of BOC Gases, a part of the British Oxygen Company, a global industrial gases producer with 30,000 employees on six continents, which in 2006 became part of the German Linde Group. On Friday, a company driver picked up Joe at the house for the ride to Newark airport and a flight to his new assignment in Kolkata (the city that the British called Calcutta). Colleen and Sean took the Subaru to visit Joe's parents for a month before their own flight to India. There, the Dunns would be the only Westerners among the affluent Indian residents of three premium high-rise apartment buildings in South Kolkata, near the one-hundred-acre Tollygunge Club that was once headquarters for the British Raj. They rented a cheery three-bedroom apartment on the eighth of their building's fourteen floors.

Joe is a chemical engineer. In his mid-thirties, he is heavyset, fair, and upbeat. In Murray Hill, near Newark, he was a global market development manager selling the air separation units used to make steel and reduce carbon dioxide emissions. With the move to Kolkata, he would be leading BOC's efforts to sell a unit to Tata Steel, the world's fifth-largest steel company and the biggest in India, and competing with Praxair of Danbury, Connecticut, and L'Air Liquide of Paris. This is a riskier, winner-takes-all business than, say, playing the horses. "In racing you can bet to place and bet to win," Colleen said. "In this race, you bet to win. He was told to win Tata at all costs." The contract was worth $150 million. He was given two years to close a deal.

Win or lose, Joe couldn't fathom what might lie ahead for this assignment. Another engineering company could try to recruit him. Or BOC could promote him or let him go, leaving the family to fend for itself. It could move him to headquarters in Munich, or to another country, or keep him longer in India. He was untroubled by the uncertainty. He thought less of climbing the BOC or Linde Group ranks than of building an industry-wide reputation for managing engineering projects. "You build your own career," he said. "You have to be mobile. I have no idea if I'm coming back to BOC."

Joe and Colleen grew up in fertile Relo terrain, old Farm Belt and Rust Belt communities with little more to offer bright college graduates than a bus out of town. Joe's Towanda is in north central Pennsylvania, a coal-mining, farming, and industrial community on the Susquehanna River, south of the New York state line. Joe's mother, Theresa, was still working, at sixty-seven, for the local Area Agency on Aging and was a volunteer coordinator for a housing program for the elderly. His father, Richard, sixty-eight, once taught math. Richard worked at Towanda's biggest business, a tungsten processing and lightbulb filament plant that Sylvania once owned. The German electrical and electronic conglomerate Siemens bought it in 1993 and sold it to an Austrian group in 2008. Over the years, Siemens trimmed its employment from 1,400 to 1,000.

Towanda's growth had stalled long before. Roughly equal parts English, Irish, and German, the population, at 3,000, has dropped from the 1900 peak of 4,500. The Dunns and Theresa's McDonald clan, both of Irish descent, were early settlers. Four McDonalds were listed in the phone book. Thirteen Dunns remained, but they, too, were leaving. Joe's one other sibling, his sister Marie, moved to Colorado Springs.

Joe first left town for Troy, New York, and Rensselaer Polytechnic Institute, where he got a bachelor's degree in chemical engineering. He went on to Lehigh University in Bethlehem for his master's and doctorate. With no promising careers for PhD chemical engineers at home, Joe tapped into the global economy. Everywhere the message was the same: "Unleash your potential around the world," Microsoft's Internet recruiting page urged him. "Are you able to think globally," it asked in another ad, "understand the needs of some of the most demanding customers in the world, and help build the systems that will drive the world's economy?" Procter & Gamble promised "global career path opportunities, where you will work in various parts of the world and on businesses that span multiple countries." BOC, a two-hour drive east of Towanda, asked job seekers, "Join us. BOC is one of a handful of truly global companies" promising "international assignments and job rotation programs."

North of St. Louis, Colleen heard the same sirens. Thirty-five, five foot six, with wide azure eyes, tortoise-rimmed glasses, and bobbed, reddish-blond hair that she parts in the center, she is peppy, quick-witted, and adventurous. She grew up in Florissant, a middle-class town where the population had fallen from 66,000 in 1970 to 51,000 by 2000. She graduated in 1996 from Southwest Missouri State University, now called Missouri State, in Springfield, another farming and industrial city. It lost its biggest employer, the Zenith television factory, when Zenith sent its production to Mexico. "In the college counseling office," Colleen said, "they were telling us that if you were getting a job in those days, you had to be geographically flexible."

Her parents made it easy to leave. As she was finishing college, her father, Mike Klosterman, was promoted to chief geologist at the headquarters of the United States Army Corps of Engineers in Washington, D.C. He and Mary Ann moved to northern Virginia, first to Herndon, then to Reston. Mary Ann taught fifth grade at an elementary school. Colleen, a geography major, found work making maps at SAIC (Science Applications International Corporation), a large defense consulting firm in Reston that claims 44,000 employees working in 150 cities worldwide.

Meanwhile Joe moved to northern Virginia. After Lehigh, he had gone to BOC in Murray Hill but wanted to try consulting. He left BOC after a year to go to the Independent Project Analysis Corporation, a global engineering consulting firm that evaluates large construction projects for governments and industry.

"So we met," Colleen said. "I was on a seven-week free trial with Match.com. My love life wasn't going anywhere." She submitted her profile and preferences, and Joe popped up among men that Match.com thought suitable. "I'm absolutely impulsive," she said. She sent him an e-mail, and in January 2000 they went for a date at Clyde's, a popular restaurant and bar in Reston. Two years later, Joe proposed and they married. By then he was moving again, back to BOC. "I got tired of the consulting lifestyle," he said.

With the move back to BOC and to Bethlehem, Colleen dropped thoughts of a career for herself. In 2005, after three years there, she and Joe adopted Sean, and she threw herself into stay-at-home mothering. "I've never really been anxious to go back to work, even once Sean reaches school age," she said. "I never really had much of a career path to begin with. If I stayed in the States, I would be one of those moms involved with volunteering at my son's school rather than working for pay."

First Base

In April 2007, Joe called home from a trip to Mumbai (once known as Bombay) to tell her of an offer to move to Kolkata. " 'Do you want me to pursue it?' " he asked. " 'This is going to be tough. It's a huge change.' I prepared her for hell on earth."

Colleen said, "It's a huge step in his career. I depend on my husband's career for my life." And as far as Kolkata would be, 8,000 miles from Bethlehem, she and Sean could at least expect to see more of Joe since his trips, all in India, would be short and quick.

"We decided sure," she said. It might be fun. She wanted to know Kolkata as well as Florissant. The shelf of her bay window was lined with books, among them a thick Lonely Planet guide to India, Dominique Lapierre's *City of Joy* about Kolkata, Kipling's novel *Kim* and poetry about India, *Holy Cow!* by Sarah MacDonald, *Raising Global Nomads* by Robin

Pascoe, and *Third Culture Kids* by David C. Pollack. She started a blog—*A Yankee Mom in the City of Joy*—to chronicle her life as a Relo, but would drop it after a couple of months.

Once in Kolkata, the Dunns could start touring Asia on the 750,000 frequent flier miles that Joe had banked. They would be well off financially. The company was covering their rent, their utilities, occasional trips home, their health care, their car and driver, and a nanny. With that and the rent from their home in Bethlehem, Joe figured they would set aside $100,000 over two years.

The benefits, however, did not cover some disquieting family matters. Colleen's biological clock was ticking. She and Joe wanted another child but were reluctant to try in a place with unfamiliar care and while they might move again, any day. Joe's father couldn't get on a plane to come visit; he had been slowed by hip replacement surgery and was using a nebulizer to manage his emphysema. Colleen's mother could manage 150-mile drives from Reston to Bethlehem, but she couldn't imagine a child living three continents away. Every day after school, Mary Ann said, "I talk to her on my way home. I put my little earpiece on. It's my daily shot. We're in each other's life daily." She fretted about Sean forgetting her. "He gets all excited when we're on the phone with him," she said. Colleen hoped that a webcam, e-mail, and calls through Skype, the voice and video conferencing software, would let them pretend they were just next door.

Half a year later, the Dunns had acclimated to Kolkata, though there had been troublesome moments. Her first day in the apartment, Colleen heated an Easy Mac macaroni and cheese for her and Sean's lunch. She had not yet bought detergent, and by that afternoon ants had colonized the plates. A power surge destroyed the microwave and knocked out the air-conditioning for a day. One afternoon when Colleen was out, the nanny took Sean off in a taxi to run an errand. She had to fire the nanny and hire another.

Pratap, the driver—twenty-nine and single—worked for the Dunns from eight in the morning to six-thirty at night. Mornings, he packed them into their eight-passenger Toyota Inova van, shuttling Joe to work, Colleen and Sean to the nursery school, and Colleen on errands. Colleen and Sean were learning Bengali. "I can say only a few phrases," she said, "such as 'okay,' 'good,' 'little,' and 'car is coming.'" Sean was mixing languages. "Tikka" means "okay." He was saying "Tikka Okay." Colleen liked the street food, especially one vendor's plate of spicy chicken and rice biryani. It cost eighteen rupees, or about fifty cents.

Looking for volunteer work, Colleen found the offices of Mother Teresa's Missionaries of Charity. She signed up to teach English for three and a half hours a day three days a week at the Shishu Bhavan home for abandoned and disabled children. The handicapped children's room, with about twenty-five kids in two rows of cribs and two rows of beds, has ceiling fans but no air-conditioning. The classroom is partitioned off in one corner. The class started at nine with songs in Bengali and English.

"At some point, I realized that these kids spend pretty much their whole day here," Colleen said. "If one gets sick, it's quite likely that it could spread quickly and affect everyone." One day she noticed a girl walking from the lunch table with food coating her face. Colleen started wiping it off, and a Vesuvian torrent of mucus gushed from the child's nose. Weeks later, she left the job. "I got frustrated," she said. "They told me that I would be teaching in the school, but after the first week I was no longer working in the classroom. I decided that my time might be better spent with Sean."

She wanted to slip anonymously into the life of Kolkata. She took Sean to public parks and the markets, but she is too tall, too white, and too transparently rich. She stopped to buy a bunch of seedless white grapes and was asked for 100 rupees, or $2.30—more than she knew Indians paid. She tried to haggle but failed. She went to a no-haggle, fixed-price market and got them for 83 rupees, about $1.90. In markets, she recoiled from the flies circling displays of meat and freshly caught fish. "I found myself picking the meat out of my food," she said, so she gave up her chicken biryani.

She wanted friends. She joined the Kolkata International Women's Club, a philanthropic association of expatriates. "But a couple of the women I thought were great moved back home," she said. "It hit me about the whole relocation thing. It's part of the lifestyle. The people you are close to move away. You can't get too close. It breaks your heart when you have to move away.

"You do miss your family back home," she said. In June 2008, she and Sean, by then three, returned to the States for a two-week trip to see grandparents. Visiting with them one afternoon, Mary Ann seemed well settled in her orderly and airy corner town house with neatly mulched shrubs in a sedate Reston subdivision. She had just retired from teaching. Mike had retired from the Corps of Engineers and gone to work consulting for the Bechtel Corporation, the global construction and engineering company.

Inside, Sean was scampering room to room throwing a blue rubber ball and Mary Ann was making a game of chasing him. He calls her "Nana." She said she weeps a lot. The Klostermans' younger daughter Anne is living in Seattle, where she married a lawyer before the Dunns left for India. Their younger son John would be getting out of the air force soon and was hoping to go to college and live in the West. The Klostermans spent Mary Ann's sixtieth birthday, Mother's Day, and Thanksgiving alone.

"At first I thought it was a novelty," Mary Ann said. But it wore off. "We can't stay here," she said. "There's nobody here anymore. I think we all have need for a family unit. What's upsetting us most, we can't use Skype to reach Colleen. Now we talk once a week. I call them every weekend. Sean will get on for maybe sixty seconds and say nothing. That's very sad for us." Anne was urging her parents to move to Seattle. Mary Ann and Mike wanted to try, but on a house-hunting trip, they recoiled at the prices.

Moving, however, wouldn't bring them any closer to Colleen. For Colleen and Joe, the key to steady employment is relocation. "Financial security is such a worry for so many people," she said. "For us, it was simply practical to take this opportunity. It certainly helps Joe get a more globalized perspective."

Colleen's outlook shifted. "I'm more aware of the environment," she said. She was struck by the collisions between parochial and more global perspectives. "Gas prices," she said as they were peaking, "look at other countries. I'm sure they're laughing at us complaining about four-dollar gas." Mary Ann said she and her friends in Missouri, all Roman Catholic, voted Republican because they opposed abortion. But in the November 2008 elections, Colleen said she would be voting differently. "I have 'Republican' on my voter ID card," she said, "but I'm not voting for McCain. I'm voting for Obama."

At home Colleen was rearing a citizen of the global economy. Sean banters in Bengali and sings Bengali children's songs. He eats Bengali cuisine and learns games Bengali children play. His friend Mattias is the son of Chinese parents who grew up in Kolkata, migrated to Canada, and returned to Kolkata to build an export business. Another friend is Maderov, whose Rajastani parents grew up in Delhi. "Sean is going to understand what it is to be Indian," Colleen said. "He's going to have an understanding of what it is to be this or that."

Soon after her June visit to Reston, Joe met with his boss to explore the next phase of his work. His boss had been getting good feedback about Joe's work on the Tata contract, a sign that he would be getting a raise. The one question remaining was the duration of the Dunns' assignment. Joe wanted to stay two more years, but that hinged on Tata's decision. Tata signed on, just after Christmas.

Borderless Careers

The propane dealership back home, the supermarket, the appliance store, the hotel, the bank, the undertaker, the plant, or the survivors among them might still raise the hopes of young local job seekers to manage a hometown business someday, and maybe make a pretty good living. But as Siemens takes over the filament plant, Marriott becomes the hotel, Bank of America the bank, and Best Buy the appliance store, another breed of young job seekers, sent by headquarters in Atlanta, Charlotte, Dallas, or Munich, take those jobs. Rookie Relos, they stay a year or two and rotate out for the next group of rookie Relos.

Relos often start in the hinterlands of consumer-product branding, chain-storing, globalizing industries. Paid $40,000 or $50,000 a year and handed a $3,000 moving expense check, they mount the bottom rungs of ladders, which the most agile among them will climb to Alpharetta, Plano, Denver, Singapore, and on up, to the six- and seven-digit wages of executive vice presidents and chief executive officers. As a slice of the American middle class, rookie Relos are neither their hometowns' transient poor nor the elite, endowed with connections and the infinite options that money can buy. They are kids who are told they can be president if they work hard enough and get out of town.

Bradd Shore, the anthropologist at Emory in Atlanta, segments the classes by their attachment to hometowns and predisposition to move. As we toured the Relovilles north of Atlanta, Shore said a town's upper class—its entrenched doctors, lawyers, accountants, its leading stockbrokers, insurance agents, and business owners—has the means to either move out or stick around and prepare their own children to succeed them.

By contrast, Shore said, many who land in the working class—as farmhands, grocery store cashiers, mill workers, and school janitors—are too rooted or ill-equipped to go. They might not have a parent to open doors, the skills for a better job somewhere else, or even the funds for the trip there for an interview. Or maybe they don't want to shed their only real wealth: their extended families, churches, ethnic ties, and shared interests and rituals.

The remaining middle class, in Shore's view, amounts to about 70 percent of the population. Its kids have neither the choices of the rich nor the immobility of the poor. They are congenital itinerants whose families raise them to chase the American Dream wherever it leads, much as their forebears did in chasing it west. Like the pioneers, the middle class equates wealth and happiness with perseverance and mobility. "You define yourself as belonging to the middle class through various kinds of mobility," Shore said. "They see themselves as climbing. The upper class doesn't feel that. The upper class can lose some money without great peril."

Shore's colleague at Emory Drew Whitelegg, a British geographer, called Relos the "aspirational class." He said, "They're caught up in a sense of 'We've-got-to-get-somewhere, we've-got-to-get-somewhere, we've got-to-get-somewhere.'" He cited Barbara Ehrenreich's books *Fear of Falling* and *Nickel and Dimed*. "They fear falling into the proletariat." Stirred to succeed or merely survive, middle-class Relos relocate again and again.

The Web pages of twelve global companies—Boeing, Caterpillar, Coca-Cola, Eastman Kodak, ExxonMobil, Fluor, General Electric, General Motors, Hewlett-Packard, IBM, McDonald's, and Procter & Gamble—listed 315 executives on their rosters of top officers in 2008. Fifty-one were women, but with some striking exceptions, most had remained in one place. One hundred twenty-six of the 315, or 40 percent, were hard-core, serial Relos—people who had been moved at least four times. Five had been moved ten or more times. Caterpillar had moved fifteen of its top thirty-three officers five or more times.

Of the companies' American Relos, most made their first move from home to state universities, mainly those of Iowa, Indiana, Michigan, Ohio, New York, and Illinois. A small minority—fewer than twenty-five— went to elite private schools, those of the Ivy League and its cousins such as Stanford and Duke. After employers started to help paying the freight, however, about one in four went on to get master's degrees in business administration, about half of them from the business schools of Harvard, the University of Pennsylvania, Stanford, and the Massachusetts Institute of Technology.

Once on the job with global companies, rookie Relos can expect to be moved and promoted. In the mid-2000s, the global public relations firm of Burson-Marsteller listed appointments of new chief executives among *Fortune* magazine's thousand largest U.S. companies—all sorts, not just those engaged in foreign commerce. Three or four decades ago, most would have been William Whyte's loyal *Organization Man* who rose through the ranks in one place like New York, Pittsburgh, or Detroit. But of those appointed in 2005 and 2006, Burson-Marsteller's list showed a third who had worked in four or more locations.

The Worldwide ERC—Employee Relocation Council—the trade association of companies that employ Relos and other companies that move

Relos—says that half of all promotions entail a move. In a report about a 2005 survey of 136 of its members, the ERC said, "Nearly three-quarters of survey participants responded that employees who wished to advance into senior positions in their companies needed to relocate with the company at some point during their careers."

Or at many points. G. Richard Wagoner Jr., then General Motors's chief executive, started in the GM treasurer's office in New York. He moved on to São Paulo, Brazil, as treasurer of the company's Brazilian subsidiary, to Ontario as a vice president of GM Canada, to the European headquarters in Zurich as vice president for finance, then back to GM Brazil as president, and on to Detroit.

At Procter & Gamble, David S. Taylor could be a contender for the top job. This is his quintessentially Relo résumé:

Born in Charlotte, North Carolina, in 1958.

Got Bachelor of Science degree in electrical engineering from Duke in 1980.

Went to P&G as a production manager at a sanitary napkin plant in Greenville, North Carolina.

Promoted at age twenty-five to department manager in Greenville.

Sent to Cheboygan, Michigan, a year later to be operations manager at a paper mill.

Sent the next year to Albany, Georgia, to be plant manager of a Bounty towel and Charmin toilet paper plant for three years.

Sent to Mehoopany, Pennsylvania, to be plant manager of a paper mill for three years.

Called to Cincinnati headquarters at thirty-four to be assistant brand manager for Pampers sold in the domestic market for a year.

Promoted to brand manager for Pampers in the domestic market for three years.

Promoted to marketing director for all domestic diaper products for two years.

Sent at thirty-eight to Hong Kong as general manager for hair care products sold there and in China.

Promoted two years later to China to be general manager for hair care, tissues, and towels.

Job expanded a year later to encompass trying to stop Chinese counterfeiting of P&G products like Head & Shoulders shampoo and Gillette razors.

Promoted the same year at forty-one to vice president for hair care and anti-counterfeiting in China.

Promoted to Western Europe as vice president for family care products for two years.

Called back to Cincinnati at forty-three to be vice president for family care products in North America for two years.

Promoted at forty-five to president for family care products worldwide.

Promoted in two years to group president for home care products worldwide.

Many Relos make their ascents like Rick Wagoner and David Taylor, with a single employer. But others, extreme Relos, hop from place to place, company to company, vaulting like monkeys grabbing ever higher branches in the corporate forest.

After Yale in New Haven and an MBA from Harvard, W. James McNerney Jr., went directly to Procter & Gamble in Cincinnati as a brand manager. Then he went to McKinsey & Company, the consulting firm in Chicago, and on to General Electric. During eighteen years at GE, McNerney took bigger and bigger assignments in Connecticut, Maryland, Cleveland, Chicago, and Hong Kong. Outrun in the race to succeed Jack Welch as CEO at GE, he bounded to the 3M Corporation in St. Paul, Minnesota, as CEO. In four years, he was off again to Chicago to be CEO at Boeing—a company, uncharacteristically among the twelve, with few Relos on top.

It is easy to see what drives companies navigating the global economy to rear Relos. In but fourteen years, from 1990 to 2004, all countries' combined domestic economies—the value of everything bought and sold from Samsung TVs to P&G's Crest toothpaste to Boeing 777s—leaped from $23 trillion to $57 trillion. In 1999, the International

Civil Aviation Organization in Montreal said airlines carried 17 million tons of freight in world trade. By 2010, the organization predicts they will be carrying 31 million tons. The United Nations says investments by "transnational" companies—those that buy and build subsidiaries, factories, mines, oil fields, stores, and offices in countries other than their own—quadrupled to $1.7 trillion from 1990 to 2005.

Yet globalization, for all the opportunity it offers industry, has become a slippery slope for many industries' employees, Relos included. Once companies like IBM, Boeing, Caterpillar, and Kodak had world markets to themselves. But as scrappy upstarts from Asia, Latin America, and Eastern Europe came along, the American behemoths had to cut costs to compete. Many reneged on their promises of secure employment and company-paid health care and pensions in return for the *Organization Man's* lifetime of hard and loyal work. Routinely they resorted to layoffs, downsizings, mergers, and spin-offs.

Relos, like other workers, can be treated like fire extinguishers—scrapped when they're old or spent. Companies dispatch Relos to conquer markets far from home without planning what to do with them next. In a survey of employers in 2006, the accounting and consulting firm KPMG concluded, "Thirty-eight percent of employees leave an organization after completing an international assignment because there is no longer an appropriate job for them in their home country." But they're getting the message. Twenty-six percent of those who leave jump to other companies, often direct competitors.

"Holding on to key talent is like trying to keep frogs in a wheelbarrow," Carol Ashton, the chief human resources officer at the global accounting firm of Ernst & Young told a meeting of corporate human resource officers. In the global economy lately, especially in Asia, skilled engineers, production managers, and sales and marketing people are courted like celebrities. "China needs seventy-five thousand of a type of management job," Cris Collie of the ERC said. "They've got only five thousand to fill them. So they poach on competitors and you get a bidding war."

The loss of job security on the one hand and aggressive recruiting on the other have begotten a species of men and women who run their own careers. If no longer coddled by cradle-to-grave job security, they are also no longer bound by it. They shed employers as freely as they know the employers can shed them. The workers, and the companies' hiring officers, too, keep executive recruiters, or "headhunters," a button away on their BlackBerrys. A Relo might have mastered vital new software that store chains need to control inventories, so Wal-Mart's recruiter calls. He gets the job. A couple of years later, the recruiter calls again. Target needs a vice president of inventory control in Minneapolis. He doubles his money.

These workers become "boundaryless careerists." Michael B. Arthur, a management professor at Suffolk University in Boston and co-editor Denise Rousseau, a professor at Carnegie Mellon, call boundaryless careers the opposite of organizational careers—"careers conceived to unfold in a single employment setting." Boundaryless careerists depend not on an employer's promises, but on their own skills, networks of contacts, and reputations with their true employer—the marketplace.

A variation of the boundaryless careerist is the stateless careerist. Stateless careerists shed not just their towns and employers, but their countries. Of General Motors's fifty-three top officers in 2008, eleven were foreigners. Six of General Electric's top forty-one officers were foreign-born, as were sixteen of Procter & Gamble's top forty-three. Four of the P&G executives came from Britain, three from Italy, two from Germany, two from Spain, and one each from Colombia, France, Mozambique, India, and the Philippines.

With their expansion into world markets and their stables of foreign-born Relos, companies might still fly the Stars and Stripes and trade on the New York Stock Exchange. What, for example, could be more American than Pepsi and Coke? Yet Coca-Cola's CEO, Muhtar Kent, is a Turk. He succeeded Neville Isdell, an Irishman, who succeeded Douglas Daft, an Australian, who succeeded M. Douglas Ivester, an American from Georgia, who succeeded Roberto Goizueta, a Cuban. Indra K. Nooyi, Pepsi-Co's CEO, was born in Chennai, India. The second "a" in Alcoa stands for America. But Alcoa's chief executive is a German who succeeded a Brazilian born in Morocco. A Pakistani runs one American pharmaceutical company, Schering-Plough, and a Spaniard born in Casablanca runs rival Eli Lilly.

At the extreme, stateless and boundaryless careerists become autonomous freelancers. Like the self-employed electrician, they take on a task and go when it's done. "The free agent gives talent in exchange for opportunity," Daniel H. Pink writes in *Free Agent Nation: The Future of Working for Yourself.* The legendary Red Adair who stopped the world's worst oil field fires could pick and choose his customers much as Roger Clemens, switching from the Red Sox, to the Blue Jays, to the Yankees, to the Astros, and back to the Yankees, picked and chose baseball teams.

"Talent," Pink writes, "can be solving a problem—a computer contractor figuring out how to set up a company's LAN (local area network), or a plumber unstopping a clogged kitchen sink. Talent can be offering a set of niche skills that allow a large team to solve a sprawling problem. Or it can be completing a project—like the housepainter putting up a new coat of paint on the living room walls. The buyer doesn't purchase the person; the buyer rents the person's abilities."

Hobos in BMWs

Sandi and Mark Remson could decompress on the plane after a hot harried week in August 2007. Mark had been promoted to the Geneva headquarters of STMicroelectronics, a global colossus of the semiconductor industry. They had emptied their big house in Frisco, Texas, and settled Laura, a sophomore, and Brian, a freshman, at Baylor University in Waco. The Remsons and their fourteen-year-old daughter Kerry would be in the air most of fifteen hours flying from Dallas to Geneva, with a layover in Frankfurt.

Weeks earlier on a home-hunting trip to Geneva, the Remsons rented an apartment. It was less than a third the size of the Frisco house but in an eighteenth-century part of town with tight streets, sidewalk cafés, shops they can walk to, and a ten-minute drive to Mark's office. They found an international school a twenty-minute tram ride away, where in two days Kerry would be starting ninth grade. It was reassuring that, as college

Packing Up: *Kerry, Mark, and Sandi Remson (left to right) take a break while packing up their house in Frisco, Texas, before moving to Geneva, Switzerland, for Mark's fourth foreign assignment. The international assignment has become routine at many multinational corporations.*

students, Laura and Brian were fending for themselves, but at a continent and 5,200 miles away, Sandi still worried how she would respond if, for example, one got sick.

Mark is forty-nine, and Sandi forty-six. Both children of Relos, like their own children, Mark and Sandi are as rootless as hobos, albeit at the wheels of BMWs. They come from somewhere: Mark was born in Maine and Sandi in Lansing, Michigan. But they are of nowhere. They have moved through four states and three foreign countries. When the time comes, Mark tells the kids, "Don't waste money on a funeral somewhere. Put me in a box and throw me away."

Slender and six foot four, with a short and thick dark beard going gray, Mark is a boundaryless careerist whose skill is his knowledge of semiconductor production. He is senior director for manufacturing solutions at STMicroelectronics, one of the world's five leading semiconductor companies and rival of the American giants Intel and Advanced Micro Devices. Based in Geneva and of Franco-Italian origin, ST makes silicon chips for Nokia cell phones, Lexus and Mercedes automobiles, Hewlett-Packard printers, cable television boxes, and digital cameras. The chips are made or assembled at twenty-four plants on four continents.

Mark is in the top tier of Relos who manage the switches of global industry and get generous perks. He earns between $200,000 and $300,000 a year. ST pays the Remsons' rent in Geneva and Kerry's tuition. Before leaving Frisco, ST's relocation company specified the car he could get. He could have an Audi, a Mercedes, a BMW, or a Volvo, and it would cover $56,000 of the cost. He picked a BMW.

With their moves for Mark's career and no way for Sandi to get work, the Remsons find themselves a cultural anomaly: ST is a twenty-first-century company in a world without borders, yet the Remsons are a classic breadwinner-dad, stay-at-home-mom family, and purest of nuclear families. The five Remsons cling like boards of butcher block. Until Laura started college, 110 miles from Frisco, Mark and Sandi had never been apart from their kids in all their years moving.

Mark would be traveling two and three weeks a month, but he calls home every night from the road and speaks with each of the children. "It's like a dinner conversation," Brian said. Once the wheels on the car Brian drove to school were misaligned, so a tire blew out and the next day another. "I asked Mom, 'What am I going to do?'" Brian said. Sandi had never changed a tire. On the phone Mark led him through jacking up the car, removing the tire, and putting on a spare. "Brian's doing stuff I'm not there to do," Mark said. "Car stuff. Taking care of the yard."

When the Remsons landed in Frankfurt for a layover on their way to Geneva, Sandi's cell phone beeped. "911," a text message from Laura said. "Call me ASAP. It's really important." That morning Laura started having headaches that hurt more than migraines. By 9 p.m., Excedrin and other over-the-counter medications hadn't helped. "I had never experienced being sick like that," she said. "One of my roommates took me to the emergency room in the middle of the night. The doctors did an MRI. They thought I might have meningitis. They wanted to do a spinal tap." She wouldn't let them. She wanted her mother. She called, but they were still on the plane. She left the message and, against the doctors' advice, she walked out of the hospital.

Sandi picked up the message three hours later. "We told her to go right back and follow the doctors' orders," she said. Laura had the spinal tap. They found nothing. The headaches slowly subsided. "I was fine a week later," Laura said. "I missed three or four days of class. Without parents around," she said, "you have to become very trusting of professionals. I had to trust the doctors and make these decisions myself."

Mark and Sandi met in California at Humboldt State College just south of Oregon's southeastern border. They got married in 1981 when Mark graduated and Sandi was still a student. He couldn't find work in his major of forestry. His father was a production manager then at Advanced Micro Devices in Sunnyvale, California. He had entered the industry in the 1950s as it was starting up, became a Relo, and ended up in Silicon Valley.

"We heard that the semiconductor industry was hiring anyone with a degree," Sandi said. So the Remsons headed south to AMD. Mark said, "I was just at the beginning of CAM—Computer Aided Manufacturing—and that's what I've been doing since. We had no plans. You figure out what you have to do to survive. As the industry became more global, we moved to enhance the career." He stayed in Sunnyvale for six years and then moved:

> To St. Louis with McDonnell Douglas, the former aircraft company and military contractor, for two years, when Laura was born.
> To AMD in San Jose for three months.
> To VSLI Technologies in San Antonio for two years, when Brian was born.
> To AMD and to Phoenix for two years, when Kerry was born.
> To Austin for a year.
> To Aizu-Wakamatsu, Japan, for three years. The children attended Japanese schools.
> To Austin for ten months.
> To Singapore for five and a half years.
> To New Delhi for a year.

To San Jose for a month.

To STMicroelectronics in Carrollton, Texas, near Frisco, for two
years, three weeks.

To Geneva.

As products are developed at ST, Mark leads a team that finds ways
to produce them and write the software to manage production, work
in progress, and inventory. He is a rare American at ST. As a senior director, he ranks a notch below the company's top echelon of twenty-
seven officers. Ten are from Italy, nine from France, one each from
Canada, Germany, Britain, Singapore, and Finland. One is Swiss-
Italian, one French-Algerian, and one Iranian-American. Eight are career Relos, having been moved four or more times.

In Frisco, although assigned to the ST plant in Carrollton, Mark
worked on his laptop and phone at the dining room table and went in to
the office only to submit his travel expenses. He couldn't schedule his
work to suit Carrollton's hours. "When I'm in the United States," he said,
"I start at one a.m. and work to three p.m. I've got 450 people that work
for me spread across the U.S., Asia, and Europe. My one a.m. is Singapore's one p.m. and Europe's eight a.m."

Before leaving for Geneva, the Remsons bought what would be their
legal American residence, near Baylor, a five-bedroom home with three
baths, at least for the duration of Laura and Brian's time there. One room
would be Laura's, and in a year, when he could move off campus, Brian
would take one. The Remsons planned to rent the others to students,
which would cover the mortgage.

They didn't expect to live again in a house as big and majestic as the
one in Frisco, with 4,500 square feet and soaring ceilings, dark paneled
spaces, and a fireplace big enough to sit in, so they have given the children
some furniture, the washer and dryer, and the projection TV. On a day
that two United Van Lines vans waited in front of the house, Mark said,
"We told the kids, 'You're going away forever. You're not coming home in
the summer. There is no home to come home to. So think about when
you graduate college and take what you might need post-college.'"

Mark expected to be in Geneva for two or four years; the company hadn't decided which. From there he thought he would be moved to Singapore again. Either two or four years was okay with Kerry. She knows Singapore better than the United States, which she left for Japan as a toddler and to which she returned only for the short stay in Austin and the two years in Frisco. Her best friend is an Indian girl she met in New Delhi who has since moved to Australia. They stay in touch every day by e-mail. They chat about school, moving, and boys.

"Our lifestyle is probably good for one-half of 1 percent of the people in the world," Mark said. "We've been lucky because the kids could adjust. The most difficult part is your extended family—your parents, brothers, sisters. I don't know how long the kids' grandparents are going to hang on. They only see Grandma and Grandpa once a year. To get them to come out and see you is a major thing."

They had already lost one grandparent. Sandi's father in Florida died while the Remsons were in Japan. "We were helpless," Mark said. Retired from his work as a civilian intelligence officer for the navy, her father was ailing and she went to stay with him. Mark's parents came to stay with the kids. Then, just after she got back to Japan, her father died. She hurried back for the funeral and to comfort her mother.

Now they worried about Mark's father, who in his late seventies was retired and living in San Jose. His organs failing, he went into the hospital as the Remsons were packing for Geneva, and Mark went out to see him. He went again for ten days to help him and his mother, who had worked as a nurse for forty-five years. (Mark's father died a year later, in February 2008.)

Leaving Frisco, Sandi said, "I do wish I had a doctor I always went to, a best friend I always went to."

But the Remsons found a groove in Geneva. The two years were stretching to four, so Kerry, happy with her studies, basketball, and volleyball, could plan to finish high school there. Sandi joined a ski group and a walking group. In the sinking economy, ST's revenues were dropping. It announced the elimination of 4,500 jobs in 2009 and was closing its two American plants, in Phoenix and Carrollton. Yet Mark was still rolling, and spending much of his time at busy plants—in Singapore and the Philippines.

5. Body Snatching

Your first call from a headhunter is one of those minor rites of passage. While it's good to know that someone has called you, such contact is about more than just a warm glow. It could be the start of a long-term relationship that is crucial to your career. Expressing a long view is rarely easy in today's economic climate. Businesses are looking for immediate results and this pressure can make candidates and recruiters focus too strongly on short-term gain. At Spencer Stuart, consultants take a long-term approach to working with candidates—because many of them will eventually become clients.

—"Working with Recruiters," Spencer Stuart Web page

Right on cue each year, the shelves and aisles of the Michaels chain of a thousand arts and crafts stores bloom with sequins and lace to make Halloween skirts for little ballerinas, sparkles and stickers for Valentine's cards, dyes and baskets for Easter eggs, and red, white, and blue felt for Fourth of July place mats. If Michaels's inventory-management people are on the ball, everything is gone like Cinderella by midnight of the holiday, and Michaels ends the week in the black. If the inventory managers miscalculate and the shelves empty too soon or remain stocked past midnight and have to be purged at deep discounts, Michaels can end the week in the red.

"Inventory management" smells of shuffling boxes in stockrooms. But like finance or sales or manufacturing or engineering, inventory management is an executive track to a $500,000-a-year "C-suite" job as chief technology officer or chief information officer. At Michaels Stores of Irving, Texas, as at competitors A.C. Moore, Hobby Lobby, and Jo-Ann Stores, as at the grocery chains, the clothing chains, the fast-food chains, and all the other chains, corporate fortunes can rise and fall with the inventory management artistry of people like Matt Fischer, formally Michaels's senior director of replenishment. With clicks of a mouse, Matt and his team of forty crank up assembly lines, rouse warehouses, and roll out trucks. He has loomed into the sights of the executive search firms, the top-scale employment agencies called headhunters.

By August 2006, Matt, then forty-four, his wife, Maggie, forty-two, and their skinny, crew-cut boys J.C. (for John Casteen), fourteen, and Lucas, twelve, had been living near Irving in Flower Mound, Texas, for four years—high noon for a Relo's next move. Over twenty-two years, Matt had averted dead-ending his career by mining his network of contacts to move from Chicago to Cleveland, to Columbus, to Houston, and finally to Flower Mound. Now he was getting calls from the recruiters who steer Relos from company to company. They were sounding him out about moves to smaller companies' C-suites as CIO and bigger companies dangling a higher-paid C-suite job after a year or two. Michaels seemed promising, too, but he couldn't be sure. Two big private equity firms—Bain Capital and the Blackstone Group—had just bought Michaels and taken it private and were bringing in a new chief executive officer, also a Relo.

Flower Mound was a fast-growing Reloville, twenty miles north of Dallas, of 67,293 people in 2006, and many of them, like Matt, mid-career men and women who pass through town on the way to another. Almost 60 percent of Flower Mound's residents come from outside Texas. Nearly all live in homes built since 1990, and nearly two-thirds of the homes have four or more bedrooms. Family incomes and adults with at least bachelor's degrees are about twice the national averages.

The Fischers bought their house, the only one on their cul-de-sac, for about $370,000. It is a standard-issue Relo model of 3,700 square feet with gables, two stories, and a brick façade. Inside, its hub was the sprawling and casual family room with the old brown sofa that Matt and Maggie had bought after college, the only thing they ever bought on time and which they paid off in a month. Maggie, her straight dark hair in bangs and clad all day in jeans and loose shirts, sorts and irons laundry in front of the room's sixty-inch projection TV, on which the Fischers watch movies and University of Illinois football and basketball games.

Out back, the Fischers have a pool they keep open all year, and in a year they would build an outdoor kitchen with a roof, a bar, and a Jenn-Air grill. Their deep driveway and three-car garage allow room for their new Toyota Camry, a Nissan Pathfinder SUV, a pop-up trailer they take camping in national parks, and a shiny black 1997 Chevrolet Camaro with a Corvette engine that Matt bought for $8,000. "What happens is," Maggie said, "when a man has the means to buy something, women say it's a midlife crisis."

Matt, gangly and six feet tall, and Maggie, five foot ten, are loud and animated talkers, more so than J.C. and Lucas. Like Matt, the boys play basketball. They are straight-A students and Boy Scouts working on badges to become Eagles. The family's routines breached some conventions, like regular meal times and orthodox diets. One of J.C.'s fourteenth-birthday presents was a tub of chocolate-chip cookie dough. For lunch one day, he combined a fist-size dollop of dough with a side of raw carrots, and for supper that night, a can of spaghetti that he heated and ate from the pan sitting in an easy chair.

Matt and Maggie grew up in Carbondale, Illinois, a town of 29,000 and home of Southern Illinois University, and went to Carbondale Community High School. Before his parents divorced, Matt's mother was an EKG technician and school board member and his father an architect, businessman, and mayor. His father remarried and moved to Lawrence, Kansas, and his mother moved to a farm in north central Arkansas where

Making a Home: *When they moved to Flower Mound, Texas, the Fischers (Matt and Maggie Fischer, with their sons J.C. and Lucas) bought a standard-issue Relo home model: 3,700 square feet with gables, two stories, and a brick façade. A year after moving in they personalized their home with an outdoor kitchen with a roof, a bar, and a Jenn-Air grill.*

she raises goats. Maggie's father, who has died, worked as a labor negotiator for the university, and her mother as a social worker.

Matt and Maggie went to the University of Illinois at Urbana-Champaign and earned degrees in accounting. Matt, two years older, found work in Chicago as an accountant at Boise Cascade, the building materials company. In 1987 when Maggie finished college, they got married in Carbondale, and Maggie joined a small accounting firm in Chicago, joining Matt there. They never considered going home to work. Unemployment is relatively low in Carbondale, but poverty, affecting 25 percent of the families, is high, and family incomes are a third less than the national average. "There were like three hundred people in our high school classes," Maggie said, "and they're like twenty-five of those three hundred who are still in Carbondale. Everyone else leaves. We leave so we can get work. Unless you're going to work at the university or the hospital, there's not a lot of work in southern Illinois."

At Boise, Matt became a purchasing manager at a distribution center—his introduction to inventory management. He became a rookie Relo. Boise moved the Fischers to Cleveland, where J.C. was born, and then to Columbus, Ohio, where Lucas was born. Matt began learning an inventory management program called E3 that the JDA Software Group of Scottsdale, Arizona, makes for retail chains and manufacturers to keep track of the merchandise on their loading docks and shelves, tell them where and when to restock, and show them how much money they're making or losing on their sales.

Then Boise sold Matt's division to another company that wanted to make him a purchasing manager in Chicago. He wouldn't be using E3. Through JDA he heard that Victoria's Secret, a Limited Company chain in Columbus, was installing the program. They took him on. After two years with Victoria's Secret, he was earning $70,000. "I wanted a director-level position," he said, "and I wanted to make six figures." Garden Ridge, a home decorating chain in Houston, was installing E3, too. It offered him $102,000 and the job of replenishment director. "I told Limited," he said, "and they're like, 'No way,' and I'm like, 'Yeah, that's what I'm worth.'" He accepted the Garden Ridge job.

The Fischers had been living in the Houston suburb of Katy only a year when Limited called back. "They had put together a position that they thought would be good for me," Matt said. "It would have meant going back to Columbus. So I went up and interviewed with them and they made me an offer for $40,000 or $50,000 more than I was making at Garden Ridge—about $150,000, plus a bonus plan, everything, and double what I was making before at the Limited. I went to Maggie, 'Okay, what do you want to do?'"

Maggie hated Houston from the start. "We had $10,000 in damaged furniture," Matt said, "and the moving van ran into our new van and hit it." A copperhead settled in the yard of the house, near the faucet for the hose. "I screamed," Maggie said, "'You've got to get me out of here!'" First grade was hard for J.C. In Ohio he was taught spelling by learning whole words. "In Houston," Maggie said, "they taught the phonics system. J.C.

got a zero out of ten in phonics." But now that she had caught her breath and the boys were making friends, Maggie wanted to hunker down for a while.

By then Matt had mastered the boundaryless careerist's skill of artful negotiation. He thought he might be able to have it both ways—stay in Houston and get a salary close to Limited's. He went to his boss at Garden Ridge. "I said, 'You know what? I'm in a bit of a predicament. The Limited has made me just a fantastic offer. We're very happy here, we enjoy what we're doing, and we're having fun and so on. But holy cow, it's like 50 percent more salary and bonus and stuff like that.'

"I said, 'I'm asking you not as my boss; I just need some advice. I mean what would you do?' And if they said, 'You should take it,' I'd have had to seriously consider taking it. But they said, 'We'll give you $20,000 more,' so I was up to $125,000. I walked in one day making 105 and the next day I'm making 125. That's a lot less than 150, but wow, I did nothing. My job didn't change. Nothing changed and I got twenty thousand more dollars." He called Limited, " 'You know what, I just got here,' " he said. " 'We've just been here a year. My kids are just getting acclimated to school. We just can't do it.' "

Fishing and Poaching

After a couple of years, Matt was restless. He was up to $150,000 a year at Garden Ridge, but the company's revenues were dropping, and he suspected, correctly it turned out, that it was veering toward bankruptcy. "It was a small, three hundred to five hundred million–dollar company that wasn't sure what they wanted to be, what they wanted to do," he said. "I had like four bosses in five years. I'm reporting to the executive vice president of merchandising or the chief information officer or the chief executive officer. I started saying, 'We got to get out of here.' "

Matt called a former Victoria's Secret colleague. "I said, 'I'm kind of looking around, quietly.' So I get a call from this guy at Spencer Stuart." Spencer Stuart in Chicago places Relos at many Fortune 500 companies, among them IBM, Nike, Best Buy, Citigroup, Merck, JC Penney, Kellogg, Kroger, Coca-Cola, Nieman Marcus, and Wal-Mart.

"They say, 'Hey, there's this position at Office Depot in Boca Raton, Florida.'" Spencer Stuart invited him to Chicago for a chat. "It was an IT, information technology, job," he said, "vice president level in support of their merchandising group. I wondered, 'Do they want someone who is more technical, who can write a computer program, or someone who manages a system, like I do, and understands the user side?' I can't write a computer program." Nothing came of that trip or another, to the CVS pharmacy chain's home in Woonsocket, Rhode Island.

By then, Matt was becoming known around retail chains and other E3 users. He went to an industry conference in Las Vegas and gave a talk about managing seasonal products. An executive vice president at Michaels gave him his card. "He said, 'Hey, I'd like to talk to you,'" Matt said. They met at a hotel near the Dallas–Fort Worth airport. He was invited back to meet more Michaels officers.

They didn't talk salary at first. "At some point the human resources people said, 'Well, what's your expectation for the salary?' I said probably around the one-sixties, and they came back and said, 'Whoa! We're talking one-twenty, one-thirty maybe.' I said, 'That's okay. Let's talk about the bonus, the full compensation.' We came to an agreement. In base pay, I probably took a $35,000 cut. But if you looked at the end of the year, from an adjusted gross income standpoint, we actually did better because of the bonus and the stock."

As director of replenishment at Michaels, Matt felt he had positioned himself for bigger things. "A lot of it is the tools you use," he said. "I've made my career around E3, which is probably among the top two or three systems in the world at managing inventory." He also knew how to build a team. Starting with a few inventory managers he brought from Garden Ridge, he hired thirty more at Michaels. Wherever he goes, he suspects, some will follow. Michaels created a new position for him— senior director.

After four years, the Fischers had wound themselves into the fabric of Flower Mound. Matt was enjoying his work. His immediate subordinates had become his best friends. He went to car shows with them, played softball with them, and had them over for cookouts with the family. The Fischers wanted nothing to change until Lucas left for college, in six years. But Spencer Stuart was calling again. The possibility of another big step in Matt's career was gnawing at the family's tranquillity.

Near the end of 2006, a headhunter there asked what he would think about moving to Bentonville, Arkansas, and Wal-Mart Stores, the biggest private company in the world. It moves more inventory, in greater variety, than any institution except perhaps the Pentagon. They talked about it. "You can escalate your career if you want to move around," he said. "The ones who don't move around don't get the calls about Wal-Mart because nobody knows who they are. You have to have that kind of background. It's a game, getting jobs, keeping jobs, moving up the corporation.

"Maybe 'game' isn't the right word for it, but it is a game. People who play the game very well do better than people who don't. It's like anything, whether you're playing basketball or you're a professional in business. It's people who know how to give their bosses what they need and meet the requirements and the goals, or whatever, whether the goal is shooting a basketball or putting in systems and making more money for your company."

Seventy miles northwest of Washington, D.C., in the village of Berryville, Virginia, Kelly Kincannon and his wife, Diana, have restored a landmark stone farmhouse with a granite cornerstone inscribed 1782. Three stories tall, up a lane past a stone barn, through swinging iron gates, the homestead commands a vista of meadows and grazing sheep. Across the drive is another stone barn and the office where Kincannon spends most workdays rather than drive the eighty-eight miles to his firm's main office in Waynesboro, Virginia. He does most of his work by phone and the Internet.

Kincannon is a tall, courteous, good-humored, and fastidious man of sixty, largely bald, with a veneer of white beard. Away from the farm, at meetings in Washington, he wears wide-winged bow ties that he tightens into knots the size of a pea. The tools of his trade, he says, are romance and seduction. He is founder and chairman of Kincannon & Reed, a firm that specializes in recruiting executives for agriculture-related businesses like John Deere; Cargill, the global grain distribution and processing company; big producers of farm chemicals like Monsanto; and industry lob-bying organizations in Washington like the National Council of Farmers Cooperatives. The Bill and Melinda Gates Foundation asked him to find executives for a project in Africa.

Though now embedded in his Virginia estate, Kincannon spent his youth as a Relo. He spent his earliest years on a family farm near Waco, Texas, where his father taught vocational agriculture. His father went to work selling DDT across the Great Plains for a chemical company. The family moved to Eddy, Texas, to Lubbock, Texas, and to North Little Rock, Arkansas. At seventeen, as Kelly was entering his senior year in high school, his father became a district and plant manager in New Jersey for another chemical company, so they moved to Ridgefield, New Jersey.

He went back to Texas, to Texas A&M, and worked off some wan-derlust traveling in Europe. Returning, he found work selling pesticides in central Florida, a job that led eventually to work recruiting pesticide-company executives in St. Louis. His then-wife, from whom he is di-vorced, was working for May Department Stores. She was transferred to Virginia to open a mall, and he and their two children followed.

Most companies still rely on their human resources or person-nel departments to find workers for entry-level management jobs—assistant brand manager, assistant plant manager—and to help select those for promotion to the middle of the officer pyramid. But at many companies—Citigroup, Eastman Kodak, and Merck among them—the once sacrosanct, career-long allegiances of the workplace, company to worker and worker to company, have broken down, and their executives move as freely from company to company as they do from place to place.

Companies turn to executive recruiters—"poachers" and "rustlers" they call them when they lose an executive to one. Recruiters are the cata-lysts of the proliferation of Relos. They have inspired the growth of boundaryless career Relos, or stateless "floaters," as Peter Felix, president of the Association of Executive Search Consultants in New York, calls them. Without the headhunters, the only Relos would be those who are moved within the ranks of one company, a practice that persists at some companies, like Cargill, IBM, General Motors, Procter & Gamble, and General Electric.

Once, employers thought frequent job-hoppers too fickle to trust in their executive ranks. But companies are more tolerant now perhaps because they have become fickle, too. Jilting an employer is okay provided only that the job seeker shows some restraint. The search consultants association asked 152 of its 1,500 member firms worldwide how often managers could abandon their companies without tainting their résumés with the rap of serial infidelity. One hundred and eight of them— 77 percent—thought managers should stick around for at least two years, and 111 thought they ought not to change employers more than three times in a decade.

In another survey of 933 employed executives, a representative sample of a database the association keeps of 34,000 men and women who have made themselves available for recruiters to call, 69 percent said they had worked for their current company for five years or less, 63 percent said they didn't expect to stay longer than five years, and 68 percent said they had already worked for four or more companies. Eighty percent were thirty-four to fifty-four years old, 88 percent were men, and 54 percent lived in North America. All earned at least $100,000 a year and most between $200,000 and $300,000.

Five firms—Heidrick & Struggles and Spencer Stuart in Chicago, Korn/Ferry International in New York and Los Angeles, Russell Reynolds Associates in New York, and Egon Zehnder of Zurich and New York—do about a third of all recruiting. They employ hundreds of consultants, or headhunters, each, and vie for nearly all the Fortune 500 companies for clients. Hundreds of other firms like Kelly Kincannon's specialize in particular industries. Typically headhunters charge one-third of a recruited executive's first-year compensation—salary and bonuses. The average in 2008 was about $90,000.

As the global economy has grown, executive recruiting has become a big robust business. The search association says the industry's revenues worldwide grew from $750 million in 1978 to $8.3 billion in 2000. They plunged through the dot-com recession to $5.3 billion in 2003, and rebounded to a record of $10.7 billion in 2007. The economy's devastation starting in 2008 battered the recruiters. But more than in 2003, the industry expected demand from the industrializing economies of

India and China and a shortage of American executives to take over from retiring baby boomers to prime their pumps once the economy gets out of its ditch.

The recruiting process is the same across the industry. Kelly Kincannon courts "centers of influence," upstanding, credible people who tend to know others throughout a community whom he can sound out about changes within institutions and who think well enough of him to refer companies that are looking for talent. He has a research staff that builds a database of executives with their location, employer, industrial sector, and education. "A client in the crop protection business might want Harvard MBAs who live in the southeastern United States and have the title of vice president or higher," he said. With the client, he prepares a script defining the job to present to candidates and from his office in Berryville he calls the candidates.

"I rarely identify the client to the candidate then," he said. "You talk about the opportunity. You ask, 'Who do you know who might fit this situation?' And then you go silent. They'll say, 'I don't know anyone.' Or, 'What about Smith?' Or, 'Let me close my door,' or, 'Call me at home this evening.' We talk some more. I request a CV. If the CV fits, I set up an interview. Before 9/11, we did interviews in airport lounges." But with security gates blocking access, he uses airport hotels. "We spend a lot of time at the O'Hare Hilton," he said. "From the interviews, you narrow it down to three people you present to the client to interview. The client says, 'I would like to recruit candidate A, contingent upon reference checks.' If it's positive, I extend an offer."

Like most Fortune 500–level recruiters, Kincannon works for clients on a retainer. Retainers discourage poaching. If Cargill and Monsanto are both his clients, he cannot approach Cargill executives for searches on behalf of Monsanto. It's a tricky business for the biggest firms. IBM got around it in 1993 when it recruited Louis V. Gerstner Jr., chief executive at RJR Nabisco, to be its chief executive. It used two search firms, Spencer Stuart and Heidrick & Struggles, so that one would be free to poach from the other. Kincannon posts dates on his list of retained clients for the end of the retainer. If he finds more candidates for clients while the retainer is active, the date rolls forward.

Finding candidates, however, is getting harder. Kincannon was doing a search for a company in Southern California. "We have a slate of five candidates," he said. "Every one would have to relocate. One said he couldn't go for a year. Another one, after a family meeting, has withdrawn, solely because of his family. His twelve-year-old daughter won't move," he said.

The Big Leap

At noon on an August Sunday in 2007, it was 105 degrees in Flower Mound. Matt Fischer was in the pool. His son Lucas was upstairs reading. J.C. was working through a jar of kosher pickles. Maggie, in blue jeans and a bright orange University of Illinois T-shirt, was having her lunch, too—two slices of yesterday's pizza. "We're not going anywhere," she said. "I've told Matt that if he job hops, he can commute. We're not moving."

"That's what I told him, too," J.C. said. As a freshman, he took advanced placement biology and got a 4, one short of a perfect 5. "Colleges accept different scores," he said. "Most colleges accept threes. When I finish high school, I'll have AP calculus, biology, physics, and maybe chemistry and some English and history."

"Right now I'm a mom," Maggie said. "When you have kids, that becomes your priority. That's why I'm digging in. We are not moving the kids at the age that they are at. I want to see my kids get through high school and go to good colleges and get them through that."

"What I struggle with," Matt said, drying off, "is providing for you and the family the best of everything, and we're pretty good right here."

"How much is enough?" Maggie asked Matt.

"How comfortable is comfortable?" Matt replied.

"That's where I sit now," he said. "Is this fine, or is there more somewhere else and once you get there, would you say, 'Is there somewhere else that's even finer?' That's the question, and I don't know the answer. If I were to move again, I could get to whatever financial level quicker, and I could retire quicker. Do I want to work another fifteen years, or do I want to work another six years? It's not about ego or being the biggest or best or anything like that. It's more about having the means to do what I want to do. I'd like to have a million bucks sitting in the account that I can drop and go buy a nice little place in the mountains of Colorado to retire in. I can't do that yet."

The Fischers are frugal. Unlike neighbors who use landscaping services, they mow their own lawn. They don't hire a house cleaner. They don't often go to restaurants. For vacations, they take their trailer and pay $16 a night in national parks. They have the boys' college tuitions ahead of them, but on Matt's $170,000 a year they feel secure.

"We decided to go buy a new mattress," Maggie said, "and we went out and bought a new mattress. It wasn't like we had to sit there and plan it out. We wanted a mattress and just went out there and did it."

"A car," Matt said. "A car. You want to buy a car, you just go buy a car."

Still, the recruiters called. "Headhunters," Matt said, "out fishing. They all start out with, 'Matt, I'd like to network with you on a couple of positions that I've got open.' That's their line. That's probably how they get my name. They talked to somebody else, or they saw it at a conference or on the Internet. So I give them a couple of people's names. I say, 'I have no idea whether this person's interested.' That's what they do. They're people-mining. I don't give them my counterparts, the people I work with, unless of course I know somebody's interested."

A recruiter for Bass Pro Shop, a fishing and hunting gear chain and E3 user, called him and his colleagues. Bass had about 120 stores and a big Internet and catalogue business but was a third or a fourth the size of Michaels. "They're headquartered in Springfield, Missouri," Matt said, "and that's their problem. They're having a hard time getting people who want to move to Springfield, Missouri. That's what would attract me to the job. It's near the Ozarks. It's beautiful, outdoors. But the job is more of a lateral or lower move for me. I would want to be that person's boss."

The trickier call was the one the year before, about Wal-Mart. "She said, 'I'm just going to send you the job description,'" Matt said. "She sent that to me electronically. I read it and thought, 'Wow, this is pretty neat.' I replied by e-mail and said, 'This looks great.' A lot of the things they said they want are exactly me. It looked like somebody wrote it with me in mind. 'But before we go any further, you better make sure you don't have a relationship with Michaels or Bain.'" Spencer Stuart does indeed recruit for Michaels and Bain, so they're off-limits. "She came right back and said, 'You're right. I'm sorry.'"

Matt considered sidestepping the conflict by approaching Wal-Mart on his own. "I was thinking about it. 'You know what, just to find out a little more about it, should I call them directly?' I don't know if I'm comfortable doing that. Plus, am I really serious? Probably not. But there's a little bit of curiosity in you. Makes you want to find out if you're good enough to make it in that league, at that level. It's my ego, I guess. But it would be tough on the kids." Juggling these thoughts, he wavered. "I could commute to Bentonville. It's an hour flight from Dallas. I could do that weekly or whatever. Maggie didn't say, 'No way. We're not going to do that.'

"But you could tell by the look in her face. I do a lot of stuff with my kids every week, during the week, too. Yeah, I probably won't pursue it anymore. I have a great opportunity where in a couple of years I could have a vice president position at Michaels, maybe then even a senior VP position, and I could still keep my family here. I could do both. I could have both. If someone offered me $250,000—$100,000 more than what I make now—would that be enough to uproot my kids? No. It's not enough. You know what I mean? Because it's not worth it.

"I'm wasting people's time if I'm not serious about it. So I haven't done anything. I'm pretty happy with where I'm at. I'm enjoying the work. At Michaels they're saying, 'Hey Matt, we think you have opportunities here.'" A couple of months after the promotion to senior director, he said, "my boss called me in. 'Hey Matt, we want to give you $10,000 more just because we like you.'

"The other thing is, I have a good relationship with my boss. Well, do you let it slip in, 'Hey, Wal-Mart called me?' That plants a little seed in there. 'Wow, if Wal-Mart is interested in this guy, if he's that good, we better make sure we're taking care of him.' But you've also got to be in the position to move if somebody calls your bluff and says, 'Oh really? We'll see you.'"

In June 2007, Michaels hired a new chief executive officer, Brian C.

Cornell, a Relo who arrived via Safeway, Inc., in California, PepsiCo, Tropicana, Seagram, and Gallo Wine. One of two co-presidents then running Michaels left upon Cornell's appointment. Perhaps Cornell would want to rattle the ranks and bring in new people, so competitors and recruiters thought Matt might be ready to jump.

"In fact, a lady called," he said, "and left me her name and said she'd like to talk. It's usually a recruiter calling you up. I didn't call back." She called again and left a message mentioning one of Matt's former colleagues so he returned the call.

"She said, 'Do you know where you dialed into?'" She said she was the senior vice president for human resources at one of Michaels's competitors, located in the Mid-Atlantic. He went for an interview and was offered $200,000 a year plus other compensation that might have brought his first-year earnings to as much as $375,000. He sounded out some other former Michaels executives. "One told me, 'Matt, you can do better than that,'" he said. He turned them down.

Holding on paid off. Maybe word got around that a Spencer Stuart recruiter had called him about Wal-Mart, or that a competitor had brought him in for an interview. Maybe Michaels just liked his work. "He got called in," Maggie said, in October 2007. He was promoted to vice president and was given a raise. It left him below the competitor's offer, but he was assured annual bonuses from Michaels profits and stock that might be worth more than $1 million if Bain and Blackstone brought the company public.

In the sinking economy of 2007 and 2008, both Michaels and the competitor he visited ran up losses, not profits. There would be no going public for a while.

For the moment, Matt had at least bought time for Flower Mound and the boys. Lucas was starring in middle school plays. He was taking pre-AP math and pre-AP science and had made the school's "All A" Club for kids with straight A's. J.C. finished his freshman year ranked seventh in a class of 794. As a sophomore, he made the varsity basketball team. He became an Eagle Scout. He had a girlfriend. He got his driver's license. An uncle gave him his old Pontiac Vibe. He was plotting the course of his life. "Be a lawyer because I like to argue," he said. "Get a house. Get a better house. Get promoted, get promoted, get a better house, get a better house."

Maggie, too, was steeped in the life of Flower Mound. She had enough of the winter cold in Cleveland and Carbondale and the swampy heat of Houston. Matt said, "I'm in a position where I don't want to say we've made it. But we make enough to live comfortably. I could maintain this lifestyle and be happy with it. I mean, we don't drive BMWs and Mercedeses. We have a Toyota Camry. It's very nice just to be comfortable."

6. The Next Move

An astute real estate agent knows her customer will be transferred, so she wants to put the customer in a house that's up to date and resalable. That real estate agent wants to get that second commission. More real estate commissions have been paid on a house in the Village Mill subdivision that has been sold and resold than the house cost to begin with.

—Jim Cowart, builder, Atlanta

In the early 1960s, the British writer Anthony Sampson described the wealth of the upper class as a subterranean river, with springs now and then revealing class excesses and customs and continually replenishing itself to nurture later generations. The Relo economy works in much the same way, unremarked and undefined, through a labyrinthine network of commercial activity serving a corporate class of global vagabonds.

Relo careers change the way people settle and live, not just how they work. From the golden ghettos of Alpharetta and Roswell in Georgia to Frisco and Flower Mound in Texas, to Westernized apartment blocks in Singapore and Kolkata, Relos migrate across a separate and autonomous universe of their own. They sustain an industry that collects more than a billion dollars a year managing their moves and catering to their special needs.

Builders conceive homes, developers subdivisions, and bankers mortgages designed for Relos. Household names among real estate firms like Prudential and Coldwell Banker appoint and train agents to cater solely to Relos. Pre-schools crop up in Relovilles to give toddlers an edge in applying to select private schools, and bands of scavengers sweep up possessions abandoned by Relos in a hurry to move or dismissed from their jobs and recycle them through flea markets and thrift shops.

No business does more to cater to Relos than the relocation management firm. According to the Worldwide Employee Relocation Council, by 2007 employers were spending $32 billion a year to move people within the United States and immeasurable additional billions to move them abroad and subsidize their housing, tuitions, cars, and summer visits home. For some employers, the moves are straightforward. They grant employees a budget—typically $70,000 for top executives, $45,000 for mid-level managers, $3,000 or $4,000 for new college graduates—and leave the Relos to tackle their moves themselves.

But for half of all large companies, a relocation package has become a significant recruiting tool and too complex and costly to leave to employees. Cris Collie of the ERC said companies spend an average of $62,000 to move a household within the United States and more than $100,000, sometimes much more, to move one abroad.

The Relo Economy

To control costs and expedite moves, employers turn to any of approximately fifty relocation management firms, most less than twenty years old and providing a wide variety of services. There's Cartus, Sirva, Inc., Prudential Relocation, GMAC Global Relocation Services, Primacy Relocation, Weichert Relocation Resources, Paragon Relocation Resources, RELO Direct, Graebel Relocation Services, Relocation Strategies, Lexicon Relocation Resources, and Altair Global Relocation of Plano. Most have grown from specialized services for home buyers: Prudential Relocation and Weichert Relocation Resources are extensions of real estate firms.

Cartus Corporation—the industry Goliath—bills itself "the premier provider of global relocation and workforce development solutions worldwide." In a typical year, Cartus moves 130,000 employees for 1,200 clients, including nearly half the Fortune 500 companies. Some of those companies transfer more than a thousand employees every year; Procter & Gamble, for one, transfers about 3,500. A subsidiary of the privately held Realogy Corporation of Parsippany, New Jersey, Cartus is a diversified real estate services company that operates under the brands Coldwell Banker, Century 21, Better Homes and Gardens, ERA, and Sotheby's International Realty. It refers Relos to 800 real estate offices it owns or to 16,000 local, independently owned, franchised offices. In return for customer referrals from Cartus, staff training, use of the brands and brand advertising, the franchisees accept Realogy's scrutiny of their accounts, follow strict criteria to standardize the offices' image and services, and pay Realogy royalties, fees, and half their home-sale commissions.

Vicki Butcher is the high-spirited director of relocation for the 23-branch and 250-agent-strong Century 21–Judge Fife franchise that serves the Relovilles surrounding Dallas. Butcher knows the travails of relocation firsthand. Now in her fifties, she and her husband were moved every two years over the course of their twenties and thirties. She chafed at the disruptions, and she considers the towns north of Dallas the hardest for making friends. She feels she is on a mission to manage her clients' moves better.

Cartus typically sends her information about five or six relocating buyers each week. Butcher calls them, assesses their needs, and assigns them to agents from her Cartus-trained A-team, made up of twenty-five relocation specialists. "We try to find every detail about these people," she said. "We know as much about them as we possibly can because if we can make a good match, we can close that transaction."

Rival firm Sirva, based near Chicago, was formed in 1999 through a merger of the Allied and North American moving van companies. Borrowing heavily, it then went on a binge acquiring moving companies throughout Europe—giving it claim to being "the largest and fastest-growing worldwide relocation and moving services company." Winning clients like 3M, Dell Computer, and Johnson & Johnson, Sirva, with Prudential, became arguably the second-largest relocation firm, after Cartus.

In the Atlanta area, several major employers, including a pharmaceutical company and a leading bank, turn to the local office of Lexicon, based in Jacksonville, Florida, and an agent for United Van Lines. Bob Packard, the company's vice president for business development, works out of Lexicon's new office in Marietta, which caters to Atlanta's sprawling Relovilles. "We sell ourselves as an outsource extension of a company's human resources department," Packard explained. Lexicon administers each employer's relocation policy and builds its business by ensuring that Relos settle into their new jobs within days, hours even, of leaving their last.

To manage a move, Lexicon assigns each Relo family a "relocation counselor," most often an empathetic, college-educated woman who advises employees long distance via phone, fax, and e-mail. "That's someone who knows their story," Packard said. "They'll manage the whole process." The counselor steers Relos to mortgage lenders and real estate agents and lines up appraisals to help guide Relos in selling their homes. She sets up house-hunting trips and household storage and temporary housing to cover gaps between the last assignment and the next. She is expected to be an advocate for the Relo, good at resolving conflicts, including a Relo's dispute with his employer over moving expenses or with the moving company over damaged furniture. Beyond the basics, when an employer allows, she researches doctors, schools, car dealers, job placement services for spouses, and furniture rental for short-term assignments. She will help ship the pets and the boat if the employer covers that.

Relocation firms sometimes charge employers a fee for the counselors' help but often nothing at all. The firms make money through

commissions or referral fees from the real estate agencies, moving companies, and other services the firms arrange for their clients. Of the average
$62,000 for the employer's domestic relocation cost, about $11,000 goes
to the moving company. Most of the rest covers the real estate transactions like closing costs, title insurance, and temporary housing. (Renters,
who tend to be young and single, cost much less to move—the ERC says
about $20,000.)

During the spirited market of the 1990s into 2007, Relos didn't need
much help to sell their homes. Within days of listing them, most collected
sizable gains from selling for more than they paid. Move upon move, sale
upon sale, Relos' real estate windfalls became a powerful incentive to keep
relocating. They could plow their money into bigger and better houses
than they could have imagined owning, and into college tuitions, luxury cars, or retirement nest eggs that grew fatter and faster than their employee 401(k)s.

In 2007, the tables turned. Home prices stopped climbing and in
some towns dropped below what many Relos had paid—a disincentive to
move. The employer or the relocation firm called upon third-party ap-
praisers to set a realistic price for homes, and Relos were given sixty or
ninety days to try to sell them for more. When they could not, the employer bought the house for the appraised value, or it paid the relocation
firm a fee, typically 8 percent of the value, to buy the house and assume
the risk of reselling it.

With most Relos in secure and vital jobs, well paid, and holding substantial equity in their homes, not many got caught in the foreclosure epidemic and holding mortgages exceeding the depressed value of their
homes. And when the appraisal prices fell below what Relos had paid, employers often reimbursed them for the difference so they would get on
with their moves or gave them compensating bonuses.

In buying Relos' houses, employers and relocation firms took the
brunt of the stagnating market. With few houses selling, they would hold
them for months, making payments on their mortgages and keeping them
heated, lighted, and landscaped—only to watch their value continue to
sink and finally sell at a loss. "What we're seeing is employers getting a
real shock when they find out that transferees own property well beyond

what employers would think based on a transferee's income," Packard said. "You thought they might have a $350,000 house, and you find out it's a $1 million house."

For most big, multibillion-dollar-a-year companies, eating Relos' losses from home sales was still a minuscule cost of doing business. But for the relocation firms that thrived, like Relos themselves, on buying houses and selling them fast, the market turned precarious. Realogy, already laden with debt incurred when Apollo Management, a private equity firm, took it over in a leveraged buyout for $8.5 billion in April 2007, ran up big losses from its swelling inventory of slow-selling homes.

From a net profit of $365 million on revenues of $6.5 billion in 2006, Realogy plunged to an $841 million loss on revenues of $6 billion in 2007. That led to speculation in late 2008 that Realogy might default on its debts. Richard Smith, the company's chief executive, told his investors in a telephone conference, "We are in the midst of one of the most protracted housing downturns in the history of our nation." He added, "We are not immune."

Sirva was in deeper straits by the end of 2007. After making its foreign acquisitions, Sirva claimed to be moving 300,000 households a year in forty-five countries for corporate, government, and individual clients. It went public in November 2003 at $18½ a share, and within a year the stock surged to $26. But by late 2007, it had dropped to ten cents, and the New York Stock Exchange delisted it.

Sirva, like Realogy, had been battered by debt and inventories of Relos' unsold homes—800 of them by the end of 2007. But that wasn't all. Sirva had been charged with falsifying its financial statements, including reports to the Securities & Exchange Commission, in a class action lawsuit. In June 2007, the company announced in a press release an agreement to pay $53.3 million to settle the suit.

Top management resigned. Sirva sold its Continental European businesses and dropped its biggest customer, Uncle Sam. The company's new president and chief executive, Robert W. Tietken, uttered the B-word. "I want to make it perfectly clear," he told investors and securities analysts, in November 2007, "that we have no plans to file for bankruptcy." In February 2008, the company filed for Chapter 11 bankruptcy protection.

Four months later, after a massive reorganization and appointment of a new CEO, it resumed business as a private company.

The Agent

The driver's-side windshield wiper of her silver Lexus SUV staggered and groaned against blasts of rain, the vestige of a Florida hurricane. Tina Davis fit a plastic grocery bag over her hair and darted into J.R.'s Log House, a big bustling watering hole at a highway intersection in Duluth, Georgia, a Reloville adjacent to Alpharetta.

Davis is a close-cropped blonde in her fifties, subtly made up and all business in a black linen shift. An agent of Coldwell Banker since the start of the go-go years in housing, she specializes in Relo referrals from Cartus. She gets them coming when they buy in north Fulton County and going when they sell and move away. At the top of the market, from September 2003 to September 2004, her firm sold 175 houses to people moving into the area and 150 from people moving out.

Over her regular breakfast table at J.R.'s, Davis settled down to wrangling over her cell phone, and an hour later picked up her new clients, Paul and Carla Kooistra, who were coming to her from a Coldwell Banker office in St. Louis. She would have to hustle to make her work pay. "I have to pay twenty-five percent of that commission to that agent and ten percent to our referral department," she said. "I had them sign an exclusive agreement with me."

Paul Kooistra travels the nation selling payroll systems to Fortune 500 companies, and when he isn't on the road, he works from home. On some level it didn't matter where they lived, but he proposed the move to be closer to customers and relatives. The Kooistras wanted a house with room out back for their children and their dogs. They wanted a room for each child, and Paul needed a room well removed from the din of the house. "I've got to feel I'm out of the house and in an office," he said.

Davis, part deal maker and part therapist, could sense their desperation. The Kooistras had made an offer on a house, only to have that deal fall through. "They have two little girls; they're two and three," Davis said. "She's pregnant. They want a house to move into the moment they leave St. Louis. They don't want to go over $285,000, but I've pulled up two 290s because you never know what they'll sell their house for."

She called an agent who had a house to sell. " 'They've just got to buy," she told the agent. "They have to have a move-in." But the owner wasn't allowing appointments that day, and the Kooistras had only two weeks before they vacated the house in St. Louis. Davis made another call: "Is there a chance I can see it at ten-thirty-ish?" Another: "Is your house still available? Somewhere around twelve, plus or minus an hour?" Appointments confirmed, Davis splashed off to Walgreen's for three $5.29 umbrellas.

Relo families have a particular mind-set, which can be rewarding for agents like Davis who know what they need and how they think. "Most of the people will tell you how long they'll be here," she said. "It's as if they're being molded by their companies. They do not expect to spend more than two to four years in any one place and don't want to have to make costly improvements. Over fifty percent of our transferees purchase new homes. One of the biggest considerations for any purchaser is resale. They want the same features in every house. If they don't get new, they want the most updated house they can get for their money."

For sellers, Davis's list of Relo-worthy features is like a litany:

"Granite counters, stainless steel appliances," she said.

"Maybe don't take the cabinets out. 'Faux' them. Paint them and caress the look of some age into the paint.

"Bathroom floors. Tear out the tile and do limestone. Granite on the countertops.

"All the brass-colored light fixtures have to go.

"All the doorknobs and locks have to be changed to brushed nickel, brown tone.

"Then obviously the carpet. It's amazing how many houses are fifteen years old and have the original carpet."

To buyers, Davis serves as a wider-ranging counselor. "I try to get them comfortable with the area," she said. "I sit down with a map and show them the communities. I get a lot of information up front: ages of their kids, special needs."

On the first visit, she drives them past North Point Mall, then tours the subdivisions and the schools. Before she circles back to the office, she said, "They've got to see a house. The big things the women look for are the laundry room, the master closet, and the pantry," while "the men's hot buttons are the basement and the yard."

No matter how much they might like a house, Relos don't always have complete freedom of choice, since some of their employers will end up buying their house when they can't sell it quickly. Rather than get stuck with an unconventional or poorly built house, they want the common-denominator houses that have made John Weiland a wealthy man. Even if the schools near a house are the best in the area, or the commute is short, most corporate transferees are told they can't buy synthetic stucco because it is susceptible to water damage. To keep things simple, sometimes any stucco is taboo. Houses with leaky basements and unauthorized additions and older houses can be off-limits, too.

Davis stopped to pick up the Kooistras. She handed them the umbrellas and printouts for six houses she wanted to show. Leafing through them, Paul paused over one. "That's stucco," he said.

"It's hard stucco," Davis said.

"You know stucco better than we do," Paul said—but he was skeptical. "Might be difficult to sell, though."

One basement smelled moist.

"That musty smell bothers me," Paul said.

Though it was raining, the floor was dry, so the moisture must have come from the walls. "I wanted this house to work," Davis said. "But it doesn't feel right."

So it was on to the next house, an "old" 1997 colonial listed at $259,900. "It's got plantation shutters," Davis said. With her foot, she tapped the base of a column beside the front door. "But see this wood rot?"

Back in the car, Paul wondered how they would acclimate to Reloville. "We lived in an old neighborhood, with huge trees. This is all so new."

"Our house was only ten minutes from anywhere we wanted to go," Carla said.

But, they acknowledged, it was just 1,100 square feet, plus the basement, and the standard-issue Relo homes of greater Atlanta were at least twice that size—built for the mid- to upper-level managers trading up in the boom.

The next stop was a subdivision called Hampton Place, in Duluth, and a house listing for $279,900. "This is nice," Davis said, entering. "Look at the moldings." The kitchen had a new wood floor.

Carla caressed the wraparound kitchen counter. It looked like granite. "Formica," she said. "That has to go."

Down the hall from the kitchen, with a door to a bathroom, Davis came upon a home office. It had large windows. "Hey, Paul," she called. "You've got windows."

The backyard stretched thirty to forty feet to some woods, which were part of the property. A section had been fenced in, perhaps for a dog run. The woods backed up to a nature preserve. "Now that's a private backyard," Paul said.

Down to the basement: "It does smell nice and dry down here," Davis said.

Carla nodded. "I like this house. I'm a little worried about the things that need updating. The carpet upstairs."

They settled back in the car while Davis called the seller's agent. "Do they have a place to move?" she asked. "Could they be out in a fairly quick manner?" Hanging up, she reported, "They had a contract, but it didn't work out. They're ready to move out in a hurry."

On the drive back to J.R.'s, the Kooistras wondered about the neighborhood. A busy commercial strip seemed a little close. "We didn't make an offer," Carla said. "We decided we weren't comfortable in that area."

Davis took them around the next day, and the next. They lost one house because hours earlier another corporate Relo beat them to it. Then she found a two-year-old, 2,462-square-foot house with four bedrooms and three baths just northeast of Duluth, in Suwanee. It had a room near the kitchen for an office and a big backyard. They bought it for $265,000.

Davis likes to form a bond with her buyers. "If there's not a bond formed, then something's askew," she said. "I watch the families. I give kids phone cards at closings so they can call their old friends. They need friends. The parents need friends. These people really need to feel connected. 'I've got to make my family feel this is a normal life'—that's what they say."

The Caretakers

The move from one city to the next involves more than the services of a Tina Davis and a change of address. Relocation has inspired a global niche industry of special services, like Tokyo's Relo Group, which manages relocated workers' homes in their absence, and Relo Deli, which helps Relos new to Japan get cars, driver's licenses, and furniture.

Kids often need tutoring, especially Relo kids adjusting to new schools, so in shopping strips in every Reloville there's a franchised tutoring service—a Tutoring Club, FasTracKids, or Huntington Learning Center. Without local connections to call upon to steer tots into elite private schools, parents can turn to the Crème de la Crème pre-school chain of Colorado. A branch in Alpharetta serves six-week-olds to five-year-olds. It opens at 6:30 a.m. and closes at 7 p.m. to accommodate parents with busy schedules. "They want their children to get ahead," said Elise Ezor, a former banker who, with a partner, started Crème de la Crème's Atlanta-area schools in 1985. "They are people who are very transient. They don't have the networks to use to get their children into private elementary schools in Atlanta. We have a very high acceptance rate for kids getting into private school."

Relos need somewhere to stay until they can get into their new homes, so near every Reloville there's a plush Oakwood, AMLI, or Marriott ExecuStay with one- to three-bedroom furnished apartments sometimes equipped even with toothpaste and shaving cream, and leased by the week or the month. Oakwood alone has fourteen buildings in the Relovilles of Plano, Texas, Highlands Ranch, Colorado, and Alpharetta, Georgia. Relos also need a place to stash their stuff, so they turn to PODS (for "portable, on-demand storage"). A company in Clearwater, Florida,

PODS Enterprises delivers a dumpster-size metal box to Relos' driveways, where anything from sofas to books can be packed and hauled away for storage or shipment to the family's next driveway. For pets, there's Pet Air (offering "corporate relocation services" with "red-eye flights available to many cities"), PetRelocation.com, Animals Away, and Happy Tails Travel.

Once they've found their homes, Relos can furnish them on the fly at chains like Rooms To Go, Kids Room Stuff, or CORT Business Services, a furniture rental company. CORT's clients include relocating families on brief assignments who store their possessions rather than bring them along. "Wherever you're heading, we'll be there," CORT's Web site promises. To make the experience as seamless as possible, CORT also offers "settling in" services, from apartment searches to identity theft cleanup.

For a more personal touch, Relovilles sprout decorators who speed Relos through customizing a new home so they can feel it's their own. In Alpharetta, Gerry Burge helps with paint, curtains, rugs, and pillows. But now and then a mover-and-shaker will call. One couple bought a house in the pricey St. Ives subdivision. "He was coming here from California," Burge said. "He needed instant acceptance. He needed to look like he belonged in Atlanta. He knew that he wanted to entertain in this house and it needed to look well done. He was used to walking into a furniture store and buying everything that went into a room right there."

And, of course, Relos need their houses cleaned—on the way in, while they're settled, and on the way out. New to town, they depend on franchises familiar from other Relovilles. Near downtown east Plano, in a lot beside a large, creaky white house that was once a single-family home, women in navy blue Maid Brigade T-shirts head off to the subdivisions in small white Maid Brigade sedans. "We start at eight here and we're at the houses by nine," Linda Ramirez, the manager, said. "We have thirty-eight to forty-five girls, eighteen to twenty teams a day of two girls, sometimes three, and five or six people in the office. We do a lot of movers. We do a lot of move-in and move-out."

Relovilles also need self-storage businesses. They cater to Relos who don't have attics, or whose subdivision homeowners associations won't let them keep RVs, boats, and motorcycles at home. In the rush to the next job, or losing a job in a downsizing and leaving town, they stop paying the storage bills. If the payments lapse for fifty or sixty days, the balance due can exceed hundreds of dollars. After the requisite warnings and fines, the company auctions off everything except personal papers, family pictures, and Bibles.

Once a month, around 9 a.m., James, his wife, Sue, David, Sam, Mike, and Harold gather silently outside the office trailer of the Public Storage franchise on Highway 9, which runs through Alpharetta. It's a ritual for the district manager, who is also auctioneer, to unlock the gate in back and lead them into the lot. They pass the RVs and boats and move on to the lanes of storage units with metal roller doors. Some are just big enough for a refrigerator, some for a couple of cars.

"Some people lose jobs," Mike Crews, who buys for a Barnesville, Georgia, thrift shop, said. "Some people are in jail, or they lose a job and can't pay the rent. I sell a lot of bedroom suites, washers, and dryers. You find jewelry once in a while, gold necklaces, TVs. You buy them sometimes, and they won't work."

The scavengers risk buying pigs in pokes. Public Storage won't allow them into the units, so when the auctioneer raises a unit's door, they size up the contents on the basis of what they can see from outside with their flashlights.

The auctioneer pulled up the door to Unit 768. It belonged to a small business, or an employee of a big business who worked from home. Tags on the file cabinet read "Confidential," "Payables," "Vendor Files." Scattered about are a photo scanner, a ten-year-old computer, computer monitors, and a copying machine as big as a Volkswagen Bug.

"Ten dollars?" the auctioneer began. "Twenty-five?"

David, crisp in a white button-down shirt and pressed jeans, took it for twenty-five. "Can you imagine how much that copier cost?" he said. "Five thousand dollars, brand new." A corporate leftover.

"It's a young, transient area is what it is," David said. He would resell most of his purchases at public auctions. "People moving in and out.

Sometimes it will be left there because the guy doesn't want it. I bet twenty percent are like that. A lot are just sad people."

On to Unit 110. A treadmill, stacks of baseball cards, framed pictures, an empty beer bottle, plastic coat hangers, a belt, a leather jacket, a necktie printed with a Christmas motif. "This is a man unit, not a chick unit," Sam said. David bought the lot for ten dollars.

The auction over, the men cleared out their units and swept them clean within a day. As the others filtered out, James, who owned a thrift shop, turned back to his prize, Unit 405. He ran his hand over a couch. "Leather," he said. Stepping over racks of clothes and moving boxes, he found a love seat matching the couch, a stereo system, a seven-piece dinette set, four stainless steel mag wheels, three vacuum cleaners, a television set, and a box spring and mattress. "You look in that unit, and you think it's ratty," he said. "But that's a good unit. You've got an entire house. Should bring nine hundred, twelve hundred dollars."

The Churn

Comings, more than goings, stir up Relovilles. From 1990 until 2006, the population of Collin County, north of Dallas, nearly tripled from just over a quarter of a million to 700,000 people. Excluding births, that was about twenty-five more families arriving a day than leaving, and most came from out of state, many on a Relo assignment. When they arrive, Troy Olson is there to greet them.

In his early thirties, single, fit, and six foot three, Olson grew up on his family's dairy farm in Taylor, Wisconsin, and graduated from a junior college in Lacrosse. He started out selling pagers and telephones for a company in Minneapolis that soon transferred him to Phoenix to build a sales team there. He was twenty-two and had never been on a plane. He discovered the real estate market there, so he got an Arizona real estate sales license and sold homes. Scouting around the Southwest for a still-livelier market, he came upon the Collin County suburbs churning with Relos.

Olson got a Texas license and joined the Century 21–Judge Fife office in Frisco, next door to Plano. "A lot of people were moving to Frisco," he said, half of them from out of state. "Property taxes are low, and the schools are excellent. I could kick-start my career in a city where I knew nobody. In my first full year, I was able to close twenty-two transactions." Vicki Butcher at Century 21 put him on her A-team of relocation specialists. In his busiest months, he would help a Relo buy or sell a house every week or two. From his base in Frisco, he covered the neighboring Relovilles of Plano, McKinney, Allen, and Prosper.

Relos wouldn't seem a lucrative source for a good living. In 2006, the typical seller of a Frisco home with the median value of $230,000 paid a 6 percent commission, or $13,800, to the two real estate firms representing the seller and the buyer. Each firm takes half of the commission, or $6,900, and gives each agent half, or $3,450. Then, for referring the Relo buyer to him, an agent pays Cartus, the buyer's relocation firm, 35 percent, so he clears $2,242.50. In meeting his A-team quota of eighteen sales a year for the median value of $230,000, Olson would earn $40,365—less than the nationwide median for full-time working men in 2006 and far below the $70,612 for men in Frisco.

Olson won't say what he actually earns, but in a hot Relo town he does better than that. His Relos spend more than the $230,000 median for their homes. Well into 2008 and the recession, the ebb and flow of Relos had slowed, but prices—and with them his commissions—were still creeping up. He shares in the commissions and referrals to Cartus for the three or four homes a year that Relos leaving town ask him to sell. And he regularly beats the A-team's quota for houses he sells to Relos.

Olson can also sell more houses, faster than most agents, because Relos require much less work than other buyers. When they receive notice to move, they move, often within weeks. "With a corporate relocation buyer, you don't have to worry about 'lookie-loos,' people who you put in your car and just drive around," he said. "You know the customers are coming. You know they're approved financially. You know they're going to close. They don't have to worry about the costs of the transaction because the employer covers them. It's a win-win for everybody—the client, the broker, the agent, the relocation firm."

By 9 a.m. on a February Thursday in 2007, Olson had gathered printouts for Mike and Mary Yon, both fifty-nine. Career-long Relos, they had retired but been referred through Relo channels by the reloca-tion services of USAA, the large insurance and financial services com-pany that caters to active and retired military personnel. Themselves children of globe-hopping military families, the Yons met and married in Japan. Mike became an officer in the air force, serving as a weapons system operator on fighter jets. Mary taught school. Over twenty-five years, they moved eight times—on average, every three years, to Japan, Spain, and Holland, with periodic stints at a base in Alamogordo, New Mexico, where they eventually built a home. The Yons' roots are their kids and their memories. When they decided to relocate one last time, to the Dallas area, family was the draw. "This is their last house," Olson said. "They have a son and grandkids in Frisco, and they want to be close to them."

As retirees, the Yons were paying for the move themselves. They set a maximum price of $425,000, which meant they could afford a 3,000-square-foot house with four bedrooms and three baths—enough to ac-commodate Mary's mother, who planned to live with them for part of the year, and visits from their daughter in Tennessee. They had already re-ceived a $12,071 estimate from United Van Lines to ship their furniture as well as Mike's prized 1987 Toyota Supra. When they arrived at Cen-tury 21's conference room in Frisco, Olson hurried them into his new black leather–upholstered GM Denali. He wanted to make a deal that day: he had eight other Relo referrals coming in the following two weeks.

Olson and the Yons headed to a development called Waterstone. The house rambled over almost 4,000 square feet and listed at $375,000. Two bedrooms downstairs, a three-car garage, a media room, and abundant kitchen cabinets—meeting several of their specifications, which Mary logged on her house-by-house checklists. "The house is wired," Mike said approvingly. In the back the Yons admired a deep swath of undeveloped land. "There might be a lake there someday," Ol-son said. But there were no guarantees the site wouldn't be developed with houses, and they were out in ten minutes.

The next stop was twenty minutes away in Prosper, a mass of subdi-visions nearly all built since 2000. A house on Willow View Drive was priced at $380,000. They ran down the checklist: "It meets all the criteria," Mike said. "I would buy this house right now." Mary agreed. But after a look at the backyard, they reconsidered: a long, tall wooden fence separated the yard from a cornfield, which, given the rapid building in the area, could soon become a horizon of rooftops.

The day was a bust. Back at Century 21, Olson collected six more houses to show them the next day.

"Today's the day," he announced as they began day two. They considered a stucco house with twelve-foot ceilings, a marble floor in the foyer, and a noisy arterial road out back, for $400,000, reduced from $475,000. Then a house built in 2002, on the market for $397,000 for just nine days, with a view of a pond—but without a first-floor bedroom for Mary's mother. Several houses and hours later, the Yons made an offer for the Willow View house in Prosper, despite the cornfield, and started their drive back to New Mexico, only to hear from Olson in the evening that they had been outbid.

In March, the Yons returned to Texas and found a four-year-old house in a 5,000-acre master-planned community in McKinney called Stonebridge Ranch. It met the criteria on their checklist, except it lacked a double oven. It cost $30,000 more than they got for their house in Alamogordo, but that was to be expected in a Relo-driven market.

For the Yons, the relocating was over. Mike joined a sixty-member monthly luncheon group called Romeo, for Retired Old Men Eating Out. The couple bought season tickets to the Dallas Symphony Orchestra. Their son and his family sold their house in Frisco and moved into Stonebridge Ranch.

By early 2009, the Relo business had slowed for agent Olson, but not as much as for most of the country. "As far as Relo 'in and out,'" he said, "I have four Relo listings and am working with two Relo buyers right now."

7. Ghosts' Town

Edge City's problem is history. It has none.
        —Joel Garreau, *Edge City: Life on the New Frontier*

Off the Dallas North Tollway, in the shadow of the monumental white mushroom of a City of Plano water tower and against a sky streaked with transmission lines, stands a new subdivision of stately $500,000 to $1.5 million homes. It is a five-minute drive from the sleek corporate battle-ships that have made Plano, with 266,000 people in 2006, America's biggest Reloville: Frito-Lay, JC Penney, Countrywide Financial, AT&T Mobility, Dr. Pepper Snapple, Computer Associates International, Capital One, Rent-A-Center, Electronic Data Systems (H. Ross Perot's first company)—and the North American headquarters of global telecommunications giants Alcatel-Lucent of Paris, L. M. Ericsson of Stockholm, and Huawei Technologies of Shenzhen, China.

The subdivision was christened Avignon, for the medieval home of popes. By late 2007, builders had completed the first twenty or thirty of the Plano Avignon's planned 200-plus abbreviated castles, some reigning imperiously over large lots, some attached town houses. Three town house models, called Old English, French Country, and Mediterranean, were open. Each occupied a small, 5,625-square-foot lot with a sliver of community-maintained lawn in front, and in back, protected by a wall for privacy, each had room for a small patio and a bit of a pool.

The houses are built of illusion. The Old English model's sales agent pointed to dark oak floors that seemed to have withstood centuries of bootwear. "The secret is, they're hand-scraped," he said. When the floors are being laid, he said, "you'll see four or five guys on their knees lined up, all bringing their planers across. You get that old distressed look.

"That mantel—it was nice polished oak. We took it out of the box it came in and took it in the backyard and took a chain and started beating it. That's the distressed look.

"That other mantel—it's not real stone; it's manufactured. It's more lightweight than real stone would be so we don't have to spend as much time on engineering."

A block or two from the homes is the Palais, a spacious community center with a pool, fitness facilities, rooms for entertaining, and Avignon's special attraction, the office of the concierge, the latest evolution in suburban amenities. The concierge's mission is the pampered sequestration of Relos. By relieving them of the quotidian chores of shopping, running errands, and mingling in the affairs of the city, the concierge protects Relos from gathering Plano moss before they roll on. "They will wash your car and wash your dog," the mayor of Plano, Pat Evans, said. "They will get tickets to the Dallas Cowboys. They will order dinner for you if you're having a dinner party, and practically shop for your wife for her birthday."

Avignon developer Lane Paschal, gray-haired, wearing a white windbreaker, stood on the front porch of the Palais conferring with the supervisor of a crew laying cement. He said the tract's most likely buyer is a senior executive with grown children and a home in some other city, Boston or Miami or San Francisco, who is sent to Plano for two or three years to take on an important assignment. The executive, Paschal said, tells his wife, " 'We'll come out here and get us a house and live in it for a couple of years, and we'll move back.' That's their thinking. 'It's not permanent. It's temporary.' The wife, she's going to be reluctant to come out here, and one of the things that corporations are going to do is use housing, and special housing like this, to draw her here."

Plano's abundance of global corporations and their well-paid itinerants bring the wherewithal to support these houses. The Census Bureau reports that Plano's 2007 median family income of $84,492 made it the nation's richest city among those with populations of more than 250,000 and the eighth richest among cities of more than 65,000. (The neighboring Relovilles of Flower Mound, Frisco, Allen, and McKinney ranked, respectively, first, third, fourth, and eleventh.) In a survey of sixty-nine cities with more than 250,000 people, the job information Web site Salary.com deemed Plano the best place in America to get rich and raise a family.

But Relos exact a social and community toll on Plano. They are too new to town, or too likely to leave soon, or too confined to neighborhoods close to their companies to get involved. Fifty years ago, people interacted through their neighborhoods and local associations. Instead, Relos' neighborhoods become their Internet-linked networks of friends, fellow professionals, global corporate colleagues—connections they carry wherever they go. They participate in their children's schools and sports, but they have no basis for knowing the neighbor a couple of houses away.

Statistics don't capture these transient populations with much precision. But the 2000 Census found that 41 percent of Plano's residents over five years old had come from outside Collin County since 1995, and that 53 percent were born out of state. And few stick around. Seven percent of the people in Plano are over the age of sixty-five—more than the 5 percent level established when baby boomers began retiring, but just over half the elderly population nationally.

With so many people new to the city, voting in local elections is lower in Plano than in more established cities, participation in civic clubs and organizations other than kids' sports leagues and PTAs is low, and philanthropic support is strikingly low. In 2003, the leading monitor of charitable giving, the *Chronicle of Philanthropy*, examined donations of taxpayers earning more than $50,000 a year in all 3,091 U.S. counties. Using Census Bureau and Internal Revenue Service data, the *Chronicle* found that of the 254 counties in Texas, Collin County, of which Plano is the principal city, ranked 236.

Mayor Evans is a buoyant and stylish sixtyish woman with short gray-blond hair. She is a child advocacy lawyer, a landscaping business owner, and a former public school history teacher. Near the end of her third, term-limited run as mayor in 2009, she is the antithesis of a Relo. She and her stockbroker husband, Chuck Evans, grew up in Abilene, Texas, and moved to Plano in 1972. She has served on the boards of more than twenty local charities, civic organizations, and government commissions.

The Evanses live on a surprising street for Plano. It is winding and affluent like many in the wealthy 75093 zip code. But these homes look ageless, some pompous and some relaxed, but no two are alike, and the neighborhood manages without new subdivisions' decorative regimentation, so no two are alike. The Evanses' house is a wide yellow-brick ranch set low and deep on a three-acre lot with gardens, grassland, and a creek in back. Inside it's an expanse of tiled floors, skylights, and wide, curtainless windows.

Mayor Evans said Plano's companies are no more magnanimous than their Relo employees in their support of the city. "The tough part is, the companies are making their money out here," she said. But their founders and chief executives live in Highland Park, Dallas's richest community, or much farther away, in New York or California or Paris. In the 1980s, a bank opened a big branch in Plano. "They dived right in," she said. "They participated, they sponsored. They got involved with our symphony and the African American museum. They were here like three years before they got bought by someone else who's not as involved."

Plano, like many Relovilles, is more a satellite office than a headquarters town, more a pit stop for executives on a Relo track elsewhere than one where they start and build a company and develop a proprietary attachment. Frito-Lay, Plano's first big employer, is, like the foreign global companies in town, owned by outsiders—PepsiCo in Purchase, New York, Oracle Corporation in Redwood City, California, Raytheon in Waltham, Massachusetts, and Capital One in McLean, Virginia.

Big names come and go: Southland Life Insurance Company, Fina

Oil & Chemical, and Arco Oil & Gas came and went in the 1980s and '90s. Countrywide, based in California and taken over during the 2008 subprime mortgage bust by Bank of America in Charlotte, North Carolina, seemed poised to go next. Ross Perot, the billionaire founder of EDS, sold his company to General Motors. GM later spun it off as a private company, and in 2008 Hewlett-Packard of Palo Alto, California, took it on.

Perot, more than anyone else, built today's Plano. In 1979, he catalyzed its growth after buying 2,667 acres of blackland prairie for his Legacy Office Park on the northwest side of town, near the site that became Avignon. In 1985 EDS moved much of its business, and later its headquarters, from Dallas to a 362-acre site in the park. After selling EDS to GM, Perot started another, competing company, Perot Systems, eventually putting his son Ross Jr. in charge, and moving it to Plano.

But for all their business in Plano, the Perots have lavished their considerable philanthropy—including $50 million in 2008 for a new Perot Museum of Nature & Science—on their hometown of Dallas. "We can't get Perot Systems to give us a thing," Mayor Evans said. "And his son's explanation is, 'All my sisters and father and mother live in Dallas, so they give to the Dallas Symphony.' I consider Plano EDS's hometown. They've been here forever. But you can knock on their door forever, and you cannot get a response."

It's a complaint I had heard in Georgia, too. Subdivision-segregated Relos only cross paths with the old and the poor through their windshields, or when they're being waited upon. At the offices of North Fulton Community Charities, an umbrella group serving cities including Alpharetta and Roswell, the director, Barbara Duffy, said, "We want services, but we want people who provide them to live somewhere else." She added, "Our biggest challenge is opening the eyes of the residents so they see that there are other residents who live in the same community and are often what makes the community function. Unless they can see the need, they see no reason to help. If we can't understand people who are different from us we are never going to solve problems in our community."

Mayor Evans and her fellow planners want more for Plano than offices and houses. They want to make Plano a "destination city," a diverse and durable home for current residents and aging Relos to sink roots in, one which will attract visitors whose taxes for entertainment, meals, and hotel rooms would supplement revenues from the homes and office parks. Their linchpin would be a world-class performing arts center, one big enough for Broadway shows that would mark Plano's coming of age as a city positioned to rival Dallas and Houston.

But it might never happen. Back in 2001, the city council proposed building a $35 million center, and voters, leary of spending their taxes to support it, shot it down. Half a year later, the mayors of Plano and the neighboring Collin County cities of Frisco, Allen, and McKinney, the county seat, proposed an even-classier $85 million regional performing arts center and established an Arts of Collin County Commission to oversee it.

The commission engaged a celebrated architecture firm from Oregon that designed a 2,100-seat glass and limestone theater with classrooms, rehearsal rooms, fountains, and biking and hiking trails, and later, with more money, a smaller theater, an outdoor amphitheater, a sculpture garden, and a visual arts museum. It recruited an executive director and staff and, as its president, George "Robbie" Robinson, a tall, amiable, and much-admired figure in Plano who was once, like Mayor Evans, named "Citizen of the Year." Robinson could get anything built. A PhD civil engineer for the U.S. Navy, he masterminded construction of the military base on the Indian Ocean atoll of Diego Garcia, a Herculean project. In 1980, Ross Perot drafted him from the navy to build his Legacy Office Park.

A landowner donated a 118-acre site in Allen, near the intersection of the four cities. The four cities would contribute $19 million each through bond issues, or $76 million. Private individuals, philanthropies, and corporations would cover the rest. Construction of the first phase was planned to begin in 2006 and finish in 2008. However, McKinney, amid converting its 130-year-old county courthouse downtown to a much smaller performing arts center and building roads and infrastructure for its fast-growing population, declined to contribute its $19 million and repelled subsequent appeals to reconsider.

Still, the other cities pressed on.

The project seemed feasible enough. The smaller panhandle city of Amarillo, where family incomes are half Plano's, was already building a $32 million, 1,300-seat performing arts center that drew so much in private contributions—$30 million—that it needed only $2 million in taxpayer support. The city of Dallas, where incomes are also half Plano's, was planning a performing arts center about four times the size of Collin County's to open in late 2009. By September 2008, private benefactors had kicked in $325 million toward the goal of $338 million. Plano's own Ross Perot and his wife, Margot, pitched in $1 million.

Robinson discussed the center over breakfast at his sumptuous, 36-hole Gleneagles Country Club in Plano. Confident that McKinney taxpayers could be brought around, he had begun the initial phase of fund-raising, soliciting people and companies for contributions of $1 million and more. But he spoke cautiously, too. "People have got to feel this project is real," he said. "There have been a couple that weren't, where they started to design a theater, and it didn't take root."

Relos would be hard to tap. "You get people who are here for a short time," Robinson said. "By the time you're beginning to make friendships, you're relocated someplace else. People don't get the local papers. They're not aware of what is going on in the local community. Some do get involved. But when you come to ask them for money, they know they're not going to benefit from it, so it's harder to get them to contribute."

By the end of 2008, the project had raised only one major corporate gift—$1 million from the AT&T Foundation—and $9 million from other sources. That left them $15 million short of their goal of $85 million. Robinson had retired from the commission. The Arts of Collin County's executive director had left to steer a similar project in Asheville, North Carolina. "Debut of shovels at arts hall is delayed," the *Dallas Morning News* reported. "Lack of funding pushes back groundbreaking of Collin County project." Year by year, the center's promoters began speaking of something smaller. The date to begin construction slipped to 2010.

If not with philanthropy and charity, Plano's global businesses have still done the city a service. They brought the jobs that lifted Plano—Spanish for flat—from a prairie of grasshoppers and cattle. The city reached a near perfect balance in its sources of tax revenues—48 percent from businesses—clean, nonpolluting office businesses—and 52 percent from homes. With business carrying nearly half the tax burden, Plano provides pothole-free concrete roads, richly landscaped parks and playing fields, and some of Texas's top-ranked public schools and best-equipped police and fire departments.

But by 2008 the old balance was in doubt. The jobs of thousands of Plano workers, many of them Relos, were on the line following the travails of Countrywide and the sale of EDS. The city had to contend with competition from young, neighboring Frisco for business, blurring the city's prospects for growth.

Most of Plano's housing is growing old, and only 5 percent of the city land remains for new housing. Frisco is awash with new upscale homes, including a subdivision with million-dollar Old World palaces with architectural features rivaling Avignon's. The city has built the region's biggest outdoor shopping mall, bordering northwest Plano, and with generous tax incentives it has brought an immense, in-your-face IKEA store to within sight, and a two- or three-minute drive, of Perot's office park.

To defend Plano and attract relocating businesses, Mayor Evans persuaded the city council to raise property taxes for the first time in fifteen years and create a $6 million development fund. It might help. She snared Capital One when it was looking around Dallas for a site for its automobile finance subsidiary. Plano gave the company $670,000 in road and infrastructure improvements, a cash grant of $100,000, a waiver of $270,000 in city fees, and a property tax cut through 2017. In return the company agreed to repay $200 for every job that fell short of its goal of 1,000 employees.

Two Cities

They occupy opposite ends of the same city—east Plano abutting Interstate 75, about twenty miles north of Dallas, and west Plano abutting the tollway five miles away. East Plano was once about all there was of Plano.

The east side developed late in the nineteenth century around a railroad hub and today is a stop for a commuter train to Dallas. It became an early Reloville, a sprawling bedroom suburb for electronics companies such as Texas Instruments and Rockwell-Collins in neighboring Richardson. Subdivisions emerged of brick ranch houses and modest two-story precursors of the west's châteaux.

Plano grew from 3,700 people in 1960 to 72,000 in 1980. But as Richardson matured, companies moved west to Perot's Legacy Office Park, and their Relos followed. Today the two ends of town stand in stark contrast, two cities that in effect mirror two stages of Reloville life—one established and middle-aged, the other doddering.

Both the east and west ends of Plano have downtowns. The west end's Legacy Town Center, set in the middle of Perot's office park, is stucco-and-latte chic, a brassy expression of the new urbanism, with 3,000 low-rise, tony apartments and town houses, a multi-star Marriott hotel, top-scale boutiques, cafés, and restaurants, well-camouflaged parking, and music blasting from wired and lighted sidewalk trees.

East Plano's downtown, like many throughout the vast, depopulating Great Plains stretching from Plano into Oklahoma and beyond, holds on as the home of the city's official business, conducted in a dramatic curvilinear, concrete city hall. The Chamber of Commerce remains downtown with some indigenous businesses, like the Queen of Hearts Magic Emporium, Nee Nee's Tea Room, Two Brothers Cigars, Plano Barbers, Jewels and Jeans, and Kelly's Eastside, a lively spot for burgers and steaks. The city is also gussying up, paving an intersection with brick and itself bowing to the trend of new urbanism with three- and four-story brick apartment buildings with stepped rooflines, balconies, and green awnings.

But much of the downtown and surrounding subdivisions remain haggard. In Relo time, they aren't just growing old: they are old. In the heart of west Plano, the 75093 zip code of Plano West High School, the 2000 Census found a median family income of $124,851, more than twice the $60,538 of the expiring Reloville surrounding Plano East High School's 75024 zip code. The median value of a house in west Plano was $280,300, and in the east, $103,800. The west's poverty rate was 1.9 percent and the east's 6.9 percent.

East Plano's decline has been hastened by the indifference of a population that moves in and out too fast to care for a home's bones. "There's a preference among Relos for newer properties," said Frank Turner, Plano's assistant city manager and the city's planner for nearly thirty years. Towns with rotating populations of transients fear other towns with newer housing like Frisco. "Americans want things easy," he said, "and I think glitz often wins. That's especially true of the person who says, 'I'm only going to be here five years.'"

Turner is a cerebral Tennessean, a Relo himself who came to Plano via city hall jobs in Kansas, Georgia, Virginia, and Galveston and Austin, Texas. Nearing sixty, balding, with a trim gray mustache, he keeps an impeccably ordered office except for a bookcase stuffed with studies and books on urban planning and suburbia, from scholarly to pop. We drive west from Fifteenth and K, the center of the old downtown, past vintage suburbia's parades of ranch houses, driveways, and lawns and out along wide flat corridors of menacing, seven-foot brick walls that shield block upon block of newer homes built in the last twenty years. "Relos are risk-averse," Turner said. "They're drawn to developer amenities. It's car shopping. Keeping houses maintained doesn't seem part of the mind-set. I think we have a culture of unschooled homeowners with a lack of commitment to a place over a long period of time. They're willing to change the oil, but they know they're not going to keep it to one hundred thousand miles."

"You know the theory of cognitive dissonance?" Turner asked. "When people are disrupted, like those who had been rich in Cuba and fled with nothing, they're driven to try to restore their former status. Relos," disrupted by moving, "will seek the same type of house in the same type of community they left," he said. "It's in their cultural

DNA. Developers have learned the patterns. Very rarely will a developer try to go counter-market."

As affluent Relos vacate neighborhoods, homeowners associations, which ride herd on residents to keep up their houses and protect property values, have lost clout. Newcomers—rarely Relos—decline to join the associations and pay association dues. "Most often they become derelict neighborhoods, junk neighborhoods," Turner said. In another decade, he said, the neglect in the east could metastasize to the west. The west's older subdivisions, dating back to the 1980s, could lose out to brand-new homes a few minutes' drive away in neighboring Frisco. "It's an easier decision," Turner said.

Yet in the east, I happened upon glimmerings of rebellion. Brick ranch houses along Amherst Drive in east Plano's Dallas North Estates subdivision have deep eaves to keep back the sun and front-yard trees big enough to cast wide and soothing shadows. They were built in the 1970s for white-collar workers, including pioneer Relos, at companies in Richardson and Dallas. Like new Relo housing, they weren't constructed with much thought to lifetime use. They stand on slabs poured over a terrain of clay and loam. The slabs contract in dry seasons and expand in wet, so they crack and leak. The early settlers, some still around and retired, found they could wrap the slabs with soaker hoses and water them like plants. At much greater expense, they stabilize the slabs by putting piers under them.

Young families, less affluent than the west's Relos, can afford these homes. The homeowners association folded with the exodus of Relos to the newly developing west, so on Amherst Drive, as in Alpha Park in Alpharetta, the houses speak for themselves. Their lawns are maintained, but with no association around, they are out of sync—some mown one week, some another week; some weed-free, shaved to an inch, and edged, some not.

A For Sale sign stood in front of the forty-year-old house at 1619 Amherst Drive. The flyer from the box attached to the sign post said the house measured 1,703 square feet, had three bedrooms, a remodeled kitchen with granite counters, a two-car garage, and a large backyard. The original price of $164,900 had been scratched out and reduced to

$154,900. At the house to one side of 1619, heirs of the first owner had torn down the original and built one that mimicked the homes in west Plano. The house across from No. 1619 had been remodeled. Another house nearby, evidently the home of an ailing first-wave settler who now had little money, was turning to junk with untended landscaping and rattling windows, but the city had put up a sign saying it would be tidied up.

The owner of 1619, Brian Ostrander, was from Arlington, Texas, near Dallas and Fort Worth. Thirty-two, he was a salesman for the pharmaceutical company Amgen, of Thousand Oaks, California. He traveled a lot throughout the Southwest but refused to move to cities closer to customers. He and his former wife, who lived in the area, had a nine-year-old son who spent six months of the year with each parent and without changing schools. Rather than move, Brian worked from home. In Plano, 8,707 people—6.3 percent of the employed population—worked from home in 2006, compared to 3.9 percent of all American workers.

Brian was selling the house and moving up—but not away, not even as far as west Plano. For a little over $300,000, he and his new wife, Sunny, a veterinarian, were relocating a couple blocks to a twenty-years-younger, two-story house, twice the size of their ranch. "I want an older neighborhood to get older trees," Brian said. A luxuriant crape myrtle stood outside the front door. Driving his boy to school would be quick from the east. Sunny's work was fifteen minutes away, and she had joined a city committee that supports the animal shelter. "The city is trying to prevent communities from degrading," Brian said. "We get very good city services here."

Lost Souls

Relos tend not to bond with their churches any more than they do with their towns. The Meadows, about thirty miles south of Denver and across the highway from the quirky downtown of the Douglas County seat of Castle Rock, is a master-planned community of 3,000 homes aspiring to be a city of 11,000. Standing at a quiet crossroads

Trading Up: *With each wave of new families seeking a resale-ready house for the next two- to three-year job assignment, Relovilles rise—while others fall. Brian Ostrander chose to work from home rather than relocate and took advantage of a Relo-heavy market to sell his home in east Plano for another one with better features.*

in the Meadows is the New Hope Presbyterian Church and its steeple, a staggered stack of stone and a needle that pierces the prairie heaven.

The Reverend Russ Kane, fifty-one, tanned and leathery in blue denim, is the pastor. He came to the Meadows in 1996 when the population numbered in the hundreds. He found an epidemic of malaise among the Relos. "It struck me after about six months in that there was just free-floating grief everywhere around," Kane said.

"Other people were sad, but there was loss. It was the loss of being moved. It was the loss of not having friends. It was the loss of, when people talked about home, it wasn't here. They spent vacations going back home, not to new places. They wouldn't commit to the new community. For two years they would regularly come to church but wouldn't join because it meant abandoning their old church. The people were generally fairly positive. But that's not the issue. There's just this sense of loss. That affected people deeply in their ways of making connections."

Pastor Kane grew up in Los Angeles County, married, and graduated from San Diego State University and Fuller Theological Seminary in Pasadena. He was assigned a church in the San Fernando Valley, then one in rural Sunnyside, Washington, in the Yakima Valley, and then to Castle Rock. "This is one of the toughest places to develop community that I have ever seen," he said. "People move here and they think they're the only outsider because they don't know anybody so they assume everybody else knows everybody. And it's a great surprise to find out that nobody knows anybody.

"I've never been in a community where school spirit is so low," Pastor Kane said. "It's because nobody had any history here. Why would you root for this team when you grew up with some other team? Attendance at football games here—I've never been in a town that had such poor attendance. People who work in student government, whether it's a dance, whether it's a rally, getting students to go 'Rah Rah' for my school is like, 'This isn't my school. I just got moved here.'"

Only a third of the 150,000 adult workers who live in Douglas County work in the county. From the Meadows, they commute to offices off Interstate 25, a beaded string of strip malls and Relovilles from Denver to Colorado Springs and beyond. Exits spill into the towns of Parker and Lone Tree and Highlands Ranch, the nation's largest homeowner association–controlled community, with a population of 90,000, whose corrugated panorama of rooftops a Denver city councilwoman famously called "one big smush of beige puke." South of Highlands Ranch comes woodsy Castle Pines, with two elite golf courses and the gated, $800,000-plus homes of retired and senior executives, and then Castle Rock.

From some distance, forming the squared-off top of a majestic butte, Castle Rock's rock looks like an abandoned medieval fortress. Nearby, the Meadows is laid out in clots of small lots with houses that sell for an average of $330,000. Like the roads and the landscaping, the houses look pristine and brand new. Streets dead-end at three- or four-board barriers that say "Road Closed," which means the road has yet to be built.

Except for its schools, churches (nearly all Protestant), and a community center called the Grange, the Meadows is a bedroom community without a core. It will soon have one, however, with a town center of shops and offices close enough for some residents to reach by foot.

The Meadows town center presents a dilemma for the 125-year-old county seat—yet another ragged but spirited old downtown, but with a distinctly Rocky Mountain culture. Downtown Castle Rock spreads east from the rock and the interstate for a mile or two along Perry and Wilcox streets. Two-story buildings house county and city offices, law offices, local banks, and real estate agencies, art and framing shops, a locksmith and a plumber, two chiropractors and a foot clinic, blue-collar bars, and decades-old eateries like the B&B Café, which serves green chili and milkshakes, and the Castle Café, which offers buffalo meat loaf and pan-fried chicken.

A block off Wilcox Street there is a restored, high-Victorian home that serves as the office of the Castle Rock Chamber of Commerce. Pam Ridler, the chamber's president, says that Meadows residents don't stop to appreciate the restaurants and entertainment downtown. "People will read the *Denver Post,* but they don't read the local newspapers," Ridler said. "We try to make a more cohesive community. We try to get them involved, to know that we have a great downtown, but that's difficult because they're not connected." The Meadows Town Center won't help. "What it has done," she said, "is segregate the community."

Ridler nevertheless senses that some people who might have expected to leave want to stay. They like living with Douglas County's hiking and skiing and sunny dry summers, and, like people in Plano with easy access to the Internet, they are opening businesses at home. In Douglas County 7 percent of all employed adults work out of their homes—almost twice the national average. Ridler says 54 percent of the chamber's member businesses are based in a home. "They don't have storefronts," she said. "Many, many of them are technology based. 'I can trade commodities from home. I can develop software from my home. I can do all that kind of stuff.'"

But home workers are still far outnumbered by the Relos commuting south on the interstate to the Colorado Springs military bases and the regional offices of Hewlett-Packard, Allstate Insurance, and Verizon or north to the Denver area and Lockheed Martin, IBM, First Data Corporation, and Qwest. Among those workers, the churches have noticed needs quite different from more settled parishioners'.

"People are looking for meaning even if they're in a place for two or three years," the Reverend Cindy Bates, the senior pastor at St. Andrew United Methodist Church in Highlands Ranch, said. "I think people want something more than just, you know, their work, and that's hard to do when people move around so much.

"But the churches can be very effective in helping people make connections, not only with other people, but with worthy causes or meaning or purpose. We see young families who are beginning to raise children, and there aren't grandparents and extended family to help raise those children, so we see families coming and saying, 'We're starting to raise a family and this is a big responsibility and we need help with this.'"

Pastor Bates has also noticed that relocation has stranded many older people, often retired parents who followed their relocated children to Douglas County. Then, when the children are relocated once again, the parents, by then older, can't follow. "It's extremely hard," Bates said. "But it also makes the church—I'm not saying I'm happy for this—but for many of those people the church is that much more important because that's the family that cares."

Pastor Bates has seen a refreshing phenomenon among grandparents whose children have moved away: grandparents informally adopting the grandchildren of grandparents who are far away. "You kind of have families becoming families for other families when you have all this relocating going on," Bates said. "We try to have some intergenerational programs here so grandparents can be grandparents even when their own grandchildren aren't living nearby."

As they try to attract new parishioners, both Kane and Bates said denominational loyalty among Protestant churches, much as it has eroded everywhere, is even less an issue in Douglas County. Less than half Pastor Kane's members grew up in a Presbyterian church. "They didn't come here because it said Presbyterian on the sign," he said.

"We'll get a lot of people who walk in the door and walk out because, 'it's not my kind of music,' or they'll stay because, 'yup, this does feel comfortable.'"

He treads lightly with the church shoppers. Relos often don't know how long they will be around so they balk at making commitments or making themselves known. They put twenty dollars in the collection plate but won't write a check or make a pledge. To accommodate them, Kane stopped handing out name tags. "If everyone's got a name tag, and you don't, you are now an outsider," he said. "Or if you've got a name tag and you don't want to put your name on it, you just stand out like a sore thumb. Old churches, I think some still do this, they say, 'Will all the visitors stand up.' Gosh, that's the worst thing you could possibly do to folks.

"You want to be friendly, but you don't want to be intrusive. We will have people who come and sit in a pew and won't identify themselves for a year or two years. If that's the level you want to be known at, then that's the level you'll be known at."

But once they do get hooked, Relos can be a boon. "Many people who get moved here want to do something that matters," he said. "And they are willing, for as long as they're here, to give themselves to something that makes a difference. 'I want to be part of the women's crisis center.' 'I want to be part of Habitat for Humanity.' 'I want to develop a grief ministry.' We try to help them do that. They don't want to sit around finding out what to do. If they're here, we want to grab their attention."

8. Trailing

> *Many of these men, who rush so boldly onwards in pursuit of wealth, were already in the enjoyment of a competency in their own part of the country. They take their wives along with them and make them share the countless perils and privations that always attend the commencement of these expeditions.*
>
> —Alexis de Tocqueville, *Democracy in America*

Moving again would be a headache for Sara Carroll after two and a half years in Roswell, Georgia, but it would be an opportunity, too. Sara could undo the mistakes of the first move, from Seattle, like buying the house on Babcock Court in the Summerhill Farm subdivision that left her strapped from breakfast to dinner in her Honda minivan with her two toddler daughters. Pushing the girls in their stroller, she could venture only a couple of blocks because the sidewalks stopped at the subdivision entrance, and the road beyond didn't have shoulders.

Her husband, David, worked fifteen or twenty minutes away in the Alpharetta offices of AT&T Mobility, the cell phone company. He was a middle manager and a director of finance for the network division, and, like Sara, thirty-six. At 10:30 one morning at the end of October 2007, when Atlanta's northern suburbs changed from golf shorts to jeans, Dave called from the office. There was an opening for a business operations director, or BOD, in the Greenbelt, Maryland, office, which covered Washington, D.C. At home that night he wanted to talk over whether to put his name in the hat.

Sara was already plotting a move. Months before he called, they discussed holding out for a BOD position that they expected would soon open in Alpharetta. That job would have allowed them to stay in Roswell another two or three years, but she wanted to get out of Babcock Court regardless, and buy a house in a neighborhood where she wasn't so confined. She knew Dave would recoil. Now perhaps she could put the thought aside. She was up for adventure, and little in Roswell would be holding her back.

Sara got giddy mining the Internet for information about Greenbelt. She found that the AT&T office was just a twenty-minute drive to the White House and the Washington Monument. They could take afternoon trips to the Maryland Zoo and the National Aquarium and spend weekends on the oceanside boardwalks and beaches of Delaware. Family and friends, all in the West, would come to visit. So as not to press her luck, she decided she wouldn't get carried away when Dave came home.

Dave felt that to get ahead, moving was compulsory. A BOD job would expand his skills. It would take him out of the office more, a good thing, and position him for another move up, or out. But much as he and Sara liked to ski, Dave didn't like living in places where it could snow. Home for dinner, he warned Sara that it was too soon to say whether he would be invited to apply for the job, much less be offered it. There would be other contenders. But he was ambitious, and Sara knew he was respected at work. "He's a GSD guy," she says. "He 'gets shit done.'" She assumed he would get an offer and would believe he had to accept it. She started a journal to chronicle her family's second relocation.

FRIDAY, NOVEMBER 2, 2007. *I did a search on the Internet for housing and demographic information around Greenbelt. Bestplaces.com and other Web sites gave me a little more insight about the area. I take these things with a grain of salt. What do they say about Seattle, Roswell, Fargo, and other places I've lived? The idea of living in Bethesda, Maryland, seemed very romantic until I found out we could only afford a 1,200-square-foot house on a major road.*

Dave suggested that she create a list of new home criteria to help guide their search. Sara filled it with the qualities missing in Roswell: a great pre-school and an elementary school nearby, so that she could walk the kids to school. "Sidewalks!" she wrote. She wanted a house on a quiet cul-de-sac and a neighborhood pool, supermarket, and café, walking trails, a library, a zoo or botanical garden or arboretum. She wanted a balance of urban and suburban amenities.

WEDNESDAY, NOVEMBER 7. *Dave and I discussed what I'd found on the Internet. The discussion led to: "We are not 'urban' people. We are a two-dog, one-cat, two-kid family. It doesn't matter if you can walk to the coffee shop or how far it is. You don't have time to sit and drink it anyway. We are a minivan-driving, suburban family and our girls will probably play soccer. We need to live somewhere that fits our lifestyle, not one that fits what you would like our lifestyle to be." Okay, so we're not urban people. I'll live in the suburbs. But I want to walk Dakota to her elementary school.*

After leaving Seattle, Sara had reached the threshold that Texan Kathy Link crossed when she gave up her career as an editor and settled into the role of supporting actor: the trailing spouse. By staying home, Kathy had freed her husband to travel much of the week and get on with his own Relo career in finance and banking. She turned to volunteer work and managing the hectic lives of her vagabond family of five.

Sara loved her work as a civil engineer, moving whole beaches and bays, and she was valued enough by her firm in Seattle that it was willing to pay her fifty dollars an hour for part-time telecommuting assignments wherever she lived. But she would get out of the way of her breadwinner husband and make a new career managing a household and their children. "This is all," she might have told the feminists of her mother's generation, and "this is plenty." "In my former life, I'm an engineer," she said. "Now I'm a mom." What she hadn't counted on was the downside—how confining and shallow Relo living would be and how much moving would fray her ties to family and friends. In Roswell, she had not made a single close friend.

Sara is five foot six, purposeful and direct, with straight shoulder-length wheat-blond hair and a child's Ivory Soap skin. She is a runner. The daughter of a police officer and a nurse, she grew up in the blistering heat and arctic gales of the northern Great Plains in Fargo, North Dakota, in a house with her parents and brother, one bathroom, three acres, chickens, horses, and a cow. She was good at math and handy with tools. She wanted to be an oceanographic engineer. She went far away, 1,300 miles, to Texas A&M, to get bachelor's and master's degrees in civil engineering. She looked for an ocean and moved to Seattle. For nearly eight years, into her thirties, she worked for an environmental consulting firm and specialized in dredging rivers and cleaning up waterway Superfund sites.

Sara met Dave on a ski trip. She joined his co-ed soccer team, and when he won a trip to Hawaii at work, he invited her along. They got married on a boat in Puget Sound in August 2002, and a little more than a year later she left work. The next day she found she was pregnant with the child they would name Dakota for Sara's home state.

Dave is taut, six foot one, balding with a deep widow's peak, and, like Sara, a runner. He is deliberate and firm with the children. They call him Papi. He is a second-generation Relo, the son of a forest manager. "Each promotion was another forest," he said. The last of four children, three born in Mammoth Lakes, California, and he in Ojai, California, the Carrolls moved to La Cañada, California, when Dave was four, to Salt Lake City at nine, and to Santa Barbara at fourteen. With eight formative years in one place, the moves were easier for him than for his older sisters and brother.

Dave loves work. Through high school and the University of California at Santa Barbara, he worked twenty to thirty hours a week, starting as a supermarket bagger and reaching the highest-paid union jobs there. He graduated with a double major in environmental studies and economics and moved to Seattle to work for an environmental firm. After seven months, the firm lost a contract, and he was let go. Adept at finance, he became a business planner at a department store chain. He left for a similar job at Cingular, the mobile phone company that would later merge with AT&T Wireless. "There I realized you have to be prepared to move if you want to move forward, financially speaking," he said.

"I work, and once I'm there I like to do it very well. There's no shortage of work and no shortage of opportunity. I never feel like I have it mastered because there are always new things to learn. The technology changes every sixteen months. I believe in the people I'm working for. I feel loyalty to them and getting the business where it needs to go."

But no job is safe, he acknowledged. "I have a skill set," he said, "but can I sell it on the street?" He felt he had to be willing to move to develop his skills. He managed a staff of five but wasn't sure he would make a good leader. "I don't know that I have the listening skills," he said.

THURSDAY, NOVEMBER 8. *Dave called in the morning and said his boss told him they may fill the position in D.C. with some "twisted copper" guy, a land-line, old AT&T person, to get the merged company more integrated with new technology guys. Bummer!! But, a vice president who was at a meeting with Dave asked him if he was considering the job.*

"What did you tell him?"

"I told him we are considering it. I said 'we.' "

"Well, okay. So I guess 'we' haven't made a decision yet."

"I sent you my résumé. Can you do a quick check?"

"I guess this means we're going? It's what you want?"

"Yes. Because if I put my name in, I'm going to do everything I can to get this job."

Trade-Offs

The Carrolls had moved to Roswell in the summer of 2005. With Dakota, then one, two dogs, and a cat, they had taken a leisurely, ten-day drive from Seattle, stopping in Yosemite National Park for the Fourth of July, at Mount Rushmore in South Dakota, and at the St. Louis Arch. At dusk, on the tail end of Hurricane Dennis, they pulled into the seven-year-old house in the crook of the Babcock Court cul-de-sac. Kim Roden, the real estate agent, had left the lights on for them.

The house was bigger and newer than the one in Seattle, and they bought it for the same $397,000 they got for the old house just a day after putting it on the steamy market. The new house was stucco and stone, painted Relo beige, with dark green shutters. "This is what you want if you're here only two years," Roden told them. The Carrolls' furniture wouldn't arrive for two days, so they ordered pizza and slept on the floor.

Almost two years later, on a drizzly Easter Sunday morning, the Carrolls had put their stamp on the house. Sara's yellow pansies bordered the landing by the front door. Dave and his cousin Kevin, an area contractor, had rebuilt the basement and installed a bathroom there, and in back Dave built a deck overlooking a deep wooded ravine. The house was spacious inside. In the small, carpeted living room, Sara had filled a floor-to-ceiling bookcase with her classics of American fiction. A combined kitchen and family room took up the back half of the first floor.

Dave drove in from the shopping strip carrying a pink plastic basket for Dakota. Fitting pieces of a puzzle together on the living room floor, her blond curls in a red Easter bow, she would soon set off to the subdivision's community center a couple of blocks away for her first Easter egg hunt. Their second child, Sienna, ten months old and named for the city in Tuscany the Carrolls visited on a vacation, took Dave's finger to pull herself to her feet. Rather than crawl, he thought she would go straight to her feet. Dakota had started walking at eleven months.

By now, the Carrolls had established some routines. Two or three evenings a week after work, Dave went off on a three- to five-mile run. Sara took the girls to gymnastics classes on Tuesdays and Dakota to pre-school Monday, Wednesday, and Friday mornings. Mondays she took Sienna to "Mommy and Me" classes to learn to play with other infants. She edited the newsletters for her homeowners association and the Alpharetta-Roswell Newcomers Club. She took the girls to the YMCA, which provided eight hours of free child care, and recruited a babysitter. She made a desk of a door placed atop two filing cabinets. She would break away from the kids to work for her firm for eight to twenty hours a week.

> SATURDAY, NOVEMBER 10. *Dave brought home the actual job description and the relocation package guidelines. Because of the soft housing market, particularly for stucco houses in our subdivision, I went straight to the buyout section where the company says it will buy your house for a price realtors give it if you can't sell it. I'm somewhat worried that with the higher cost of housing in Maryland, we're going to go backwards . . . I think we need to run the numbers and figure this out if we're really serious about trying to sell the house instead of just waiting for the buyout. We'll have a ninety-day period to decide.*

Around Roswell, Sara had found a monochromatic community far removed from coastal, polyglot Seattle's. "At parties," she said, "it's like the splitting of the Red Sea. The guys go and talk about sports. The women chitchat. I don't remember that at home in Seattle. I could spend a lot of time there talking to somebody else's husband, and it doesn't seem weird. Men here, it seems all they really talk about is sports. Dave now feels he has to watch *SportsCenter* at night on ESPN, the sports recap for the day."

She discovered a Reloville mommy culture. Mothers gathered in groups like her own Mothers for Pre-Schoolers, or MOPS. In Roswell and two thousand other towns, they have also formed MOMS Clubs, support groups for stay-at-home mothers that help them meet others who are moving to town. "Tennis Moms are the ones in little white skirts," she said. Room Moms help out in the kids' classrooms, Party Moms run class parties, Team Moms get cookies, juice, and bandages for their kids' games, and Trophy Moms get the trophies. On the Internet, moms join busymom.net, operationmom.org, agnosticmom.com, groovy-mom.com, hotmomsclub.com., and, for Relo Moms in particular, a Yahoo! group called Moveable Families.

Sara and her Relo neighbors, lacking long ties to a place, collected mementos to track their gypsy lives. From house to house, they pulled their tools and pictures and glue in cases on wheels and gathered together to "scrapbook" and "crop." Scrapbooking became a big business, with hobby chain stores, including Michaels, and Creative Memories, a leader of what the company calls the "memory celebration industry." Sara's group met one Friday each month, from 6 p.m. to midnight, for dinner and scrapbooking.

But outside Atlanta's Relo-friendly neighborhoods, around coifed and tailored suburban career women, childless or from two-earner families, Sara felt the stigma of the barefoot-and-pregnant stereotype. She had her years in Seattle as a civil engineer but decided she wanted mothering more; she could manage as a stay-at-home-mom with a husband with a good career and her own part-time job. But against a half century of growing demographic odds, she had resurrected the breadwinner-dad family, an institution that shrank from representing the choice of half of all women with children under eighteen when the Carrolls were born to the choice of one in four.

"I feel I'm being judged by the way I look, how I dress, what I'm driving," she said. "I'm struck by how made up these moms are when they are dropping their children off at pre-school. It's hard to get past the superficial and into who people are. Sometimes I have an issue with the materialism. My husband is very frugal. He says he's not. He says, 'Look at all our furniture.' We always buy three-year-old cars after the leases expire on them. Our TVs we got when we were in college."

What troubled her most, however, was the void that dogged Kathy Link in Alpharetta, Sandi Remson in Frisco, and Colleen Dunn in India. She didn't have a woman nearby for an intimate best friend, and her parents and brother were far away, in Texas. "You can't make best friends every two or three years," she said. "A best friend is different from a pretty good friend." One criterion is history—a friendship dating back to a hometown or to high school and college or to years of idle time with other mothers at the playground. Another is trust. "You can't be completely open with a neighbor because you think you're being judged," she said. A third is empathy.

"When you move around a lot, your husband has to be your best friend," she said. But he cannot stand in as an all-weather best friend, not least because some agonizing issues involve the marriage, or don't, in women's experience, typically resonate with men. "Having babies, post-partum depression," she said. "I believe I had it with both of my daughters. 'How did I get here? How did I get into this? Could I just leave?' That's something you could say to your best girlfriend." Her most empathetic female connection was her mother, whom she called two or three times a week.

TUESDAY, NOVEMBER 13. *Dave talked to the guy who left the position he would take. He said it's a great team, and by the way, the office is moving to Hanover, Maryland, near the Baltimore airport, in April. I searched our big 11 × 17 map. Dave tells me most of the folks in the office at Greenbelt actually live in Columbia, which is not too far from the new office in Hanover. I'm going to be out in the boonies again. What the hell. Oh, but look, there are some big parks. Crud, the town center is a mall. Oh, a river. I wonder if it's brown like the Chattahoochee. Ohhh! Big state park. Good, good. But if we're going to be in the 'burbs, I'm definitely going to be within walking distance to Dakota's school, even if there's three feet of snow on the ground.*
THURSDAY, NOVEMBER 15. *I created a little spreadsheet this evening with different interest rates, house prices, and percent down payment. I'm pretty sure our mortgage will go up. I guess I need to put together a budget for Dave to look over. Otherwise he won't want the mortgage to change. I'm tempted to put more money down (25 to 30 percent) so the monthly bill will be lower, but I bet Dave would rather put the money in the market.*

Leaving home at 6 a.m. when he's in town and getting back after the children's supper, Dave mixes with colleagues all day. He doesn't share Sara's need for close friends, but he has qualms of his own about the track he has put himself on. "You have this clock, this periodic moving cycle," he said. "What you give up is community. It's hard to commit. Before you're in, you're thinking about exit strategies. You don't want to put up a lot of pictures. You're going to have to fill the holes in the walls."

For Dave as for many white-collar workers with promise and skills, well-paid and gratifying long-term jobs are hard to find in many places. The choice comes down to moving and vying for the best jobs, or lowering expectations. With each move, Dave can count on a raise of $25,000 or $30,000 and building the family's savings for college tuitions, health care, and an early retirement. By moving to Maryland, he could expect to earn around $150,000, depending on bonuses. "But where does it stop?" he said. "I wonder. What is more money going to get you?"

"More stuff," Sara interrupted. "Titles. Accolades."

"That's where we are with everything," he said. He didn't feel trapped yet, but he thought he might. "More is more," he said, "but more is not everything. Our parents may not have had the same economic means, but they didn't have to work as much. Free time is worth a whole bunch. If I didn't need to earn money, I'd be a jack-of-all-trades. I don't like being educated in one thing and not at all in another. I can't fix a motorcycle. Most of my dad's generation could. I'd play an instrument. I'd pick up a language. I'm a finance guy, but could I do somebody's taxes?"

SUNDAY, NOVEMBER 18. *Dave called from the hotel in Maryland, and we talk about roads and towns. As we talk, he gets in the car and drives to a gas station and picks up a map of Howard County. It's funny, how we're talking on the phone and I'm particular about the type of map he should get. I'm thinking, "You have a camera on your phone. Just take a picture of my choices." Boy, this is going to be fun. While he's driving around, I'm on the Internet checking out the county schools and the SAT and more importantly the AP test scores . . .*

The realtor gave him printouts of forty homes to weed through on the plane. I asked him what the price range was. Shocking!!!! $500K to $625K. He said most houses less than ten years old with four bedrooms and two-plus baths are in this range. We talked a bit about creative financing. Dave mentioned that some of the executives that move often just do interest-only loans because they're only in the house for a short amount of time. Dave says our plans for the bonus and stock incentive programs would probably need to be reconsidered. While we talk, I check the Internet. $417K is the magic number for a mortgage. Anything over is a jumbo loan with a higher interest rate.

Moving a Family

Dave got home at 9:30 p.m. the next day, after Sara had put the children to bed. The momentum toward moving felt irreversible. In Maryland Dave had an interview with the area vice president–general manager, a man with whom he had worked on some projects but had never met. They clicked, and he told Dave he had the job.

But Dave wasn't sure. Four days earlier, AT&T Mobility had completed the acquisition of Dobson Cellular Systems, a big and largely rural cell phone competitor, and AT&T was reviewing its own positions to see whether Dobson employees should be considered for some of them. It was a false alarm. Two weeks later Dave called from the office. He had run into the chief operating officer of the network division. "He told Dave he had the job," Sara said.

Barely three weeks had passed since Dave's first call in October, and Sara, for all her enthusiasm to start anew, thought she would get depressed, as she had upon leaving Seattle. She loved Seattle's diversity and young bustle. She loved being single there for so many years, and then being newly married, having Dakota, buying their first home. More than two years after moving to Roswell, she still called Seattle home. But Roswell, her first stop as a deracinated Relo, had at least lived up to the claim of so many suburban towns—"a great place to raise a family."

She had settled into a church, the family's first, and started the girls in Sunday School.

Sara was most troubled about losing Melisa, the babysitter she found only that September on Craigslist. Melisa was especially attached to Sienna. She brought the girls Mickey and Minnie Mouse dolls from a trip to Disney World. To help her find work, Sara would hound her networks of MOMS, MOPS, and scrapbookers. Her other worry was selling the house and the possibility that it would sit on the market for months.

TUESDAY DECEMBER 4. *So, I've come up with this grand scheme. I'll rent an apartment here in Roswell/Alpharetta. I can get a two-bedroom for $700 to $900 a month. I'll stay here with the girls until May, when Dakota finishes pre-school and we sell the house. We'll leave most of the stuff at the house, so it looks lived in, but it will always be ready for showing.*

I tell Dave. He gives me the "You want me to be away from you and the girls for how many months???"

"Okay. It would suck for you."

Dave asks how are we going to look for a house in Maryland if I'm here in Roswell? Good point.

FRIDAY, DECEMBER 7. *I told Melisa this morning and it just killed me. She said not to worry about it and I told her we may have some friends that could use her help in February/March with their newborn. I told her I may not be working much in January, but will still need her help with having the house always ready for showing when we put it on the market and having time for all the paperwork with the move.*

MONDAY, DECEMBER 10. *Greatschools.net: Do they really have test scores in elementary school? Yes. Crazy. I guess it's the "No Child Left Behind" thing. I hate testing elementary kids, and I hate the idea of forcing my child to memorize and regurgitate information— ABCs, numbers—at a young age, instead of teaching them to problem-solve.*

THURSDAY, DECEMBER 13. *Big Rude Awakening. We have Kim*

*Roden over to give us an evaluation on the house. Bottom Line: List
$415K to $420K and expect to get $410K to $412K. Slight problem: We bought the house at $397K. We built a retaining wall,
$8K. We finished the basement, $22K. And that doesn't include the
sweat equity from Dave, his cousin (for the basement), or his father
(for the retaining wall) . . .*

*I told Dave as he poured a gin and tonic. "Well, we haven't
packed up yet," he said. "I haven't signed anything yet . . ." How
silly would that be? "Sorry we don't want to move and take the
other job because we're going to lose money on the house. We've decided to stay here in Roswell." I suppose Dave could tell his boss that
"my wife is mental/psycho/bipolar."*

WEDNESDAY, DECEMBER 19. *I definitely feel more comfortable
with the home-searching process this time around. The Internet
and the search engines have made searching and eliminating home
choices so much easier . . . I need a wall map of the area so we can
start putting in stick-pins: the Y, schools, library, church, trails . . .*

Sara and Dave e-mailed Mark Leone, a real estate agent in Ellicott
City, Maryland, with their criteria for a house:

> Basics—three to four bedrooms; two to three baths; $550–
> $650K. Open kitchen to living area. We have children and
> dogs, so cul-de-sac, low-traffic street. Usable yard. We do not
> anticipate staying more than five years, but we are looking at
> the school districts for resale. Sara would like to be near one
> of the parks and close to the elementary school, but it's a
> lower priority.

They took a house-hunting trip to Maryland. Leone met Sara at a
hotel in Columbia to show her around while Dave went to his new office. He showed her a $648,000 house with vinyl siding. It was a "Relo
Special"—disposable. At a corner of the garage, siding abutted a post
planted on the foundation slab. The bottom three inches of the post

were soft to the touch. "Wood rot," Leone said. "You can see it on a two-year-old house. This builder used cheap pine."

In the car, Sara traced their route on the map she had laminated at home and marked the locations of five more houses they saw and the schools and shopping areas nearby. Far back on a cul-de-sac, too long a walk from an elementary school, they came to a two-story brick house built in 2000. The real estate slump had caught up with it. The sellers bought it new for $341,000, and they had put it on the market six months earlier for $703,000, a price consistent with the neighborhood's appreciation at the time. Since then they had dropped it to $669,000. A similar house across the cul-de-sac hadn't budged from $719,000 in four months.

The house Leone showed Sara had a deep front lawn and a driveway long enough for four or five visitors' cars—a desirable feature for a cul-de-sac house. It overlooked a big backyard with a play set that would stay and, beyond that, a dense woodland that could not be developed. It was vacant inside, spotless, freshly painted, with nothing to show of its previous use except some nail holes from pictures and some impressions in the bedroom carpets from bedposts. Sara walked from room to room, pausing in each, assigning bedrooms for children, including a third she hoped to have within a year. It met her acid test for a suitable house, one with enough daylight in all the rooms so she could read without lights. "I'm in love with this house," she told Leone. "I would buy this house right now." She called Dave.

Dave came from the office. He looked suspicious. This was a lot of money. He had not yet resolved how he would raise it all. He set off alone, without Sara or the agent, to examine the lawn that he would have to mow and the backyard where he wanted privacy and room for the children and pets. Inside he strode through the rooms, checking appliances and faucets.

"Good family room," he said at last. "No wasted space." He stopped in the dining and living rooms. "Lots of nail holes," he said. He examined a large sunroom addition. "Nice house . . . I like this house . . . This is like a home, and there's no one in it." They offered

$640,000, and it was accepted that day. The bank would make them a mortgage of $512,000, so they would make a down payment of $128,000, or 20 percent.

But the slump had also swept Roswell. To break even on Babcock Court, the Carrolls needed $427,000—the $397,000 that they paid and $30,000 for their improvements. They asked $424,000. Five months later, in May 2008, they would sell it for $384,000. With incentives for selling it from AT&T and Altair, their relocation company, they got $404,000, so they lost $23,000.

Months before, having packed the van with the girls, the pets, and her mother, Gigi, who had come along to help, Sara set off on the twelve-hour drive to Ellicott City, resolved to shake the anxieties of her stint in Roswell. "I've decided that I need to stop trying to find people like me and that I just need to be me," she said.

A successful life, she said, did not preclude moving. "A successful life, for us, is having good family relationships—with my husband and children. That makes life. Whatever Dave does with his job, he is also a father, an athlete, a TV watcher. My husband's a very good worker. He's been able to pick where we want to go. Dave's career-climbing. You get to a point where you're not climbing anymore, and then you stop moving." Dave was not there yet.

She made one last visit to Babcock Court, by then bared of its contents and voices, and composed a credo of the Relo spouse.

FRIDAY, FEBRUARY 22, 2008. *As I walk around the house, I think about the saying, "If walls could talk." I used to think that it was associated with a house that has seen a generation grow up from when the kids are little, go to high school, then off to college, then back for the holidays with their own little kids. I think about what this house has seen. Not one family but many. I like to think we've made the house better than when we got here. And I think that's the way we need to go through life. Every place we go, everything we touch, and everyone we meet should be better off when we leave than when we arrived . . . Is it easier to live in a place and you know you won't be there long and*

Buying in: *After showing Sara Carroll several "Relo specials"—houses that are considered re-sellable if also disposable—real estate agent Mark Leone (center) walks her and her husband Dave around in Ellicott City, Maryland. They bought a better one built in 2000. It was spacious, bright, sat on a quiet cul-de-sac in a good school district, and had come down in price because of the slump in the housing market—a perfect fit for Sara's real estate checklist.*

still get engaged in the community—to live like you were dying? It's probably easier to leave no trace, like you were camping.

The Silent Question

Employers call relocated wives "trailing spouses," and lately, to accommodate unmarried and gay couples, "accompanying partners." They might occupy a different universe from the Betty Friedan archetype of mid-twentieth-century suburbia. But in most Relo families, the husband's career still rules. Wives move at their husbands' behest and mothball careers in fields to which few in previous generations felt they could even aspire, like business, law, medicine, and civil engineering.

Twenty-first-century women make up a little more than a third of the students at Harvard Business School—three times more than in 1975. The American Medical Association reports that 27 percent of the nation's physicians are women, two and a half times their number in 1980. Almost half of all law school students are women, twice the level of the 1970s. Seventy percent of women with children at home go to work. Women earn 81 percent as much as men, but slightly more working women—51 percent—hold high-paying management and professional jobs.

As their access to the workplace has opened, more women take jobs requiring relocation. In 2007, the relocation management firm Cartus surveyed 184 companies in twenty-five industries with 83,000 Relos. It showed that 21 percent of the primary breadwinners were women. A survey of 136 employers who move about 25,000 workers a year by the Worldwide Employee Relocation Council and Prudential Relocation found that women accounted for 30 percent of the employees moved in 2003—almost three times the 11 percent in 1986. But young single women accounted for most of the increase, and from 2005 to 2007, women's advances stalled at the 30 percent level.

The ERC survey also showed that, of employees on long-term assignments of a year or more, 47 percent were married men and 15 percent were married women. Further, 61 percent of women employees who turned down an offer to move cited adjustment difficulties for their children, compared with 29 percent of the men. Forty-six percent of the women who declined a move said their husbands would have to quit their current jobs if they agreed to the move; half as many men refused moves because of their wives' jobs.

Although women have achieved greater employment equality, Kenneth G. Dau-Schmidt, a labor law professor at Indiana University, and Carmen Brun, an international lawyer in Washington, D.C., write that "women suffer a larger share of the conflict between career development and childbearing, including: forgone work experience and training, the depreciation of skills during periods of childcare, and the undertaking of more flexible, but less remunerative, employment that will accommodate childcare." The doctors and lawyers among them don't have much of a choice: to practice in a new state, they need a new license—and sometimes they move on before they can qualify. Men lose something, too. "As women strive to gain jobs with flexible hours," Dau-Schmidt and Brun write, "men will be left to shoulder a disproportionate share of the inflexible jobs and lose opportunities to be with their families."

There might be something else behind working women's reluctance to move: salary discrimination. Women are less likely than men to get a raise as an inducement to change employers, which often leads to a move. In several studies in the 1990s, Jeanne M. Brett, a professor at Northeastern University in Evanston, Illinois, and Linda L. Stroh, a professor at Loyola University in Chicago, examined differences in wages and work experience among men and women managers at twenty Fortune 500 companies. "It is surprising to note," they concluded in one study, "that female managers who changed companies between 1989 and 1991 received no greater compensation than their female peers" who remained behind. However, "male managers who changed companies between 1989 and 1991 benefited greatly from the move." Women who jumped ship, in fact, ended up earning 4 percent less than their peers who stayed behind. Men who jumped ship earned 12 percent more.

There are some benefits. The luckier Relos live in fun and exotic places with many diversions—Miami or San Francisco, Paris or Bangkok or Rio de Janeiro. Those working abroad in the higher echelons of their companies can also get the big perks of luxury cars, large subsidies for housing, free private school tuitions, servants, country club memberships, and first-class travel.

But psychologists speak of a bleaker existence for many trailing spouses. "As women, we talk," Dee Brodbeck a clinical psychologist in Castle Rock, Colorado, said. " 'I can't open up to my husband. He wants to tell me what to do.' Men solve problems by action, women through discussion. Moving a lot, you don't have time for the cycle of ups and downs you need to make a good friend. You don't have time to stop, heal, adjust."

Dr. Brodbeck, a court-appointed child and family investigator for dysfunctional families, said of the women she treats that "they feel trapped. They want to go back to their extended families. Many are homogenized vanilla folks. They've lost their sense of uniqueness. They try to become what they think everybody else is. You learn not to prize things a lot. The big houses. I can't imagine how you can consider eight thousand square feet homey. They create a façade for themselves."

Relo family clients tell her, " 'We've been broken for a long time and can't get fixed.' Often it is the woman who is violent. There will be a history of substance abuse. With women it is wine, with men beer and hard liquor. They're desperate. Some women may want to go home to heal, and they are not allowed to. Infidelity is high in that group. The traveling father. They both do it. With women, I see the use of an affair as an exit strategy. They've got to have a reason to leave. Another exit strategy: addictions."

Relo wives complain of stress and feelings of loss and anomie. "They do-do-do-do for the kids," Howard Drutman, a psychologist in Roswell said. "Everything is very structured. Father's not around much. There's not a lot of romance going on. Women come to the point where they say, 'That's it.' They lose self as a woman, as a sexual being, as having a romantic marriage. The guys think everything should be taken care of at home. They throw more money at it but they don't necessarily contend with the wife's emotional needs. 'That's the wife's problem.' "

A dearth of intimate friendships with other women might be the toughest consequence of frequent moves. Every Relo wife I spoke to brought it up. Through schools, clubs, playing fields, and kids, the wives make some friends. But they don't make best friends. A fear of making friends and then having to shed them might be a reason.

"Global nomads," writes Eileen L. Lawlor, the general manager of an Irish relocation firm, "learn what to ask so that they can get to know people quickly. They also learn how not to get too close—how much distance to keep so that when a relationship ends, as their experience tells them it will, it does not hurt too much. Both the ability to make friends and the tendency to enforce a certain distance are global nomad survival skills."

9. Rootless

Migration gives the illusion that things can get better—if only you move far enough west; if only you find out where the good jobs are. You can start over by moving . . . Americans assume that if people are moving around they must be moving up.
　　　　　　　　　—James M. Jasper, *Restless Nation: Starting Over in America*

Ashley Cottrell, age eleven, and her sister Kasey, ten, were playing Capture the Flag in the backyard of their house in the Providence Oaks subdivision of Alpharetta, Georgia, like it had always been home. In fact, it was the girls' third home, following Indianapolis, where they were born and their father, Phil, and their mother divorced, and Sussex, New Jersey, where his company had first moved them. By May 2004, they had spent half of their short lives in Alpharetta. They trick-or-treated among neighbors each Halloween, learned to ride bikes on the suburban streets. They knew everyone at Alpharetta Elementary School.

Phil came to the door and called, "Come on inside. We need to talk."

The girls froze. "Oh-oh," Ashley said. "We're in trouble." There would be trouble, though not of their doing.

"I have some news," Phil said. He paused. "I am going back to school, and we'll be moving to Pittsburgh."

Kasey started wailing, then laughed. Ashley rose. "I'm going to call my friends," she said. She fled to her room where she stayed for two hours, crying and making her calls.

The following Sunday, during the Memorial Day weekend, a "For Sale by Owner" sign stood in front of 2175 Providence Oaks Street, a nine-year-old, two-story, brick and gabled house with green shutters, four bedrooms, and a basement. (Phil bought it for $250,000 and was asking $350,000; in that boom-time summer, he would sell it in two months for $349,000.) Phil was sitting alone at the entrance to the garage facing a listless cul-de-sac, waiting for someone to stop by his moving sale. He is amiable enough, deliberate and unexcitable. His second wife walked into the garage carrying their nine-month-old daughter. She looked over the sale items, mostly the older girls' clothes, and went back in the house without a word or a nod.

Rite of Passage

As he gazed over his family's leavings, Phil seemed pleased with his Relo career to date. Living in Alpharetta was quite different from growing up in his hometown of Valparaiso, a middle-income city of 27,000 in the northwestern corner of Indiana. "I was a latchkey kid," he said. Both parents worked, his mother as an executive secretary at a savings bank, his father as an accountant for an oil company. Both were home in the evening. "Here, Mom doesn't work," he said. "When I'm not traveling, I'm home all day. I do most of the cooking. When I travel, I make sure there's the right food for my wife to throw together quickly."

Phil's field is sales information—the data about shoppers' behavior that companies and store chains collect and mine. After high school in Valparaiso, he attended the University of Chicago, then transferred to Indiana University–Purdue University in Indianapolis to study distribution and marketing. Enrolled there part-time for seven years, he married and worked at DowBrands, a part of the Dow Chemical Company that made Saran Wrap, Ziploc bags, and Fantastik, the household cleaner.

"They needed someone who could type and knew Microsoft Word, so I got my first job, as an office assistant," he said. Ashley and Kasey were born, Phil earned his bachelor's degree, and DowBrands made him a manager of sales information.

Over six years in the company's Indianapolis office, Phil watched well-paid young managers sweep in and sweep out to bigger jobs. He realized there was no going back to Valparaiso: it just couldn't offer the spectrum of careers and opportunities he could find if he were willing to go anywhere. In Valparaiso, he said, "you can start as a store clerk at the bottom of the hierarchy, and you can be promoted from within. But you can't be assured of that. You limit yourself." He spoke like a textbook on tape. "Not moving suppresses your wages and career potential in today's global business environment."

Phil joined the tide of young managers moving out. DowBrands sent him to its office in northern New Jersey. He and his first wife were divorcing then, and she was given custody of the girls, then ages six and four, when schools were in session, while Phil was to take them during vacation breaks, but they reversed the arrangement. Phil and the girls had barely settled in Sussex when in 1998 Dow sold DowBrands and put Phil out of work. He found a similar assignment at Eastman Kodak, which packed him off to Georgia. He and his second wife had met by then, and they soon married.

Two years later, "Kodak was not doing well," he said, "so I wanted out." He had come to know ACNielsen, the market research firm based in the Chicago suburb of Schaumburg that conducts analyses of companies' data and sells it back to them, and a Kodak client. Nielsen took him on as an RMS—a retail measurement services consultant.

For Nielsen, Phil did much of his work by telecommuting. From home in Alpharetta, he scrutinized the corporate data for market share and consumer trends and met with clients and colleagues on conference calls. He flew to meetings—to headquarters in Schaumburg and to clients like Kmart in Detroit and Winn-Dixie in Jacksonville. He estimated that he spent 50 percent of his time traveling. "I'll do one, two, three trips a week. As long as I live close to an airport, I'm in good shape." Working that way, he said, "corporations don't have to pay five-dollars-a-foot rent for offices. I have an office here in my house. We all work out of our houses. My boss is working out of his home in St. Louis. The vice president in charge of the whole division works out of his home in California. It's all virtual now."

At thirty-five, Phil had reached the career-ladder rung at which ambitious young managers vie for the opportunities that can propel them to a "C-suite"—the top executive plateau made up of chief executive officer, chief operating officer, chief financial officer, chief marketing officer, and assorted other chiefs. For that, he and the girls would have to move again. "Relocation is a rite of passage," he said, conjuring the Relo variation on the American Dream of ever-better jobs, wages, and homes. "You cannot get to the top level of organizations without relocating. It's impossible. I would like to have European experience. I don't think anybody can get to the C-level without global experience."

To position himself to move up, at Nielsen or anywhere else, Phil decided he needed a master's of business administration from a top business school. He singled out computational marketing, a core discipline at Nielsen and the backbone of much of its market research, and identified the Tepper School of Business at Carnegie Mellon University, in Pittsburgh, as the field's high temple. So he was moving to Pittsburgh for three years, where he would enroll at Tepper and telecommute full-time for Nielsen. Carnegie Mellon's tuition came to $135,000; Nielsen would contribute up to $15,000 and Phil would have to take a student loan for much of the rest.

Unlike Ashley and Kasey, Phil had no particular fondness for Providence Oaks or Alpharetta. It was simply a place to park. He chose the subdivision for its proximity to well-regarded Alpharetta Elementary, nothing else. "There are people in this subdivision—I don't know them—ten, twenty families who get involved," he said. "Most of the rest of us keep to ourselves. Several took advantage of the increased equity in their homes and moved to the next level. But that's not the rule. Most are corporate relocations. They come in on Relo and go out on Relo."

For that matter, he couldn't be sure that he would stay at Nielsen. He wondered if, once he had his degree and began the long process of repaying his student loans, Nielsen would come through with a bigger salary, a bigger job, and full coverage of his relocation expenses for the next post-MBA move. He started sending his résumé around, discreetly.

Meanwhile, he would have to show that he would be around for the girls. Their mother, in Ohio, was challenging the custody agreement. "She says I'm not spending enough time with the kids," he said. "She's trying to get full custody." Nielsen agreed to let him keep working at home while letting him cut back his traveling.

That September, the family moved to Gibsonia, Pennsylvania, an affluent suburb twenty miles north of Pittsburgh.

Dislocated

On a Monday in early February 2007, it was dry, sunny, and hovering above zero in Gibsonia. The schools were closed. Six inches of shimmering ice-coated snow paved the hilly Treesdale development's wide lawns and yards. Salt, ground to dust by the cars, had turned the roads and the semicircular driveway a chalky white. The house was barely six years old when the Cottrells moved there two and a half years earlier, and by then it had already seen two previous owners, presumably also Relos.

At 5,000 square feet, brick with beige trim, the house was more than twice the size of the one they had left in Alpharetta. Tall oak double doors with leaded glass inserts opened to a cavernous echo chamber of space with glossy, uncarpeted oak floors. It felt big enough for a church but was only half furnished, with few curtains or pictures hung. A wide expanse of glass overlooked two decks and the backyard. On the first floor, the walls were painted light beiges and grays, except for the rich cherry paneling, matching the desk and cabinets, of Phil's wired home office. Three pairs of shoes had been doffed in the foyer so Phil and the girls could minimize housecleaning. Money was tight, and he had let the maid go.

Ashley and Kasey, fourteen and thirteen now, were finding their way at the area schools, wide, low-slung, unadorned buildings that looked indistinguishable from their brick-and-mortar kin across most young and affluent suburbs. Blond and animated, a sophomore at Mars Area

Senior High, Ashley was earning A's and B's in her classes, including two advanced placement courses. She was on the honor roll and scoring above grade level on national tests. Kasey, her deeper blond, spectacled sister, is more pensive and shy. An eighth grader at Mars Area Middle School, she was getting B's and a few C's.

The girls said adjusting to their schools had been tough. "Academically, it's fine," Ashley said. "But socially, it's difficult. A lot of kids have lived here their whole lives. They were raised here. I wasn't raised in any one place." She's indifferent to sports. She can't work herself up for the Mars Fightin' Planets and the football culture that permeates the school. She had not found a satisfying extracurricular outlet.

"I think they should have more drama programs, more creative programs," she said. She likes to write and writes in her journal every day. She and a few other kids are ignored in school. "We're called 'ghosts,'" she said. "Other kids don't notice us unless they need to. We drift through the hallways. We're not really in a clique because we can accept other people. When someone comes up to talk to us, we will talk to them. But in a clique, we would alienate everyone else."

What Ashley wanted most was a serious girlfriend. "In Georgia, I was the second-most popular girl in my class," she said. "I had over a hundred friends. Some I could walk with at school but they weren't someone I would want over to my house. I had three best friends. My first friend was Courtney. We would overnight weekends at each other's house. We would go to the mall, share intimate secrets with each other. We called each other sister." After some time in Gibsonia, she had made two pretty good friends. She kept in touch with Courtney, but her outlook was brightening a bit.

Boys had entered her life. On the Internet, she came across one who lived in Philadelphia. While they never actually met, she bugged her father to move to Philadelphia—they'd be moving eventually, anyway. She later shifted her attention to a boy at school. His mother would drive them to movies, and Phil would pick them up when he wasn't in night class.

For Kasey, the social transition had been tougher. "Sometimes I laugh at my life. Sometimes I'm like *grr*. Moving here was a horror. I'm not that social. I get scared around new people. The first few days were embarrassing. I didn't know how to make friends. I want to make a good impression, but I usually mess up and I become the geek in the school. Most of the people have never lived anywhere else, so they don't know how hard it is to move.

"My teachers don't like me. I don't do sports. I paint, I draw, and occasionally I write my own music, but then I forget it. I do have several friends here now. In Alpharetta I had tons of friends, like Ashley. I've lost contact with most because they moved, too. One friend I keep in touch with, Rebecca, Becky. We send letters. Occasionally I talk to her on the phone. In the summer we go and stay in Alpharetta for a week. Each of us sees our friends and we spend at least one night at their houses. It took me two years to get a best friend here. She's almost up to the standard of Becky. She gives good advice and follows some advice I give her. It's really nice to have her when I'm in need."

With a half year to go at Tepper, Phil had taken on a new marketing assignment at Nielsen that he thought might work out well. "I'm launching a new product, a database platform," he said. The job required little of his former nationwide travel—the weekly trips he would take from Alpharetta. Nielsen felt the work was best done at headquarters in Schaumburg, he said, so he explored settling there. "I draw a circle around Schaumburg and target all the schools within thirty minutes and pick the best in that range and I'll let my daughters interview at them." But Nielsen hadn't mandated a move, and he felt he had to stay put for the girls.

In *Restless Nation*, James Jasper asked, "What do kids lose by moving? A 'place' in the local culture; in the pecking order; including friendships which reinforce that place. They are still figuring out how to have their first identity, and are hardly ready to start over with a second." Apart from military families, there hasn't been much scholarly examination of the effects of multiple moves on Relo children like the Cottrells—those who move again and again because of parents' jobs—or studies that differentiate between children who move great distances and those who move within a community. Two researchers for the National Center for

Allergy and Infectious Diseases, Gloria A. Simpson and Mary Glenn Fowler, found in a 1988 survey of 10,362 school-age children that, compared to children who had never moved, those who moved three or more times "were 2.3 times more likely to have had emotional/behavioral problems, 2.2 times more likely to have received psychological help, 1.7 times more likely to have repeated a grade, and 1.9 times more likely to have been suspended or expelled from school."

Howard Drutman, the family psychologist in the Atlanta suburb of Roswell, said many Relo patients, more than most, contract the upscale suburban affliction known as "affluenza," the subject of a 1997 PBS documentary that defined the condition as "the bloated, sluggish and unfulfilled feeling that results from . . . stress, overwork, waste, and indebtedness caused by dogged pursuit of the American Dream." To compensate for frequent absences, Drutman said, parents buy their kids off with toys. Among the 200-some Hondas, Toyotas, and a few Chevrolet Blazer and Ford Explorer SUVs in the seniors' parking lot of Reloville Alpharetta's Milton High, I counted five Ford Mustangs, seven Mercedeses, a Saab, seven Volvos, three BMWs, and a Lexus.

At home in Gibsonia, Phil had mastered the executive machinery of a hands-on job and was bristling to take one on. His office was a cozy sanctuary dedicated to work. "I'd never had a serious office," he said. "I always had to share." On the desk were two flat-screen monitors, on the credenza behind it a laptop computer and a multifunction printer, and to one side of the desk another printer. He had made lists and filled files. He had two land lines plugged into the phone, one for family calls, one for business.

The office spoke of another, personal dimension of Phil. A glass-enclosed cabinet displayed his collection of agate, fossils, pink jade, and Herkimer "diamonds"—brilliant six-sided quartz crystals that come to points at each end—that he mined in Herkimer County, New York. On a shelf, he kept a long row of genealogical books. "We emigrated from England in the 1600s," he said. "We're a founding family of Richmond, Virginia. We moved from Tennessee to Indiana on Christmas Day in 1832."

The office seemed more than a pit stop for the strategizing, bound-aryless careerist who had moved from Valparaiso to Indianapolis to New Jersey to Georgia and to Gibsonia. It was the refuge where Phil began confronting a hostile economy and the limits of a Relo career. He thought he might value something more. Rootless and striving for fif-teen years, and almost forty years old, he said, "I've been looking back in Indiana. I would like to buy the old homestead. It was built in the 1830s." He would keep shooting for a C-suite job. At fifty-five maybe, maybe sooner, he thought he could move to the homestead and retire or telecommute.

But that was a while off, and Phil was hitting some bumps. His sec-ond wife, who helped care for the girls, was preoccupied with their daughter, then three. That and Phil's absorption in work and his two nights a week in classes shattered the intimacy of their marriage. "We agreed fairly amicably to split," he said, and his wife moved with their daughter to her mother's in Ohio. "The marriage dissolved as a direct result of this move," he said.

After they left, Ashley and Kasey were happy to have bathrooms of their own but felt lonelier. Most days, one or the other would call their mother, also in Ohio. "I'd like to move to my mom's," Kasey said. "I want to be closer to my mom." So another shoe dropped. A caseworker advised the court that Phil wasn't home enough for the girls and that their mother should have full custody.

"They're conflicted," Phil said. "They would like to live with their mom because they don't see her very much." He settled on going to Schaumburg just one day a week and working at home the rest of the time. "The desire is to do the job remotely because of the kids," he said. He skipped classes on Kasey's birthday to take the girls to dinner, but it was hard to juggle gestures like that with his job and his classes. "Bal-ance has been the hardest thing to deal with," he said.

Phil's career planning took a turn, too. Soon to have his MBA, he hoped for a bigger assignment at Nielsen—the same goal he had set upon leaving Alpharetta. He applied for a job that would lead to vice president and eventually a shot at the C-level. Then earning around $100,000, he said, "There's the question of how much more I am going to make. I

The Cost of Relo Life: *Several years commuting for his job and taking classes for a master's degree in business administration did not reward Relo Phil Cottrell as soon as he hoped. Faced with changes at work and at home, Cottrell decided to sell his spacious five-bedroom house, but ran into the moribund housing market of 2008.*

want to get an entry-level vice president job, a 25 percent increase in salary, and a small bonus."

He was turned down, however, perhaps because he wanted too much, too soon, or because Nielsen was then focused on bigger management changes. Six private equity firms had bought the parent company, a Dutch conglomerate, the VNU Group. They renamed VNU The Nielsen Company, hired a new chief executive, and began slashing the global workforce by 4,000 people, or nearly 10 percent. "Jobs are being cut at the top, removing layers of management," Phil said, "so there are fewer jobs to take." So it was with other companies as the economy slowed. They'd encourage him to get in touch in a year or so.

In January 2008, the family court judge ruled against Phil and awarded custody of the girls to their mother during the school year. Two weeks later, Ashley and Kasey moved to their mother's home in

Ohio. Around the same time, the real estate market pummeled the house, by then pointless to keep with just Phil haunting its 5,000 square feet and, as his biggest asset, the source of his retirement nest egg. He had bought it for $674,000, almost twice what he got for the house in Alpharetta, and listed it for sale at $989,000, a price then in line with neighboring houses. He dropped it to $939,000 as the market declined, then to $899,000, and $799,000, and still there were no takers.

Finally, around Thanksgiving, Nielsen let him go. "I became one of those lucky many," he said, to be laid off in the stalling economy. His severance pay and unemployment benefits gave him some breathing room. But losing the girls would be costly. He would soon be paying child support for all three. With the economy sinking, a company in New York that scheduled a job interview called to cancel. A company in Chicago that looked promising kept putting him off. In early March 2009, his outlook brightened. A company in San Francisco that met his criteria wanted him to come out for a second interview, but he tried to keep cool. "I want to make sure that the career moves in the direction it has to move," he said.

Meanwhile, another corner of his life perked up. He had, as he puts things, "a friend I would be considered to be dating."

Fighting Back

During the three nights of Thanksgiving weekend in 2007, four seventeen-year-old and two eighteen-year-old boys who attended a new high school on the edge of a swirl of Alpharetta subdivisions went "car hopping." They broke into 150 cars. They took golf clubs and anything electronic, including laptop computers, navigation systems, DVD players, and iPods. They were from Windward, Alpharetta's largest subdivision with three thousand homes tucked into smaller, mini-subdivisions off the shores of a 195-acre, man-made lake.

Relo-packed upscale Windward produces a disproportionate share of the city's home-grown hooligans. For more than a year in 2000 and 2001, eight thirteen- and fourteen-year-old boys terrorized the neighborhood, slashing tires, breaking up outdoor Christmas displays, and setting fire to houses that were under construction. They were charged with more than a hundred acts of vandalism and arson.

"They're a bunch of spoiled brats," said Jim Matoney, Alpharetta's municipal court judge who lives on the shore of Lake Windward. "Their parents knew about it and wouldn't do anything about it. They're just bored, overindulged kids." In another case, kids got in a boat with paintball guns and picked off houses around the lake, including Matoney's. "Mine got pretty well scorched," he said.

In a 1993 study of 9,915 six- to seventeen-year-olds for the *Journal of the American Medical Association*, Dr. David Wood and Dr. Neal Halfon, pediatricians at the University of California, wrote, "Frequent relocation was associated with higher rates of all measures of child dysfunction. Twenty-three percent of children who moved frequently had repeated a grade versus 12 percent of children who never or infrequently moved." In a more recent 2006 survey published in *Sociological Quarterly*, Dana L. Haynie at Ohio State University and Scott J. South at the State University of New York at Albany reported that more than 7 percent of adolescent girls who moved during the previous year reported attempting suicide, compared with 5 percent of girls who had not moved. In another study, they said movers tended to be drawn to the wrong crowd in school. They noted, "Our findings imply that relatively deviant adolescent school networks may be particularly welcoming to new members and that, once mobile adolescents become embedded in such networks, they tend to adopt the violent behaviors of their members."

The Alpharetta Police Department is a classy operation fully equipped with new cruisers and spiffy uniforms, which it hands down to poorer police departments in rural Georgia. The city is rich enough to have built a new, forty-eight-prisoner jail that, after more scrutiny, it found it didn't need. In arguing for bigger police budgets at city council meetings, the department's biggest fan on the council often warned of "criminal activity surrounding our borders" and of "growing gang activity around our borders." The Alpharetta police may indeed be succeeding in keeping out crime and the gangs from the city to the south, Atlanta (which has seven times Alpharetta's rate for violent crime, twelve times its robbery rate, and almost twice its rate of property crime), but it has been less effective in foiling the crime and gang activity that bloom in the mulch of the city's own immaculate subdivisions.

No one can say how many suburban kids who get into trouble with vandalism and drugs are Relos or how many Relo kids are troublemakers. Neither the police nor the Census Bureau keeps track of how many places people have lived before moving to their current home or who employs them. But there's little doubt that vandalism and teenage drug abuse are often common in young, well-educated, and affluent suburbs with global employers nearby—in towns like Alpharetta and Roswell, Georgia; Plano, Frisco, and Flower Mound, Texas; and Castle Rock, Parker, and Highlands Ranch in Douglas County, Colorado.

Moving from Arkansas via Connecticut, James and Jane Lee bought a house on Hampton Crossing, in Windward. Jane came first. "The day I got here, the power was out," she said. Accustomed to outages in Connecticut, she didn't think anything of it. But as evening began, the neighbors' lights came on, and hers did not. It turned out that a neighborhood boy had broken into the electrical service box outside the house and turned off the power. He also destroyed the satellite dish. "The car in the driveway," James said, "he put a rag in the gas tank and tried to light it. You could see the scorch marks." Jane said, "When we found out he did it we didn't press charges. He was thirteen at the time. 'We'll let it pass.'"

How deep-seated the abuses are is another question, because the victims, like the Lees, are reluctant to complain about neighbors. "We caught somebody who vandalized a home," Gary George, the Alpharetta police chief, said. "We had the kid. But the homeowner wouldn't file a complaint. The kid's mother wrote the owner a check."

Chris Lagerblood, then a sergeant in Alpharetta and later the police chief in the new neighboring city of Milton, said, "The victims fear retribution from a fifteen-year-old and don't want to report it. The kid might throw eggs at the house, then fire a BB gun. They fear retribution. That happens very frequently."

In Relo-packed Douglas County, Colorado, Undersheriff Tony G.

Spurlock sees similar behavior. "The ones that are committing the criminal acts are the ones that are relocated. They're not the ones with strong family ties or ties to the community. Most drug abuse happens at home. This isn't like New York City or L.A. and Denver. It isn't like that. They'll go into a house, and they're safe to make deals, and a patrol car could drive by fifty times and not see any difference," he said.

To drink and use drugs, Spurlock said, "they're not going to bars because they're too young. Dad's out of town. Mom's wherever. They have this network. They go to one kid's house, and when the parents are back, they move to another house. The only time we get involved is when the parents call us—when they can't handle it themselves—or if there's an unfortunate tragedy."

Dr. Lisle Gates, a career high school administrator in his sixties, was appointed principal of Douglas County's Castle View High School, in Castle Rock, when it opened in 2006. He is a tall, bald, brick of a man, a star wrestler as a youth in California and later a wrestling coach. For a decade, he was principal of Highlands Ranch High School. "I would say most schools in the south metro area—Columbine, Chatfield, Cherry Creek, Highlands Ranch, Castle Rock—have more than their fair share of Relos," Gates said.

Executives from Lockheed, First Data Corporation, or Sherwin Williams moving to the area congregate in the new housing around these schools. In Highlands Ranch, Gates said, "I had an assistant to do nothing but talk to new families. I would have 250 to 280 kids, out of 2,000 or 2,200, walking in the door at the beginning of the school year who weren't there before, and in June there were probably 180, 190 who were leaving. Of them, 30, 40, 50 were miserable.

"These were kids who were so pissed at Mom and Dad for 'jerking me out of my school and forcing me to come to Colorado.' Their agenda was to make life so difficult for Mom and Dad that they would let them move back home and stay with an aunt or a grandparent. The parents of fifteen or twenty of them would say, 'Okay you can move back to Grandmother.' This was more true of junior and senior kids than of freshmen and sophomores. They weren't disciplinary problems.

They were just hurtin' kids. Dad is traveling all week. You got to know that his wife is hurting, too. You drive a kid home and there isn't any furniture in the house."

Gates's Castle View High had been opened little more than a year when it was struck by a form of substance abuse called "pharming." Kids mined parents' medicine cabinets for prescription painkillers, sedatives, and tranquilizers and mixed them with one another and with over-the-counter medications. Worse outbreaks of substance abuse have struck the Relovilles north of Dallas, especially Plano. As Plano was becoming the nation's biggest and fastest-growing Reloville in the 1980s and '90s, it also became the prime-time symbol of suburbia's travails with transient, disconnected, and suicidal kids.

Heroin hit the Plano schools—often in the form called "cheese" that students mixed with antihistamines like Benadryl, ground to a Parmesan-like powder, and snorted. In the late '90s, twenty kids, most students in Plano's affluent schools, died from overdoses. After arrests of twenty-nine distributors, including recent Plano high school graduates, heroin use simmered down. But in 2005 and 2006 at least three more Plano teenagers succumbed to overdoses.

Meanwhile teen athletes in Plano picked up on professional ballplayers' use of performance-enhancing drugs. In July 2003, Taylor Hooton, a seventeen-year-old, six-foot-two varsity pitcher for Plano West Senior High, hanged himself from a belt on his bedroom door. He had added thirty pounds injecting anabolic steroids and became depressed when trying to withdraw. His father, Don Hooton, an international sales executive with Hewlett-Packard who had moved the family to Plano four years earlier, left his job to run a national foundation, named for Taylor, to stop the drugs' abuse and proliferation.

Drug dealing in Relovilles' churning, affluent subdivisions is harder to spot than it was in the days when kids would drive to the big cities to buy. At noon on a Wednesday in April 2007, Jeffrey C. Garner, a deputy and an investigator for the Douglas County sheriff, snaked his big black and unmarked Chevrolet SUV through the compact middle-income subdivision in Highlands Ranch called The Hearth. It was a short walk from a high school and a middle school. Not a soul was afoot outside.

Garner paused half a block from a typically beige, two-story clap-board house with a two-car garage close to the sidewalk. A week earlier, after a neighbor called, the sheriff's office checked the home's electric bill. "The power usage is going through the roof," Garner said. "Then we checked the water usage through the sanitation department, and that's going through the roof. The home is rented so we talked to the landlord and asked him if he wanted to go in and check his property. Well he went in there and found that they had two dead bolts on the door leading to the basement. So we know that they're using the house as a marijuana grove."

Across the street was another, innocuous-looking house. It looked vacant. "We've got some people in there watching this house," Garner said. "You'll see people coming to the house and blowing the horn. The garage door opens and the guy backs in so you can't see their license plates and the door closes so you don't know what they're doing." By biding their time before raiding the place, the deputies hoped to catch a drug ring. "We've got a lot of license plates we're following up on," Garner said. "Some of them we know are active drug dealers."

Three weeks later, the deputies crossed the street to the house. "They weren't Mexicans in there," Garner said. "They were Anglos from the area, in their twenties. There were five or six of them. We ended up bust-ing them for marijuana growth and distribution."

Choosing Resilience

Yet psychologist Howard Drutman has also noticed an adventurous segment of Relo kids who thrive on moving. Like Amber Howard, daughter of the UPS family in Canton, they seize upon a move to turn a new leaf in school and reinvent themselves. They have a quality that therapists call hardiness. According to Drutman, "There are a lot of variables involved in making people strong. People who are going to make it as Relos have personalities that will allow them to handle all the variables they go through in a move.

"A move is chaotic," he said. "A person who has these hardiness values—friendly, positive attitude, doesn't have anxiety or substance abuse—they're going to make it." In an analysis of families that lose jobs, the American Psychological Association found that hardiness is key to surviving and managing stress. "Hardiness," the association said, "enhances performance, leadership, conduct, stamina, mood and both physical and mental health."

Ariana Koblitz could be one of Drutman's hardy adventurers—to the extreme, in mastering not only new places but different cultures as well. Sociologists call her a TCK, a "third-culture kid" from nowhere and everywhere. Not yet twenty, Ariana speaks the five languages she learned while living in five countries. She is dry, direct, self-assured, and unassuming.

Ariana's father, Donald Koblitz, grew up near New York City, went to Columbia University for his bachelor's degree, and graduated from the law school at Stanford University. He met his wife, Becky, who is Japanese and was an undergraduate there. Don worked for the State Department in Washington, D.C., while Becky got a law degree and then was transferred to Berlin. Once fluent in German, he left the government for the German office of a Texas law firm and became a lawyer for Volkswagen. After living in Berlin, the Koblitzes moved to a fishing village in what had been East Germany, when Ariana, their oldest child, was six. In 2005, with three children near or in their teens, the family moved to Beijing, where Don was named general counsel for Volkswagen in China.

At six months, Ariana started speaking German, which she calls her mother tongue, at a pre-school she attended with five German toddlers. She learned English at home. She went to the bilingual—German and English—international school in Berlin, and to Paris for a year in the ninth grade to learn French. Barely settled in Beijing, she left to spend a year in Saitama, a small town west of Tokyo, and live with a Japanese family, go to a Japanese school, and learn her mother's language. Back in China for two years at the International School of Beijing, she learned enough Chinese to speak colloquially.

Every July, the Koblitzes return to the States for a visit. In 2007,

Ariana, then nineteen, had decided to go to an American college, so they were touring campuses. During a stop in Washington, D.C., Ariana and her sister, Avril, thirteen, said they had resolved to call themselves American, and they spoke with the inflections and vernacular of American teenagers. But they saw themselves as stateless. The surnames of the friends Ariana listed on her Facebook page were Cheng, Flores, Raj, Xie, Ren, Westlin, Tseng, Lam, Pan, Saeta, Duemler, Rööler, Uebelgünn, Poon, Park, Ellis, Surendra, Harandi, Khavarian, Terminet, Garvey, Yu, Duke, Hung, Cane, Beider, Northagle, Ang, Chin, Michel, and Smith. "I'm an international," Ariana said.

As internationals, the Koblitzes make a point of living in the belly of whatever country they're in, away from the apartment buildings and Western compounds—the foreign Relovilles—of big global cities. "Dad approached each of us," Ariana said. " 'What do you think of living in Beijing . . . ?' I said, 'As long as it's in the city.' " They found a place in an old part of town where Ariana needed only to step out the door, on occasion over garbage rotting in the streets, to see how others live and to practice Chinese with neighbors and peddlers. "Seeing a place with someone who lives there," she said, "is a million times better" than the compounds.

There are challenges, Ariana said. In Saitama, her classmates ignored her. She was a misfit. They called her a "ha-fu," someone of mixed race. As she stumbled learning Japanese, she hoped that at least one classmate would engage her and help her along, but none did. Then, midway through the school year, she finished first among the girls in a school-wide, thirty-kilometer endurance race. Her teacher called her to the front of a student assembly to congratulate her, and that broke some ice.

Applying to colleges, she recounted her brushes with language and cultures, and some lessons she learned. In her essay for Stanford, she wrote of the California artist Kip Fulbeck's Hapa (for "half" in Hawaiian) Project, head and shoulder portraits of people of mixed race, with a space on the canvas to answer the question, "What am I?" "If he had asked me," Ariana wrote, "I suppose I would have written: 'a daughter of three continents still learning about who I am.'" In September 2008, Ariana was accepted for early admission to Stanford.

Like Ariana Koblitz, Mark and Sandi Remson's three kids, Laura, Brian, and Kelly, come across as self-assured and competent. They're too tall and athletic to be bullied. They play basketball and volleyball, and like Sandi they are long-distance swimmers. At dawn every day in Frisco, Texas, Brian swam laps in their pool. He made the varsity swim team at Frisco High. He wore the team T-shirt and two members became his best friends. At Baylor University he was playing water polo.

But it is travel that most defines the Remson kids and sets them apart. They have climbed mountains in Nepal. They toured the Killing Fields museum in Phnom Penh that recalls the genocide of the Khmer Rouge, which killed 2 million fellow Cambodians in the 1970s. They saw the Cu-Chi tunnels in Vietnam where the Vietcong hid from the U.S. forces they eventually routed. "Some are still intact," Laura said. "We could lower ourselves into the tunnels and crawl through them."

After so much of their youth spent abroad, in Japan, Singapore, and India, Brian and Laura's perspectives clashed with what they would hear in Frisco classrooms. "When you go to a place like Vietnam where things happened, you get a different view," Laura said.

"I try to explain what it's like living in India," Kelly said. "I have to explain that I didn't live in a hut. You don't feel at home in your own country. You feel a loss."

Brian said, "I would say I'm from Texas, but coming to Frisco, I consider myself a TCK," who doesn't identify with any country. "I like going out and seeing different cultures," he said. "I've lived overseas my whole life. This is my first time in public school back in the United States. On Facebook, they ask for your hometown, and I type T-C-K."

Routinely, the Remson kids are reminded of how different they are. Laura started high school in Singapore, moved to India for her junior year, and to Frisco as a senior. On Senior Day at Frisco High, the day before graduation, the seniors lined up to enter the hall according to how long they had been in Frisco schools. "Laura spent the whole ceremony outside," Sandi said, "until she marched in last."

TCKs' social and emotional crutch is their immediate families. "An expatriate family really is the ultimate of nuclear families," Barbara F. Schaetti and Sheila J. Ramsey write in the Employee Relocation Council's *Mobility* magazine. "Grandparents, aunts and uncles, cousins, neighbors, teachers, and friends, all those who surround a family with support and a community of relationships are necessarily left behind when a family moves abroad. Father, mother, children, the immediate members of the nuclear family, must look to one another for the support provided other families by their external community. When that support is absent, the risk to expatriate family members of serious family dysfunction can be extreme."

Hardy third-culture kids often feel they reap at least one big benefit from their moves: being enriched by mixing with other cultures. Michael Gerner, a school psychologist, and fellow researchers compared 1,071 students attending American schools in Bangkok and Cairo and a public high school in Belle Plaines, Minnesota. "U.S. adolescents who live overseas," he writes, "rate themselves more culturally accepting, more interested in travel, more interested in learning other languages, and more interested in following an international lifestyle in the future than do U.S. adolescents who have lived only in the United States."

But upon entering American colleges, third-culture kids discover that their worldliness marginalizes them socially. "They must set aside a major part of their identity from peers who cannot relate to their overseas experiences," Gerner writes. "Difficulty forming new friendships with peers who do not share their unique overseas experiences results in feelings of alienation and social separateness. There is no readily identifiable social group to which they can belong."

Yet the Remson kids seem little enough scarred by their moves to keep going. Laura adapted easily to Baylor. She is tall, five foot ten, and plays basketball. She loves the variety at Wal-Mart. After years of slim pickings in India and Japan, she was ecstatic about the selection for women of her height. She made friends quickly, too. "My social life is good," she said. "Overseas, your social life is very fluid. You never know how long people are going to live there. You never know if it's two months or two years."

But she was ready to get back on the road and persuaded her parents to let her go to Rome for her junior year. "At times I get restless," she said. "I'm not used to staying in one place. I get this moving itch. I've experienced Waco. I'm ready to find a new place. You put yourself in a new place and see if you can adjust." She might put herself in many new places. Soon she would take the Foreign Service exam.

10. Family Duty

The Western sense of place has been undermined by the new global economy, which has unleashed the greatest movement of people since the nineteenth century . . . thus once again undermining the fixed meanings of home.

—John R. Gillis, *A World of Their Own Making*

By Monday, January 22, 2006, the sod around the new stone and clapboard, pastel-hued homes of the Seasons at Laurel Canyon, in Canton, Georgia, had gone dormant and brown. It was flu weather, too bleak and drizzly to go for a walk. The moving van had unloaded their belongings two days before, and Arthur and Bernice Friedman, he seventy-two and she sixty-seven, were fighting mean winter colds. It was a dismal start for a couple who had become "collateral Relos"—late-stage vagabonds who uproot themselves, not for a job but to follow their unrooted children. A few months before, the Friedmans' daughter Terri, her IRS-officer husband, and their two children moved from Maryland to Cumming, twenty miles from Laurel Canyon.

Two blocks from the Friedmans' house, Linda Vandergeest was

having a red sofa delivered. In jeans, sprightly and chatty, a widow for twenty-five of her sixty years, she had left lifelong friends in Orange County, California, to try living in Georgia. Richard Boivin and his wife, Beverly, both in their late sixties and avid skiers and golfers, had driven down from Stratford, Connecticut, where they had lived their whole lives, to check on the house they would move into in a week. In a navy blue windbreaker with "Palm Beach Fire and Rescue" on the back, Steve Bloom, sixty-one, divorced, and lean as a lifeguard, had mothballed his 43-foot motor home and stopped in the Seasons's sales office to ask when the clubhouse pool would be finished. All, like the Friedmans, were collateral Relos, and in their cases, all were following relocated daughters.

Unlike the dutiful daughter who stayed around in Valparaiso, Fargo, or Carbondale as her parents aged or came back when they needed her, Relos invite their parents to come along with them. As collateral Relos, the parents give up their ties to a town, and their place at the stove and the head of the table, to join the kids. They get the guest room, or a "casita"— a little house, maybe with an elevator—adjoining rich Relos' homes. Or like the Friedmans, they get a low-maintenance, one-story house with wide doors for wheelchairs, stepless entries, raised toilets, and walking trails nearby with shallow inclines in one of the "active adult" subdivisions like the Seasons that have been sprouting up around Relovilles for retirees and collateral Relos.

It is easier for the parents to pull up stakes than it used to be. Many can take still-unimaginable gains from selling homes they bought decades before the late-2000s relapse in real estate prices. They are also better off than ever. The poverty rate among people over sixty-five has dropped from one in three a half century ago to one in ten. Health is less of an obstacle, too. A sixty-five-year-old man can expect to live seventeen more years, two more than in 1980, and the number of the elderly hobbled by chronic disabilities has dropped from one in four in 1984 to less than one in five.

It is impossible to determine just how many people become collateral Relos, but no doubt they make up tens of thousands of the more than 300,000 people aged sixty to seventy-five who move out of their home states each year. They run one big risk as they age and the kids keep moving: finally too feeble to move, and far removed from their old homesteads, they can end up in a Reloville assisted-living facility, where they know not a soul. It is a risk that collateral Relos are willing to run as an alternative to rarely seeing children and grandchildren, thousands of miles away, who can't interrupt hectic lives to visit them.

The Seasons at Laurel Canyon is a new active adult retirement community of 192 occupied, single-family homes, with eventually perhaps five hundred more, in rolling woodland an hour and a half's drive north of Atlanta. Unlike the retirement havens of Florida and Arizona, the Seasons can't boast of a desert or ocean or mountains, a predictably benign climate, or amenities like golf-cart trails to doctors and shops. The appeal of the Seasons is its proximity to younger Relos.

Levitt & Sons, which built the post–World War II Levittowns for baby boomers' parents, originally developed the Seasons based on the idea that the boomers, entering their sixties, might follow their children to new Levittowns built especially for them. In the housing crash starting in 2007, Levitt was hit hard, along with a number of builders, and the company had to bow out of the Seasons after filing for bankruptcy that November. At Laurel Canyon, Levitt left about fifty houses in various stages of construction, with roads incompletely paved and a half-finished community clubhouse. New buyers were stuck with punch lists of ill-fitting doors and faulty faucets.

But with its proximity to the young Relo families passing through the north Atlanta subdivisions, the Seasons was holding on. The residents rallied, raised dues to pay the gatekeepers' wages, found a lawyer, the daughter of a resident, to represent them pro bono, and prevailed on Wachovia Bank, the biggest creditor, to maintain the place until it found other developers. Creditors also got the clubhouse completed, and the golf course was opened.

Linda Vandergeest's immigrant Dutch husband had built a big landscaping business in Orange County. Part of what kept her there for years after his death was the proximity of her own parents. "I was looking after them, a child looking after parents," she said. Once she had buried them and Heidi Herbert, the older of two daughters and mother of two boys, had moved to Canton, she said, "Everyone knew I needed a change in my life. I turned sixty and I thought, 'I need to leave my support group and give this a try.' "

Heidi stopped by to help organize the living room. "I will make it easy on you," Linda said turning to her. "I have friends whose parents lived in other states and got ill, and I watched them go back and forth, back and forth. And I said to both daughters, 'I will make it easy on you. I will move to wherever you are.' " Her other daughter is divorced and lives in Lake Arrowhead, California, with two children.

"I don't think it's fair for Heidi to get on a plane" to see her, Linda said. When she's older and infirm, she said, she will tell Heidi, "Keep it simple. Put me in a home five minutes, ten minutes, twenty minutes away. When I'm in the home I would like you to check up on me to make sure they're plucking the hairs out of my chin and basically making sure I'm okay and I'm not being abused."

That's as Heidi would have it. "I think for me, being the eldest and seeing my grandparents go through their issues, it's a priority for me to get her close and stay close." What she couldn't know, however, was when—less likely if—her husband's employer, Vodafone, the British telecommunications company, where Doug is a global accounts manager in Alpharetta, would ask the family to move again.

Linda's neighbors Arthur and Bernice Friedman have the expressive gestures, liberal politics, and fearless air of undiluted Brooklynites, which they are. Arthur has snowy white hair, glasses, a white mustache, and a small paunch. Over it, he wore a shirt depicting a bionic golfer whacking a drive to the clouds. Bernice, in gray sweats, is shorter with graying, closely cropped hair. Detachable gold balls rimmed her ears. Her BMW's Maryland license plate—soon to be changed for a Georgia plate—read "Berni," his Nissan Maxima's, "Arthur."

The Friedmans had set up their bedroom and hooked up their computers in the two other bedrooms. They had barely begun to sort through 17,000 pounds of possessions, including 300 boxes, they brought from Columbia, Maryland. They bought a house, one of the largest in the

Seasons, for $442,000—a little less than they got for their last house in Columbia. Paying much lower property taxes than in Maryland, they expected to get along well on less than $75,000 a year.

Over the years, the Friedmans moved from New York City to Harrisburg, Pennsylvania, and to Maryland. Arthur is a career salesman. Part of his e-mail address is "arthursells." He spent most of his years going store to store throughout the Mid-Atlantic selling rubbery products like waterproof baby pants and shower curtains. Unemployed after the collapse of the U.S. textile industry, he sold residential real estate in Maryland for eight years. Along the way, Bernice got a bachelor's degree and then a master's in nursing and became chief of infection control at Walter Reed Army Medical Center in Washington—"putting dirty stuff where it belongs," she said.

As the Friedmans approached retirement, their daughter and son-in-law, Terri and Michael Counts, were asked to move from Baltimore to Atlanta. Michael is a group manager for the Internal Revenue Service. In Maryland he and Terri lived only three miles from Bernice and Arthur, and the Friedmans had become deeply involved with them and their children, both under five years old at the time. "If we move out of state," Terri said she asked her parents, "would you consider moving out of state?" They had an added incentive to move. Bernice's brother lived near Laurel Canyon, in Cumming, the community where Terri and Michael found a house. "It took us thirty-seven seconds to say yes," Bernice recalled.

Three months after the Friedmans moved in, Terri and her family came over for hot dogs, and Arthur and Michael hooked up a ceiling fan on the screened-in porch. With her brother and the Countses nearby, "what we're doing is merging multiple families," Bernice said. "That's part of the reason we came down here. We had a built-in social system." It might not be a durable system, though. In four or five years, Michael might be made a territory manager, a promotion from group manager, and the Countses would move again.

The Friedmans have considered that. "It was nice the kids were moving and invited us to come along," Arthur said. But they're bound to the Seasons now. Initially, Bernice said, "I felt I was living in a vacuum, very isolated. Once it warmed up, and I went out walking, I made friends. You have something in common with these folks. Grandchildren. There are things I won't do, like the mindless card games. But I feel comfortable. I don't feel pressured. If they go anywhere else, we're not going." She will only leave in a box, she said.

Wound Down

For reading, Darlene Selby loops her legs over an arm of her easy chair beside the bay window in the back of a light and wide living room in Littleton, Colorado, near Denver. Nearly a half century since they started out, Darlene and her husband, Ed, are full-fledged, road-hardened Relos at rest. They followed no one to Littleton, and no one followed them. They have made no deep connections between themselves and a place to call home until *the* home, as they put it, where someday they might have to be leashed. They are rooted, but only to each other by their interests and recollections.

In jeans, her hair a dense white bird's nest, Darlene has a wry and skeptical look. She plays golf, but a bad hip has slowed her down. Ed, in his easy chair with a stool for his feet, looks fit enough for another stint in the navy, though his knees have gone arthritic. He has a gray 1950s crew cut and wears pressed khakis and a crisply ironed pink button-down shirt.

On an uncommonly warm November day in 2006, the living room is barren of tokens and trophies of long lives or of anything that Darlene and Ed don't regularly use. The Selbys' rugged square oak coffee table is strewn with books, among them *Life on the Color Line* by Gregory Howard Williams, Charles Frazier's *Thirteen Moons*, and others by Elie Wiesel, Alice McDermott, Eudora Welty, and Lisa See.

Darlene, who was sixty-seven then, and Ed, seventy, do not own the books, or any books. They get them at the library in Littleton. "If we do buy a book, we give it away," Darlene said. "Books are heavy," Ed said. After forty-four years of marriage, packing, moving, and unpacking at twenty-six addresses in nineteen towns in nine states, Darlene said, "I hate stuff." Ed said, "Every time we move, we say, 'Let's get rid of stuff.'"

At Christmas, the Selbys volunteer at homeless shelters, but they do not put up a tree or exchange gifts. "People give each other lists!" Darlene said, dumbstruck. The last time they moved, from Salt Lake City to Littleton, they got rid of all the silver but the flatware. They hold on to some Haviland china and unmatched crystal wineglasses in the kitchen cabinets, to a dozen scenic watercolors and oils by artists they have known, and to the tools Ed uses when they buy a house. They get good deals buying houses because they specialize in fixer-uppers, and Ed is good with his hands.

Working in the kitchen or Darlene's front yard xeriscape of desert-friendly plants, in conversation, in their diversions and expectations, the Selbys tick with the synchrony of twin clocks. They moved so much, she said, because "my husband has a short attention span," and so, as it happens, does she. "I was always ready to go," she said. "The opportunity would come up and we'd do it."

Darlene lived on a farm in Illinois until the sixth grade, when she moved to Mount Prospect, a Chicago suburb. She studied nursing at Illinois Wesleyan University in Bloomington, Illinois. Ed moved from Denver to Billings, Montana, at eleven, and eventually returned to Colorado, to the University of Colorado in Boulder, where he got a degree in mechanical engineering.

On a lark, driving separate Volkswagen Bugs, Darlene and another nurse came to Denver on their way to see San Francisco. "They were skiing here already," she said. They found work as visiting nurses, which let them ski on weekends. Ed, a lieutenant, was in Denver after three years in the navy, and met Darlene. They got married, had Mark, and the navy called him back. They were posted to Norfolk, Virginia; Virginia Beach; Camden, New Jersey; then San Diego. They had their second son, Chris. Ed was shipped to Vietnam as a guided missile officer.

Out in two years, he went to work for a company based in Milwaukee that became Johnson Controls, a multibillion-dollar maker of car batteries, car interiors, and air-conditioning and heating systems for factories and office buildings. He started in Denver and was sent to St. Louis for six months, to Chicago, where they lived in three suburbs in three years, and to Dallas as branch manager. "My parents did not understand us," Darlene said. "My father said, 'He seems like a nice guy, but he can't keep a job.'"

After little more than a year in Dallas, when Mark was in first grade, they moved to Billings. Ed's father had died and left him a blueprinting business there, so the Selbys took a break and raised the boys into their teens. Even around Billings they moved, four times. In 1984, Darlene said, "We went back to our normal lifestyle." They sold the business. Ed took a couple of years off and then needed a job.

Over the years, computers had displaced many of Ed's engineering skills, so to learn the technology he went to work for a computer company in Billings for free. In a year and a half he joined the staff. He left the company for another that returned the family to Denver. He traveled the country, making about $75,000 a year setting up Hewlett-Packard computer systems at client companies' warehouse and distribution centers, until the Denver branch of Johnson Controls hired him again and made him operations manager. In two years Johnson promoted him to branch manager—in San Francisco. "That was the stupidest move of all," Ed said. His salary was $90,000, not nearly enough to get along in the city. "And the day I took over the branch, the vice president who put me there was fired, and the new vice president didn't want me, so they fired me. He got rid of fourteen of sixteen branch managers within a year and a half."

A company that makes computer systems to manage industrial production hired him to open a branch in Salt Lake City—another luckless move. He couldn't get the business going. "I found out it was a closed society," he said. "We were there for one year. Unless you were a Mormon, you weren't going to do business in any volume. It wasn't worth it. I fired myself."

The Selbys returned to Denver. In their sixties by then, they thought of retiring. But they worried that they hadn't built much of a retirement fund, and Ed had an itch to work. He bought a Nissan pickup truck with a pipe rack on it and became an independent construction contractor. "I'd finish your basement, build your deck," he said. After five years, that job, too, ended badly. He drove a hole through his left hand with a nail gun, had four operations, and lost six months recuperating.

"Now I'm really retired," he said, but he wasn't. He wearied of frittering around the house. He found a job as the inside salesman for a manufacturers' representative for industrial companies. He went to work full-time for a year and put half his salary in his 401(k). At the end of March 2008, he retired again. "But it won't be for long," he said. He became an all-purpose volunteer at a Veterans Administration hospital.

Along the way, Darlene worked, too. She calls herself a caretaker. Wherever they moved, she took jobs as a nurse, paid and volunteer. For seven years in Denver, until retiring in 2004, she was a hospice nurse. She is active in the Assistance League of Denver, a women's philanthropy group similar to the Junior League, and in the local Newcomers Club, which helps Relos find their way in town. In Billings, she managed and helped start the Lutheran Center, a place for rural parents to stay when their children are sick in the hospital.

Over the years, the Selbys saw Relo marriages crumble and kids go astray. "The difference was, we made it the two of us against everybody," she said. "You had to be friends, or it wasn't going to work." Ed said, "We didn't have parents to bail us out. We didn't have extended family." Ed's father came from Iowa. He doesn't know where his mother came from. The Selbys feel no special need for the attentions of relatives or to be near Chris and his wife, although they are not very far—115 miles— in Steamboat Springs, or Mark, two years older, and his wife and two small boys, 450 miles away in Billings.

Once pushing walkers, they might let Mark take them on as collateral Relos—call them to Billings so he can watch over them—but they would recoil if instead he moved to Littleton for them. It cuts both ways. As a grandmother, Darlene said, "I feel like I should be more guilty than I am, that I should be up there in Billings more than I am. We go once a year. But because we raised our kids by ourselves, I don't feel any need to interfere. I raised them to be independent, so why should I be surprised that they are?"

The effects of all the moving on their children are hard to unravel. Their sons, both in their early forties, have made wholly different choices from their parents and each other. When Ed and Darlene left Billings, Mark began an eight-year, fit-and-start circuit through three colleges to his bachelor's degree. "He always wanted an extended family," Darlene said. In Billings he married into one. He became an industrial products salesman and coaches a ski racing team.

"He's never moving," Ed said.

"The oldest was never goal-directed," Darlene said. "The little one came out of the womb . . ."

"Hell-bent on making everything work," Ed said.

Wanting to study foreign languages that Billings schools didn't offer, Chris left home at fourteen on a full scholarship to a prep school, Hotchkiss, in Connecticut, whose alumni include ambassadors and philanthropists. "He always wanted to be the very best," Darlene said. He was a top student and athlete and won a prize for best all-around student. Then for his junior year, he went to Rennes, France. "He learned there was more than being the best," she said.

Chris resisted the school's encouragement to apply for the Ivy League and enrolled instead at the University of the Pacific in Stockton, California, where he was granted another full scholarship. For his junior year, he went to Japan and learned Japanese. For work back home after college, he led backpacking tours on bicycles and had no fixed address.

More settled now in Steamboat Springs, he skis, plays golf, waits tables, and works as a janitor. He married a reference librarian with a master's degree. He and his wife live in an 1,100-square-foot house. "They're not going to have children," Darlene said. "He doesn't want to work like his dad does. He would not have married his wife unless she didn't want to have children."

11. Fugitives

I saw the things that I love in this world. The work and the food and the time to sit and smoke. And I looked at the pen and I thought, what the hell am I grabbing this for? Why am I trying to become what I don't want to be . . . when all I want is out there, waiting for me the minute I say I know who I am.

—Biff Loman, *Death of a Salesman*

With the school buses and commuters gone, Jody Green could hear the cicadas courting along the asphalt roads that curl through White Columns, an affluent subdivision for athletic middle-aged families outside Alpharetta, Georgia. "People were so proud of their landscaping," she said. They paid Hispanic lawn care crews $250 to $450 a month to tame, pose, and mulch the shrubbery and make it look sculpted from stone.

Jody slowed her Jeep in front of 930 Treyburn Run. Forty-five when I met her in 2004, she is intense and handsome, with short, deep-bronze hair she had begun grooming herself. She and her Relo husband, Larry Green, built the house for $420,000 in 1998, after he left Alcoa in Indianapolis for Coca-Cola in Atlanta. Tucked at the base of a slope, the house is light gray stucco with olive green shutters, a highly pitched roof, two dormers, three gables, and a glass-walled basement overlooking Chicken Creek, where their daughter Kendall and son Mitchell played. "Larry found a vine they could swing across the creek," Jody said. "For me to have that house was like a dream come true. We really thought we'd be there forever. It was a good neighborhood. I made great friends. Larry liked his job. I became a tennis fanatic."

She turned and continued down to the hub of White Columns, the Swim & Tennis Center and the White Columns Country Club. The center has five courts and a junior Olympic pool. "If you lived in the neighborhood when we came here you could join the golf club for nine thousand dollars," she said. "Dues for swimming and tennis were eighty dollars a month. I ran the swim team for three years. It was a huge job. The children became beautiful swimmers.

"Tennis was really important. You meet someone. 'Do you play tennis? What level do you play?' It's one of those badges," she said. "Mondays, I took care of the house. Tuesdays I took tennis lessons. Wednesdays I'd usually play tennis. Thursdays, we had tennis matches. I'd finish in time to meet the kids. Fridays I'd run errands and have lunch with a friend. That was my week."

For wives gathered at the courts and the pool, decked out in bikinis and little tennis dresses, appearance was paramount. "There are a lot of people in their forties who have had plastic surgery, laser surgery, breast implants," she said. "The big graduation gift for girls leaving high school is a breast implant."

After two decades shuttling from town to town, Larry and Jody Green had gilded the American Dream, living on more than $200,000 a year in a showplace home in a showplace subdivision, with their kids doing well in showplace schools. Larry traveled many weekdays, and it was reassuring that he had reached a level in Coca-Cola's management hierarchy that probably precluded another move.

But not unlike Ray and Kathy Howard, who late in the game dug in against UPS's corporate moving culture so they could stay within reach of their kids, the Greens began to question their Relo-hewn values and lifestyle. On the trek from their hometowns in Wisconsin—Jody's

Minocqua and Larry's Wausau—to White Columns, they felt they had left something vital behind.

A lot of things, some economic, some more profound, triggered the Greens' doubts. "What woke us up," Jody said, "is I should have been the happiest woman on earth—two beautiful kids, a great community. But Larry was gone a lot. I wasn't happy. It's something to tell someone you live in a half-million-dollar house, you're in a golf club, and you're not happy."

Jody and Larry met at the University of Wisconsin in Madison. "I really had my heart set on becoming a social worker," Jody said. "I was told they didn't make money and that the work was depressing." She switched to journalism but didn't see much money in that, either. "I was told it was more important to make as much money as I could and buy a house," she said.

"I met Larry. He has a father he admires who is in advertising. Larry knew he would be in the business world. In the eighties that's what it was all about, and we bought it." They went to work in St. Louis, Larry for Alcoa, Jody for the Brown Shoe Company, and became Relos. Larry's jobs with Alcoa took them from St. Louis to Chicago, Milwaukee, and Indianapolis, where he became general sales manager for North America.

"That promotion got us to an income level where I could stay home with Kendall," Jody said, "and for the first time we moved to the suburbs." They bought a house in an Indianapolis subdivision for $305,000. Later, they moved on to Coca-Cola and White Columns.

The first jolt came when Larry, traveling the world making television commercials for Coke, was sent on a trip to South Africa. "Our charge was to understand the essence of the culture of South Africa, to find a way to talk to South Africans about Coca-Cola," he said. "We were out talking to people in townships and we went to Soweto. We were invited into a house, the tiniest little house. I saw absolute poverty. They said, 'You must stay for dinner.' They were going to go to the market to get food. I said, 'No, we have to leave for meetings.'

"Walking along the path to the car, the African colleague I was with put his hand on my shoulder. He said, 'Do you realize what happened? They would have gone to market and bought steaks. That would have been one month's salary.' I was stunned. We were strangers. I'd never seen anybody do that for somebody else. I started to think, 'What is this all about?' I learned that they don't think of pride as a personal thing. Pride is what they bring to the community. Your value and worth is what you can bring to others."

His son Mitchell would jolt him next. "Mitch was five or six," Larry said. As he would gather his clubs and pull out of the garage, "he'd say, 'Daddy, don't go play golf.'" About five foot eleven, wiry and unscarred by middle age, Larry had played on his high school golf team and at forty-six had a handicap of 9. "My dream was to become a member of a country club by the time I was forty-five," he said. "I did it sooner. I'd come home from a trip on Friday and go play golf Saturday."

To avoid Mitchell, he said, "I'd get up earlier and go sneak out. One Saturday I got up at six, and he's standing by the garage door. 'Daddy, I don't want you to play golf.' I ended up quitting the golf club."

Alpharetta psychologist Carol Cox Pursley has seen this syndrome writ large, sometimes playing out in extravagant gift-giving and sometimes in a feeling of loss and disconnection. Fifty-two and the divorced mother of a thirteen-year-old boy, she had moved nineteen times herself before arriving in Alpharetta. "I thought there'd be some southern hospitality," she said, but she "found a collection of people who've been transferred in from everyplace else. The husband is out of the picture most of the time. The wife's juggling. She's almost a single mom, but she has money in the bank. People that get transferred find it hard to find a 'home church.' They do not do well when they lose a spouse. It's all magnified when we feel isolated, with no sense of community."

Meanwhile Larry's work was changing. The Enron scandal was in the air, and Coca-Cola management had been charred by its own firestorm and investigations by the Justice Department and the Securities and Exchange Commission. "The company felt that executive management was becoming arrogant," he said. It put him in charge of coaching executives to think differently—much, as it happened, as he had been thinking himself since Soweto.

"In concept, it's how do we develop our people and our leaders— helping leaders get clear in their heads what their purpose is," he said.

" 'What do you believe in, what do you want to create that's bigger than you are?' Versus, 'This is all about me.' I fell in love with this executive coaching work.

"Then they wanted me and the guy I was working with to go run the advertising for North America. My heart wasn't in that." He left Coke and started his own coaching business. He called it Leadership Path. Coke became a client, and he thought corporate America would rush to his door. "We were going to make more money doing that than at Coke," he said.

But corporate executives only trickled in, along with other people who couldn't afford the firm's fees. "People who wanted to get off the treadmill or were out of work," he said. "So what do you do? When you're helping people, you ultimately get to the question, 'Where does God fit in?' A spiritual element started to take over."

By then, the Greens had discovered a church. "I grew up Catholic," Jody said. She had joined a Catholic church and taught Sunday School. "But I had a hard time finding a group to plug in to," she said. "Larry was raised Episcopalian, but he had stopped going to church." A friend invited her to a Christmas musical service at the steep-roofed Birmingham United Methodist Church, once a farm-family church, on a rural road that runs through north Fulton County.

In 1993, the Reverend John L. Wolfe and his wife and assistant pastor Judy Wolfe moved from a church in Roswell, which had grown from 1,700 to 6,000 members during their tenure, to salvage Birmingham United and its 22-member congregation. In 2003, when Jody first visited, the church had grown to 650 members, excluding small children, and 500 people regularly attended one of the two Sunday services. "I think it's a result of people trying to find some place to belong," Pastor Wolfe told me.

"I took Kendall and one of her friends to the service," Jody said. Taking a pew inside, surrounded by walls and a pitched ceiling paneled in golden pine, among festive young families like her own, she said, "I sat in that church and felt like God was in that church with us. I came home and told Larry, 'You need to go to that church.' " He joined. That and the soul-searching that started in Soweto threw an entrepreneurial spark. He organized a nonprofit variation of Leadership Path for clients seeking spiritual coaching and mentoring through a service he called Cloud Walk and found instant support from the Wolfes and new friends at the church. One helped develop a Web site for Cloud Walk; another organized a direct mail appeal; yet another helped with fund-raising. Drawing clients from churches across north Fulton County, contributions reached $94,000 in the first two years.

To help make up for the plunge in their income, Jody started a business around her hobby of landscaping. She bought a small, five-foot-long flatbed trailer to haul plants for $1,000 to $5,000 garden sanctuary installations—shrub and tree-enclosed backyard refuges where her clients could relax, read, or pray.

One night, she left the little trailer, with plants to be delivered the next day, in the driveway. Under White Columns' rules, driveways must be clear at night. The next day there was a letter in her mailbox from the homeowners association. "It warned if I left it there another day, we'd be fined," she said. "I thought, this is silly. I can't even have a trailer."

She began cutting back at the Swim & Tennis Center. "I think I made people mad at me," she said. "I wasn't valuing what they valued anymore, being part of the team. I didn't want to play tennis anymore. I became more involved with the church. It was almost like they thought I was choosing this over being their friends."

Mitchell, ten by then, had stopped baseball. "He started at five," Jody said. "He played at the Hopewell baseball park for two years, just in the spring. In second grade, he started playing spring and fall. Larry was coaching, and they both loved that. The next year he got on the all-star team, which meant playing all year. He did that two years. He played short stop. In the end he had the best batting average."

"It became a badge," Larry said. "How well your team does, how well your child does."

Then in the summer of 2004, they signed him up for "travel ball," which involved playing teams all over the state. "He just didn't like it," Jody said. "It was more intense, more yelling. He doesn't function well in those situations. He just really lost interest and became one of the worst players. He dropped out."

Downsizing

Though less than a mile long, Ranchette Road feels Appalachian, slicing through hollows and hills. It is barren of subdivisions' standardized mailboxes, their cul-de-sacs, gables, columns, and wide weedless lawns. No two houses on Ranchette are alike. They are nestled well back on three-acre wooded lots carpeted with pine needles and leaves.

Up a steep, tree-shrouded driveway, the Greens' seventeen-year-old brick ranch house was barely visible from the road. A small flatbed trailer and two Jeeps were parked outside. A sliver of mown grass bordered the walk from the garage to the front door. It was unusually cool for a late August morning in Georgia.

Larry opened the door into a large living room with wide windows. It felt lived in and rustic. When the Greens moved in two months before, they laid a new floor of unstained, 10-inch-wide planks of knotty pine. The television was there, and an ample brown couch, a matching easy chair, and a large square coffee table. A screened-in porch in the back, nearly as wide as the house, grazed the woods. Trees blotted out the sun, so Jody lit some candles.

"We had to downsize," Larry said. "We're going the other way." The Greens sold their house in White Columns for $551,000 and bought the one on Ranchette Road for $309,000. They relied wholly on public facilities for recreation and sports—Fulton County pools, tennis courts, and playgrounds. "We would have people come up and say, 'We really feel sorry for you,'" he said. "'You lost all this.' We said, 'This is really by choice.'"

"When I realized we would sell the house, at first I was okay with it," Jody said. "It was the logical thing to do. Then I worried if it was the right thing to do. I was angry with him. I thought whatever friendships I had would be gone. I was almost at the point of, 'Larry, go back to Coca-Cola.'"

Then Jody came to equate life in White Columns with death. "I felt I sold myself out," she said. "I felt like I was selling my soul for something I was supposed to want. When I let go, I felt such peace. I didn't have my nails done or pedicures anymore. I haven't had my eyebrows waxed in quite a while. I don't have my hair done as often.

"It's not a judgment on other people's choices," she said.

"But it is a choice," Larry said, "against the whole idea of people who turn their lives over to the illusions."

In the old house, Kendall and Mitchell slept on the second floor and Jody and Larry in the master suite on the first. Jody said, "Kendall told Larry that at the other house, 'Sometimes I felt so far away from you.' There would be times I would go to their rooms to wake them up, and I would not be in their room the entire rest of the day. Now I'm in their rooms all the time."

"When we decided to move," Larry said, "Kendall's one request was, 'I would really like to go to Milton High School and stay with my friends.'" So they decided to stay in Alpharetta and look for a place near Milton. Thirteen, a tall thin reed, Kendall could also keep up her dancing, both jazz and ballet. She had been dancing at the same studio since she was seven.

Mitchell, towheaded, skinny, and growing fast, was harder to read than Kendall. He was angry and lonely after leaving friends in White Columns and going to a different elementary school. But he liked having Larry around.

One dewy Saturday morning, a middle school soccer field had been cut in two. Three- to five-year-old boys and girls engulfed in baggy satiny uniforms came out to play serious soccer. Parents in folding canvas chairs took pictures, cheered, and goaded. "Kick the ball, Nicholas," a worked-up father shouted. "Let's go. Go go go go go!"

Mitchell and Larry drove up to a grassy vacant lot near the soccer fields to play serious football, the two of them. Hunched forward, standing side by side, they glared at a phantom phalanx of New England Patriots.

"Hut," Quarterback Larry said, gripping the ball, stepping back to pass. Mitch darted off, zigzagging, stiff-arming, turning. He missed it.

"Hut." Quarterback Larry rolled back and tossed the ball high over the line of scrimmage. Running hard, right end Larry snared it only to be stopped cold by Mitch and crumpled into the dirt.

Next they were off to a cul-de-sac in the Westminster subdivision to meet Jody at Erik and Melissa Johnson's. They were a younger Coca-Cola household with two small children. Their deep backyard extended twenty-five feet to woodland stretching another forty. "I called Jody to get some solace in our yard," Erik said. "We lead a hectic life. I need space in that life to write in my journal, to read. Melissa needs a place where she can take a break when the kids nap."

Larry and Mitch arrived, followed by Jody, pulling her trailer of gardening tools and buckets of hosta, ferns, and creeping phlox. They cleared a space for a sanctuary. Mitch dug a deep hole for a prayer tree, a post with a dozen thin chips of black slate hanging from small arms. The Johnsons can write a word or two with chalk on a chip to remind them of subjects of prayers—a child's first day in school, or someone sick. They'll install an Adirondack chair or two.

It was Jody's fifteenth sanctuary. Three years later, after selling through word of mouth, she opened a shop and formalized the business as The Garden Within. Larry, building on Leadership Path and Cloud Walk, organized Souly Business, a spiritually based nonprofit group for businessmen—only—that gathers for retreats three times a year and for breakfasts twice a month. Kendall was auditioning for the Atlanta Ballet. Mitch was getting straight A's and had jumped back into sports, including golf.

By then, the Greens had sloughed off the last vestiges of Relo life. "I would say who I was by what I thought everybody wanted me to be," Jody said. "I wanted to make people see me as worthwhile and successful, and running a good home, and playing good tennis, and having well-behaved kids. Now what you see is what you get."

Lost and Found

"Excellence in Community Living," promised the stately sign on the drive into the Northampton Falls subdivision in Canton, Georgia, in August 2004. "Forty-nine estate homes from the mid $400's–$500's."

Settling Down—For Good: *After twenty-eight years on the move—with stops in Alpharetta, Georgia; Kansas City; Florida; Connecticut; and Maine, and grueling commutes for her husband—Jeanne Strout remarried and was able to plant roots in Seneca, South Carolina, opening an antiques store she named, aptly, "Lost and Found."*

There was no community, though—no focal point, no shop, no neighborhood pool or tennis court, no post office, no public bench. It was just houses and skinny new trees on one- to seven-acre lots of bald and rolling terrain. Like Larry and Jody Green's older White Columns, nothing moved inside the subdivision in early afternoon: no cars, no feet.

Steve and Jeanne Strout's two-year-old Arts and Crafts house at 126 Northampton Drive was a swaggering eccentric among the colonial and multi-gabled fortresses that had sprung up since the Strouts, the first to build there, moved in. Painted a brown-tinted green, it had sections of rough-cut stone, deep eaves, a fat stone chimney, and square tapered posts on the porch. Yet it looked tired. Weeds had invaded the lawn and crabgrass had clawed through the year-old pine straw mulching the shrubs. In back, the filtering system of an irregularly shaped, brick-rimmed swimming pool was broken. Steve had not been around to look into it.

A blue and white Mini Cooper hurried up the driveway, and a golden retriever bounded over while another inside bayed at the door. Forty-eight, five foot six, with straight brown hair and bangs, Jeanne looked jaunty and fit in jeans and a loose embroidered white blouse. Inside, the house was awash in daylight and relaxed, though without a thing out of place in the kitchen, no breakfast coffee cup left in the sink, no sign of preparations for dinner. Home from school, Jessica, sixteen, was upstairs in her bedroom with music throbbing behind a closed door.

Canton was the sixth town and the fourth state in twenty-seven years for the Strouts. Steve was an information technology executive. They moved with his jobs from Myrtle Beach, South Carolina, to Kansas City, to Woodstock, near Atlanta, to Ocala, Florida, to Monroe, Connecticut, and to Canton. Canton was a horrendous drive—186 miles and three hours—from Augusta, where Steve worked as chief information officer, CIO, for Morris Communications, which owns newspapers and radio stations.

The Strouts wanted to stop making and remaking homes. They thought a home near a major airport could be their base no matter where the next job took him. "I told my husband, 'I have to live somewhere I'm going to stay,'" Jeanne said. She has family around Canton. Her father was manager of a commercial construction firm in Iowa, where she grew up, and twenty years earlier he and her mother were transferred to Alpharetta. Her brother lived in the area. Steve would get home on weekends at least. "I thought this would be good for the last twenty years of his work," Jeanne said. "We weren't going to move again until my husband retired. That was our plan."

So she built her American Dream house. "We were going to make it reflect what we like and who we are," she said. "I built it from nothing. I was the architect. I designed everything. I drew it on graph paper, and it was converted to blueprints with no changes. I loved this house. Your home and your grass are the focus of what you do. You're doing things to the house, the garden, the patio, the deck, the pool.

"My husband makes a lot of money," she said, "and the house is where they show off their money. People here would rather buy a new house and put in a $60,000 pool. All of them want big yards of grass. A $600,000 house here has one acre, a forty-five by twenty-two-foot swimming pool, and a media room in the basement."

But like Larry and Jody Green, she wondered what the money had bought. "How does it get this way?" she asked. "You marry someone, and you're in love with him. Then he gets this money view of how much he can earn. It starts to become his life. I had the feeling that with so much money, attention, and energy put into the house, the other stuff wouldn't matter."

Her own ideal is a more urban setting where she can walk to some shops and run into familiar people. "I compromised hugely," she said. "You just compromise when you're married. I never in my entire life wanted to live in the suburbs. But it was what he thought we had to do." In the past, she had gone along because new houses were exciting distractions. For a year or so, a new house could rekindle a marriage. Canton would be better, she thought.

Steve, who is six foot four, balding, and a bit hefty, spoke by cell phone as he drove his new silver Infiniti M45 from Augusta to Atlanta for a flight to Las Vegas, where he would meet friends for two days of golf. He grew up a Relo because of his father's job as a corporate financial officer. Like Larry Green, Steve started out in Wausau, Wisconsin. At five he moved to Cincinnati, at ten to Cleveland, Tennessee, and at fifteen to Tampa. "My father always looked to progress," he said. "It was my father's American Dream. He thought you should always try to better yourself and your family and provide opportunities to do more stuff."

After graduating from the University of South Florida in Tampa,

Steve found work paying $24,000 a year as a computer programmer in Lakeland at the *Ledger* newspaper. Four years later, for $35,000, he went to the *Sun News* in Myrtle Beach, a part of the Knight-Ridder newspaper chain. He met and married Jeanne, a news clerk at the *Sun News* and a graduate student at the University of South Carolina. They wanted to get out of Myrtle Beach, a garish coastal tourist town, so Steve went to work at a software company in Kansas City for $45,000 a year.

"I was there a year and got fired just before the company went belly up," he said. Three days after he lost the job and just after Jessica was born, he said, "We were lying by the pool outside our apartment, and we decided, 'If we're going to be unemployed, we want to be unemployed in a place where we like to live.'" They thought they would like Atlanta's northern suburbs near Jeanne's parents. The *New York Times*'s Regional Newspaper Group in Atlanta hired him for its data processing office for the same $45,000 he earned in Kansas City.

The *Times* company sent him to Ocala to direct technology and production for the company's six papers in the area. He was thirty-five and earning $55,000. He and Jeanne felt they were settling down. "It was good," he said. "Part country, part city. We were less than a mile from Jessica's school. We got her into riding horses." Jeanne was working in advertising and graphics design.

"But in mid-1995," he said, "I got a call from out of the blue from a headhunter. He wanted to interview me for a job at Thomson newspapers in Stamford, Connecticut. They wanted a chief technology officer." The job paid $125,000, and he took it. "I had all technology and production for 156 newspapers in the United States and Canada and 53 in the United Kingdom," he said. The $125,000 rose to $275,000, plus annual bonuses. "That was a life-changing experience," he said. They bought a $500,000 house in Monroe.

Jeanne, however, couldn't get her career in graphics off the ground. I had met her months earlier at Gerry Burge's Allenbrooke decorating shop in Alpharetta, fifteen miles from Canton, where she worked part-time catering to high-spending Relo wives. "I had to switch jobs every time we moved," she said. "It became apparent that I was never going to go back to graduate school."

"In Connecticut," she said, "his career crashed into high gear. He began traveling almost every week." Jessica was then eight. "It was very hard," she said, "so I stopped working." Jeanne was having bouts of depression, and Connecticut's cold and gray winters didn't help. She wanted out.

Steve was ready for a change, too. The Thomson Corporation sold its newspapers. "The intent was to put me in a holding pattern to keep me employed there," he said. They decided to build the home in Canton. Steve would keep working in Connecticut or wherever else he found work, getting home on weekends.

"I decided I can't be doing this forever," he said. "A buddy called and said, 'There's this job in Augusta'" as chief information officer of Morris, which owned thirteen daily newspapers, including the *Augusta Chronicle*, the *Savannah Morning News*, and the *Amarillo Globe-News*, as well as thirty-three radio stations. "The money wasn't quite as good, but it was reasonably good," he said. He took the job.

The commute from Canton to Augusta, however, was worse than commuting from Monroe. "He was going to come home every night for dinner," Jeanne said. "He did that for two months. After that, I never cooked dinner because there was no husband to cook it for." They decided he would rent a small apartment in Augusta and come home Wednesday nights and on weekends. That didn't work either.

"I bought a plane and learned how to fly," Steve said. I started flying every day, back and forth. It was expensive—$75 to $100 a day for fuel." Jeanne said, "He said, 'I'm under a lot of stress. I want to take a break for four or five months.'"

"What happened," he said, "was, I think the time apart when I was traveling a lot, all my focus was on things going on in the business. Very infrequently was I home more than a day or two. The time away gave me an opportunity to think about my life and reflect on our relationship. It got to the point where I thought, 'You know, I don't need this.'"

But he also began to reflect on the course of his career. "As soon as you start the movement pattern," he said, "it's kind of like the lace coming off a baseball. I'm done with this life. I think I can figure out a way to make a reasonable income without working for others.

"I do think there are some benefits to the moving. You have more awareness of the bigger part of the world. We've made a lot of good friends, in a lot of different locations." But he gave up a lot, too. "Probably the biggest thing would be the day-to-dayness of family. We were looking for that Norman Rockwell kind of purity. Having grandparents around and extended family and their kids and the closeness that that leads to. That's the trade-off."

In June 2005, the Strouts divorced. They put their dream house on the market. It had cost $650,000 to build in 2002, high for outer Atlanta then. But novelty, even a tasteful rendition of a classic design, was hard to sell in suburbs that favored Relo-oriented, quick-to-sell styles. They got $490,000.

"I loved this house," Jeanne said. "But when you don't have a family living in the house, you don't have the focus of your life anymore. It's not my dream house anymore. The whole reason we built this place doesn't exist. Do you think, now that I'm single, I have any reason to work in the yard? That's what you do together, building your little homestead. None of the parameters for living here exist anymore."

Steve agreed to provide child support for Jessica and some alimony for Jeanne. With the divorce, she said she would be living on $60,000 a year. "I'm off the treadmill," she said. "I think our whole corporate culture dictates everything, like the growth of the suburbs. It almost takes you back to the 1960s military-industrial complex."

Steve married an information technology executive from the *Washington Post* whom he met at a conference in D.C. With the newspaper business waning, she left the paper to become a consultant for Bearing Point, a global management and technology consulting firm. Steve left Morris Communications for the little-celebrated interstices of computer technology. He became president and chief executive of a management software users' group—50,000 North American clients of SAP of Germany, a multibillion-dollar global software company. "I get to deal on a regular basis with the executives of Fortune 500 companies and at the same time learn what it takes to really run a company," he said.

Steve moved back to the Atlanta area with his second wife, to Alpharetta. Eschewing the subdivisions, they built a town house downtown within an easy walk of some shops and restaurants. But he hadn't shaken all the shackles of Relo life. His office was in Chicago, where he spent 60 percent of his time and thus kept a small apartment. He was looking for land in North Carolina and north Georgia on which to build a weekend house. In ten years, he hoped to make it his first "forever house."

A week or two after the divorce, Jeanne, Jessica, and the dogs piled into the Mini Cooper and moved to Asheville, North Carolina. They found a tight little 900-square-foot house in a semi-urban neighborhood, and Jessica resumed high school. Jeanne turned to the Internet and Match.com. "Something I've come across," she said. "You have no idea how many men about forty-eight to fifty-five have gone through divorces that have thrown them off careerwise. They chuck the corporate race and do landscape design or something. My husband, he didn't want to lose his career. He lost his family."

At Exit 2, off Interstate 85, at the site of a fireworks store with walls longer than an eighteen-wheeler's, South Carolina State Highway 59 curves west, then winds through ten miles of hills, farms, and Spanish moss, past trailers, mobile homes, and scattered matchbox houses— none in subdivisions—past an enormous Baptist church. It continues on into the heart of the faded cotton-trading and textile-mill town of Seneca, population 7,652.

On the town's gentrifying historic block, Ram Cat Alley, there's Lost & Found, a two-story brick, 7,000-square-foot antiques concession mall, where Jeanne Strout opened a 200-square-foot vendor's booth and found a career. By August 2008, she owned the mall and rented out the booths. Jessica, nineteen, was studying art at a community college near Asheville.

On Match.com, Jeanne had met a Dutch divorcé with teenage children who was a marine biologist at Clemson University, six miles from Seneca. Gerry Burge from Alpharetta went to the wedding. "It was in English and Dutch," she said. "When I saw them together, I thought they were crazy about each other."

Jeanne, then fifty, her hair shorter and dyed copper orange, moved into her husband's house in Seneca. She was working seven days a week to cover her rent of $5,000 a month, advertising bills of $1,500, and other costs, and had to clear $20,000 a month to break even. She expected to top $21,000 in 2008, her second full year in business. Her husband helped out in the shop and joined Jeanne on her buying trips to estate sales and auctions. "It feels like I have a real partner," she said.

Jeanne had one more objective: she wanted another dream house. Having once built one, it proved hard to settle into her husband's old white-trimmed brick Cape Cod with a deep front yard of untended scrub and trees. It's about a third the size of her house in Georgia and located in an aging working-class subdivision with boats and a motor home parked in the driveways. "I didn't pick this house," she said. "It's as unfancy as any house I've ever seen."

12. Square One

The fruit once fallen finds the stem no more.
—Oliver Wendell Holmes, *Homesick in Heaven*

Places define people. In taking on this book, I asked Relos, "Who are you, what are you?" Some said "a mother" first, or "an electronics engineer," but they all said where they came from. I assumed that Americans are shaped as much by a place as by their parents and genes. A place—a town or a neighborhood with a latitude and a longitude, with walls, windows, and doors, seasons and soil—forms our accents and values, our preferences and references, our learning, aspirations, and diversions, our senses of belonging and continuity. Roots in a place sustain us in youth and old age. "All places are assigned to people and all people are assigned to places," Mindy Thompson Fullilove, psychiatrist at Columbia University, writes in *The House of Joshua: Meditations on Family and Place.* "The true meaning of being 'out of place' is that one has stepped out of an assigned spot."

Students leaving college can choose to go home and paint themselves into Norman Rockwell tableaux as the courthouse lawyer, the veterinarian, an officer at the bank, a teacher, the paper mill manager, the State Farm insurance agent. They stay close to family and old classmates. They join a bowling league, a church, and the Rotary Club, and get home for supper by five. The more ambitious or adventurous or desperate, without hope for lifetime jobs at home, leave. Like the homesteaders of a century ago, some settle down and build a new home place. And some, the Relos, sail off as twenty-first-century pioneers to ply the global frontiers of Procter & Gamble, UPS, and Toyota and barely taste a place before moving on.

Through families like the Fischers, the Howards, the Remsons, the Cottrells, and the Links, I saw how Relos tried to manage their lives and careers. Finally, I wanted to see how they had started out and shed their place. Many from the Heartland's withering farm and industrial towns joined a demographic effluvium known as a "brain drain." Disproportionately large numbers began as top graduates of the public universities of the Great Plains and the Midwest, those of Nebraska, Iowa, Illinois, Michigan, Ohio, the Dakotas, and Indiana—not the elite schools of the East and West that feed cities like New York, Boston, Washington, and Los Angeles. Purdue University—the public land-grant, once primarily agricultural school in Lafayette, Indiana—may be the leading supplier of Relo engineers and CEOs.

Carbondale, Illinois, had little to offer Matt and Maggie Fischer when they left for the University of Illinois in Urbana-Champaign and then for Chicago with accounting degrees. They became Relos, bounding to Cleveland, Columbus, and Houston before alighting in Flower Mound, Texas, long enough for their boys to finish high school. Phil Cottrell thought of starting out at home in Valparaiso, Indiana, perhaps as a clerk at Lowenstine's department store and climbing the ranks. But Lowenstine's later burned down, and Wal-Mart, Target, Kohl's, and JC Penney, all newer to town, import their managers, their own Relos. So where would he be now?

With 20,000 undergraduate and graduate students, the University of Nebraska's main campus in Lincoln is a wellspring of future Cottrells and Fischers. Two-thirds of UNL's graduates get jobs with Nebraska employers—public school systems, state agencies, banks, and insurance companies that keep them in the state.

But many of the other third who leave Nebraska go to work for businesses that depend on Relos to navigate national and global markets. Employers of UNL graduates include the national construction companies Olsson Associates and the Kiewit Corporation, Union Pacific Railroad, and ConAgra Foods, all based in Omaha; Target stores and grain trader Cargill, both in Minneapolis; Microsoft in Redmond, Washington; Sprint, the cell phone company, in Kansas City; Wells Fargo & Company in San Francisco; Enterprise Rent-a-Car in St. Louis; IBM of Armonk, New York; and accounting firms Deloitte & Touche and Ernst & Young, based in New York City. In a survey of 3,804 students who received bachelor's and advanced degrees in 2006 and 2007, the Lincoln campus's Career Services Center found that more graduates find their first jobs in Nebraska, but that California, Missouri, Texas, and Kansas ranked highest among other states.

Go West

The western Nebraska town of North Platte, where Kimberly Ryland moved when she was in college, is a heavy-metal metaphor for the itinerant career she was expecting to begin any day. Loaded with coal, oil, chemicals, and grain, 10,000 railroad cars a day rumble through North Platte's Union Pacific Railroad classification yard, the largest railroad yard in the world.

Track following the Platte River approaches the yard's eight-mile-long, rust-brown terrain, splits like the tongs of a fork, and reassembles to carry the trains out again with their resorted cars. North Platte, population 24,386, once home of Buffalo Bill Cody, is the big city for Stapleton, population 291, thirty-five miles north of North Platte in the Sand Hills of Nebraska, where Kimberly grew up.

Kimberly wanted to design tiny surgical mechanisms to repair organs, joints, and veins. She was getting her master's degree in mechanical engineering following a bachelor's degree in biological systems engineering. Twenty-five, a runner, eager-looking and scrubbed, she stopped for coffee at the Starbucks counter in the University of Nebraska's student union in Lincoln. "My passion is biomedical device design," she said. "I want to do research and development, and it's not in Nebraska."

Kimberly has strong Roman Catholic and rural Republican convictions. She was the last of five children, nine years younger than the fourth. In Stapleton, where just one in ten adults in 2000 had finished four years of college, four of the five Ryland children have master's degrees. Two are teachers, one is a rancher, and one is a priest. Their mother is a retired nurse and works as a janitor. Their father, who had a degree in agricultural engineering from the university, had a feedlot and raised corn on 320 acres.

"I was Daddy's little girl," Kimberly said. "I was with my dad all the time helping him build." He built much of his equipment himself, like trailers and farm implements. He had a heart condition since before she was born and wore one of the first four-lead pacemakers in the state. He died of heart failure at sixty-six. She thought that she, too, could be an engineer, but a biomedical engineer who would build a better pacemaker.

At Stapleton Public School, which had two hundred students, kindergarten through grade twelve, Kimberly was valedictorian in her class of twenty, editor of the yearbook, president of the National Honor Society, and a quiz bowl competitor. She played varsity basketball and volleyball and ran track. Pole vaulting in a state meet at twelve, she cleared eight feet, six inches. Loaded with scholarships to attend the university, she made the dean's list every semester as an undergraduate. She won the College of Engineering's outstanding master's thesis award.

Kimberly assumed that wherever she went to work, she would be moved again and again. Through college, she had paid internships with a pharmaceutical company, a consulting firm, a materials science lab, and an agricultural equipment company. "All the companies I worked with said I'd have to be a Relo," she said. "They said, 'If you want to succeed in this company, you will move every three years.' It's part of the package." As she was finishing college, Procter & Gamble offered her a job as a plant technician starting in Aurora, Nebraska. She would work there for a year and a half or two years and then be moved to another plant. It was not in her field, so she turned it down.

Women graduating from college become Relos as readily as men, but upon having children, many give up those jobs, and many, like Kathy Link and Sara Carroll, become trailing-spouse Relos. Single and absorbed in her career, it could be a decade before Kimberly is forced to confront those issues. Once she does, she intends to stay home with her children while they are small. She would move as a trailing spouse for her husband's job but, like Sara Carroll, try to keep a hand in her work from home. "I would hope employers would be flexible with me," she said. "If they can't be, I don't want to work for them."

The next week, Kimberly would go to San Jose, California, for interviews with Stryker Endoscopy, a part of the Stryker Corporation of Kalamazoo, Michigan, a maker of medical instruments with 16,000 employees worldwide. They were looking for a design engineer. Stryker offered her $65,000, nearly $20,000 more than the university's average for new graduates with master's degrees. She accepted the job, and Stryker moved her and her car and possessions to San Jose and provided a free place to stay while she looked for housing.

Starting work at Stryker in June 2007, Kimberly was assigned to a team developing disposable arthroscopes—instruments, thin as a knitting needle, that carry minuscule tools and a video camera through small incisions into joints to repair damage like torn cartilage and ligaments. She called the work a good fit. "I'm blessed to be doing what I always said that I wanted to do," she said. Stryker itself, not San Jose or her neighborhood, became her place for a while. It's a sink-or-swim environment of long hours and high expectations and, as a result, high turnover.

It is also a very homogenous community. "The unique thing about Stryker is that they try to hire mainly young people straight from college or in the first few years of their career and largely from the Midwest," she said in an e-mail. "It creates an artificial microcosm society—a large concentration of very similar young people who are new to the area. Thus our social world revolves mainly around Stryker as well as our work life." Dating is forbidden among close colleagues but not among workers from other departments.

Relocation both within Stryker or by employees recruited to competing companies had slowed with the economy when Kimberly arrived. But she assumes a move is in the cards. In starting at Stryker, she said, "I did not expect one move from Nebraska to California to be enough, and furthermore do not expect it to be where I spend the rest of my career."

At the end of her first year on the job, she was enjoying the West—the Pacific, the mountains, snowboarding. But she missed her place in Nebraska. "I've not found anyone who shares, say, seventy-five percent of my values," she said. "They don't understand what I'm saying. I miss the wide open spaces, the slow pace, the people who go out of their way to say hello."

On the Road

From the time she was three, Jennifer Schultz hadn't been much of anywhere beyond her home in a pretty neighborhood of Portland, Oregon, with soaring pine trees on large lots. But it wasn't much of a place. Her father drove a cement mixer, and her mother, who stayed home until Jennifer was a junior in high school, worked in a grocery store. She said her parents drank, and her father was rarely home. She left home at seventeen and moved in with a friend, then found an apartment, and hung out at the ten-pin bowling alley nearby. "It was my support system," she said. "I grew up in bowling alleys."

Jennifer is a small woman with straight dark hair nesting on her shoulders. At Kuhl's Restaurant, near the university, she seemed matter-of-fact and unexcitable, and, in black-rimmed glasses, studious. She said she had graduated from high school in Portland with honors in 2001, but without plans or money for college, she took a job providing technical support in a call center and kept bowling. A man with connections to UNL spotted her, at five foot one and 110 pounds, delivering strike after strike. He called Lincoln. The university gave her a 50 percent scholarship, and in two straight years her women's bowling team won the National Collegiate Athletic Association's national championships, the university's first for the team.

But in Jennifer's third year, a painful bone spur formed in her right, bowling arm's rotator cuff. It was removed with surgery, but it put her out of competition and her scholarship. To stay in school, she ran up debt, worked forty hours a week during the school year while carrying a full course load, and worked summers as an intern for a construction company and Time Warner Cable.

She majored in construction engineering, a field in which UNL excels and in which she might have had some skill. As a twelve-year-old in Portland, she and her best friend Jeff built a three-story tree house in Jeff's backyard. She thought she would find work in Nebraska with one of Omaha's construction companies, settle down, and marry her boyfriend, who had graduated from UNL and was working there.

But on UNL's career services Web site, Jennifer happened upon a recruiting announcement from the Union Pacific Railroad in Omaha. "Never in Union Pacific's 145-year history have there been as many opportunities for employment and rapid advancement as there are today," UP's site said. "With baby boomers retiring in record numbers and the intense demand for our transportation services, we're hiring in unprecedented numbers in every part of our company. We need good people. And we need them now."

Wow, she thought. She clicked on the page about the operations management program. "This is an opportunity to do work you couldn't do anywhere else," it said, "real railroad work, and an opportunity to begin your railroad career in a position of true authority. As a manager in our operations department, you'll be responsible for a mechanical shop, major track projects, or the logistics of keeping thousands of trains moving safely and on time every day."

She pictured herself in the cab of a 200-ton locomotive, a giant bowling ball rocketing down a lane of two iron tracks, scaring off cows and herding cargo across UP's twenty-three states west of the Mississippi. "I got excited after the first interview," she said. "I've always loved travel. Railroads go to places most people don't. You get to see parts of the country you don't usually see. *And* you get to learn how to drive a train. It's like a big toy railroad."

UP called her in for a second interview. They offered her a job on March 22, 2007, and wanted an answer by March 26. They would pay her $56,000 a year. She started ten weeks later. Of the fifty-five graduates entering her management program at UP, Jennifer was the only woman.

She adopted the life of an extreme Relo. In training to learn the railroad, she spent her first ten days in Omaha. She was sent to Kansas City for three weeks and to Milwaukee for six, except for a four-day stint in Searcy, Arkansas. She went back to Omaha and then to Milwaukee and Searcy and to Council Bluffs, Iowa. She spent the whole year on the road, staying in hotels in eighteen states.

At the end of the training program, she was taken off the road and promoted to assistant manager working in the Omaha headquarters. She got a small apartment. She brought her twelve bowling balls thinking she might coach on the side. But that wouldn't be for long. In January, 2009, she was promoted to field engineer and shipped to Chicago. "I'm happy," she said. "I've learned a lot."

"On the down side," she said, "my boyfriend hasn't been able to adjust to me being on the road, so we've broken up. I think it's going to be difficult to find a guy that doesn't mind moving around."

Grounded

Jesse Whidden was interested in computing, photography, cycling, finance, genetic genealogy, and geography. He was a citizen of the Internet. He edited articles for Wikipedia. He created a Web page for his hometown of St. Edward, Nebraska, and a page called Nebraska Roads depicting roads throughout the state. Asked the distance from St. Edward to, say, Laredo, Texas, he could pluck it from his brow. Applying for college, he was one of two Nebraskans his year to get a perfect 36 on the ACT; on the SAT his score was 1590, just short of a perfect 1600. He was accepted by Harvard, Yale, the Massachusetts Institute of Technology, and the University of Nebraska in Lincoln.

In April 2007, Jesse was a graduate student at UNL, twenty-five, and five foot five. His face is nearly as round as the moon. Halfway to bald, he keeps his hair short and brushed forward. At 170 pounds, he was working on shedding the twenty he had gained since posing for his Class of 2000 St. Edward Public School yearbook. He is a cheerful, fast talker, sometimes too fast to track, but he tries not to show off. "One thing I learned, for better or worse, was not to be a know-it-all," he said, "to not put up my hand to answer the question my teacher asked when I knew it. People don't care what you do as long as you're not a jerk."

Jesse was driving the 110 miles west from Lincoln and north to St. Edward to have supper with his parents, Francis Whidden, a farmer, and Virginia Whidden, who teaches home economics at the local school. Passing through barren brown prairie with crossroads convenience stores, past silent irrigation windmills, cottonwoods, and junipers, he knew the purpose of every farm implement and structure, the history of every town, the genus of bugs and bushes, the coordinates of the roads and streams.

Entering St. Edward, he knew the stories of the buildings along Beaver Street, the main drag and the town's only paved road. He passed the Tri-County Cooperative grain elevator, the city park, with a pool, tennis court, and basketball court, a new metal shed housing City Hall and the fire department, some shuttered storefronts, a used car dealer, mobile homes, ranch houses, a community library that one family paid half the cost to build, a nursing home, the Whiddens' United Methodist Presbyterian Church, Faith Lutheran Church, and St. Edward's Catholic Church, which burned down in 2000 and was rebuilt in 2002.

He stopped at his alma mater. The school had 176 students, kindergarten through grade twelve. The lockers don't need locks. A poster announcing the prom said single students would be charged $4 and couples $7. The science teacher said he teaches chemistry, physics, earth sciences, physical sciences, and biology to grades seven through twelve. Like Kimberly Ryland from Stapleton, Jesse was bigger than the school—a National Merit Scholar and valedictorian of his class. In addition to Jesse, his father and sister Jenna, twenty-two, had gone to the school, and his other sister Kalie, eighteen, would soon graduate and head to the university in Lincoln.

St. Edward was incorporated with 198 settlers in 1887, during a decade when hundreds of towns formed along the new tracks of the Union Pacific Railroad. From its peak of 1,029 people in 1930, the city's population had dwindled to 719 by 2006. A tornado in 1954 killed six people; one in 1964 killed four. In the 2000 Census, families in St. Edward had a median income of $33,750, about two-thirds the national average.

The town does have a lower cost of living that can compensate for lower incomes. Jesse could rent a house there for $200 a month or buy one for $30,000. The median property tax is $566 a year. But low incomes also isolate the townspeople from the wider national economy. Airfares, for example, or clothing or tractors or gasoline, take a comparatively bigger cut from their wages. With both parents working, however, the Whiddens live relatively well. In 2000 and 2007, they all went to Europe.

For Jesse's first two years, the Whiddens lived in a trailer. They moved to a farm, and after Francis's parents died, they moved to their home a mile out of town on 320th Avenue. As he drove up, the Whidden homestead was surrounded by comatose fields. Outside the house were the family's fifteen cats and a large black, mixed-breed dog that helps herd cows.

The house was almost eighty years old, white, two stories, with wide eaves and a glass-wrapped front porch with a hot tub at one end where Virginia soaks after school during the bitter Plains winters. Inside, walls had been removed to open the living room to the kitchen and dining room. Glass doors lead to a back deck with a grill and a view of the fields and sunsets.

Jesse's father, fifty-four, has long, center-parted, raven-black hair that sweeps past his ears and a wide lush mustache. He is a biker on weekends, when he and Virginia take daytrips on his Harley. He owns 800 acres, a bit smaller spread than the average for Boone County, and he rents 250 more. He grows corn, soybeans, and alfalfa and runs a cow-calf operation—breeding calves, keeping them for a year, and selling them to other farmers to fatten.

Virginia, fifty-three, is a strawberry blonde. Well before the 2008 presidential primaries, she had become an Obama Democrat in a county that in 2004 voted four-to-one for George W. Bush. "I'm frustrated because I don't think I belong," she said. "I would move. I'm ready to do something different." But she must teach for six more years to get her pension. She grew up on a farm and met Francis at a 4-H Club dance. "I wanted to be a lawyer," she said. "I got a scholarship to UNL. Then I thought teaching would be a good job. But what I really wanted to do was get married. Then you get to middle age, and you see a lot going by."

Supper was grilled skinless chicken, mashed potatoes with white gravy, broccoli, mushrooms, onions, rolls and apple jelly to spread on them, and a choice of milk, water, or Pepsi. Francis said Whiddens have been fishermen and farmers for twelve generations, since the 1640s, when Icabod Whidden and his sons docked in Portsmouth, Maine. "I grew up right here in this house, on this farm," he said. "I'm as grounded as you can get. You're not going to pick up your land and move it. Once you give it up, you're done."

As he spoke, a cow's woeful moos seemed so close she could have been at the table, and she almost was. She had wandered from the barn beside the house, and Francis got up to prod her back in. Farming, he continued, was getting the twelfth generation down. He ached from lifting ninety-pound calves and arthritis gnawed at his hands and arms. He was ready for something else. He said he wouldn't try to persuade Jesse or the girls to take over from him, and none intended to. "I think it would be nice to live right here and have a different job," he said.

From the start, Virginia said, Jesse was preparing for a life far removed from the farm in St. Edward.

"He read at a very early age," she said. "He was reading at three and studying math at five. He read the encyclopedia."

"It looked like he had a thirst for knowledge," Francis said, "so we provided him with books."

"I showed an interest in piano," Jesse said, "and they got me piano lessons. I also loved maps."

In the sixth grade he won the state geography bee and represented Nebraska in the 1994 National Geography Bee in Washington, D.C. (He stumbled on Gdansk.)

He got a letter from McKinsey & Company, the global management consulting firm and incubator of managers who become chief executives of Fortune 500 companies. "They wanted to know my college plans," Jesse said. After receiving his acceptance letters from Harvard, Yale, and MIT, he and Francis took a 1,500-mile trip to Cambridge, Massachusetts. Harvard had offered the most help—$40,000 a year, enough to cover tuition and most of his room and board.

"I went to a chemistry class. 'This is it?'" he said he thought then. "'This is the best in the world? Do you need this to differentiate yourself?'" Even with the scholarship, he doubted he could afford Harvard. Among other things, he would have to pay airfare to and from home.

More to the point, though, Jesse was afraid to leave his place. "My eighteen-year-old self was fearful of moving half a continent away from everyone I've ever known," he said. UNL recruited him for an honors program in computer science and management and came up with enough money.

Surely, he thought, he could go far at UNL. Three graduates had won Nobel Prizes. Willa Cather, the bard of the prairie, went there. So did Johnny Carson, the former *Tonight Show* host, and World War I general John J. Pershing taught there and attended the law school. Warren Buffett went to UNL. So did executives at IBM, Microsoft, Google, Cisco, and General Dynamics.

Jesse told McKinsey he would be going to UNL. "I never heard from them again," he said.

That was seven years earlier. He had a bachelor's degree in business administration and soon after his April 2007 visit to St. Edward, he would have his master's in finance. He considered what he would do next. He took a trip to Kansas City to see Sprint Nextel Corporation, with offices across the United States, and the Cerner Corporation, a company that sells software to hospitals and governments in fourteen countries to help them control the cost of health care.

Cerner, especially, seemed a dead ringer for Jesse's skills in computer science. But according to Cerner's Web site, the company looked for candidates for its executive development program with a business degree from Duke, Harvard, London School of Business, Northwestern, Stanford, University of Michigan, University of Chicago, and Vanderbilt University. It didn't mention UNL.

Cerner and Sprint had other openings, too, but the visits came to naught, perhaps because of the sagging economy, or perhaps because he didn't interview well or wasn't committed enough to moving to a city a 300-mile, five-hour drive from St. Edward. He stopped his search and went to work for UNL's computer science department for $35,000 a year. With eight other computer scientists, he tested state agencies' software for crashes and abuse.

"I do enjoy my job," he said, after a year in the department. But there was nowhere to go from there. Friends from UNL were marrying and leaving Lincoln. At twenty-seven, he sensed that the choice he made as an eighteen-year-old in turning down Harvard might have been a mistake. "What's past is past," he said. "I've become much more confident and independent. Living and working on my own does not bother me."

Jesse could see the writing on the wall for St. Edward, the farm, and the thirteenth generation of Whiddens. Rather than dwell on one place, he resolved to collect places again. "I have been sticking to what's known as a course of action," he said. "I need to stop doing that." He updated his résumé and began knocking on doors at companies in Omaha and Kansas City.

Jesse might find an alternative to his place in the Nebraska prairie. Maybe a corporate employer like the Howards' UPS or Kimberly Ryland's Stryker could itself become his surrogate place. Maybe the Relo children of Relos, like Ariana Koblitz, or the Remson kids, or the nomadic Pawnee Indians of the Whiddens' own Boone County, could make a place of no real place. Moving from a house in one town to another in another town, with the same floor plan, bedrooms and bathrooms in the same locations, with the same chain stores along similar shopping strips just beyond, might inspire a comforting sense of running in place.

Jesse could settle someday in one of the new retirement frontiers, like Laurel Canyon, outside Alpharetta, Georgia. He might follow Mark

Visitations: *Jesse Whidden, a top student in St. Edward, Nebraska, and the state's geography bee champion in 1994, wanted to stay close to home and chose to attend the University of Nebraska at Lincoln over Harvard. But after graduating with a bachelor's degree in business administration and a master's in finance, the first good job he could find was three hundred miles away.*

and Sandi Remson, approaching retirement after their odyssey across the globe. They speak of getting a little house somewhere, but perhaps they have already established a proxy for a place along the digital highway linking them and their kids.

Jesse resolved those questions much as Kimberly Ryland and Jennifer Schultz did. In the first week of December 2008, he received a job offer from Cerner in Kansas City. "I'll be a traveling consultant," he reported, "helping clients install, upgrade, or convert to Cerner products." He would move to Kansas City in the spring.

The illusions might be all that remain of the Rockwellian depictions of home. Among this class of serial movers, I met people who were as clearly defined as the oak in the courthouse square. Yet they and in particular their children had little notion of geographic origin, of a starting place. I think that's sad, but I can't conclude that it's bad. Without room to grow in St. Edward or Stapleton, Nebraska, these Americans, the Relos, become pioneers on the global frontier. They fly where they must on the shifting winds of a breadwinner's job. Through booms and busts, the hardiest find a proxy for place in close family ties and the digital links of a boundaryless age.

Appendix

America's Top Relovilles by the Numbers, 2007

Reloville	Percentage of Residents Who Were Born in a Different State or Country	Population in 1990	Population in 2007
United States, 2000	41.0	248,700,000	301,300,000
1. Alpharetta, Georgia	72.0	13,002	65,168
2. Huntersville, North Carolina	66.8	3,014	42,901
3. Apex, North Carolina	64.5	4,968	33,601
4. Parker, Colorado	59.4	5,450	36,975
5. Castle Rock, Colorado	60.6	6,708	37,422
6. Flower Mound, Texas	57.5	15,527	66,779
7. Frisco, Texas	55.6	6,141	84,778
8. Cary, North Carolina	68.2	43,858	116,910
9. McKinney, Texas	52.8	21,283	108,356
10. Roswell, Georgia	71.2	47,923	101,851
11. Fishers, Indiana	41.2	7,508	63,420
12. Carrollton, Texas	55.2	82,169	117,563
13. Franconia, Virginia	74.9	19,882	34,695
14. The Woodlands, Texas	58.0	29,205	62,311
15. Sandy Springs, Georgia	69.0	67,842	98,043
16. Leesburg, Virginia	63.0	16,202	36,160
17. Centreville, Virginia	72.0	26,585	53,465
18. Dublin, Ohio	43.0	16,366	41,127
19. Allen, Texas	55.0	25,380	74,462
20. Highlands Ranch, Colorado	62.0	10,181	90,843
21. Woodbury, Minnesota	40.0	20,075	52,479
22. Overland Park, Kansas	66.0	111,790	164,811
23. Gaithersburg, Maryland	74.0	39,542	56,265
24. Round Rock, Texas	49.0	30,923	81,639
25. Plano, Texas	59.0	128,713	255,591

SOURCE: U.S. Census Bureau, 2007 figures (most recent available), unless otherwise indicated. Weighted rankings based on family mobility, economic growth, median age, median family income, and median house prices.

Percentage of Adults Who Are Classified as Management/ Professional Employees	Percentage Who Work from Home	Median Family Income	Percentage of Houses Built Between 1990 and 2007	Median Value of Home
34.1	3.9	$60,374	24.6	$181,800
58.3	8.0	$108,769	66.2	$321,800
45.2	5.6	$90,739	94.0	$231,400
56.5	4.5	$91,326	80.5	$225,100
45.3	7.1	$89,174	83.1	$275,300
42.6	7.5	$88,811	72.6	$268,500
47.3	8.7	$112,725	74.7	$232,600
53.9	8.2	$106,187	91.4	$231,300
59.1	6.9	$101,761	60.8	$253,700
47.6	5.6	$87,193	79.8	$180,900
43.7	8.2	$94,666	25.5	$294,100
55.4	4.9	$101,397	84.5	$193,900
37.9	3.6	$73,025	29.0	$181,800
63.6	3.8	$106,998	49.0	$471,800
54.7	6.5	$111,997	59.5	$203,900
47.9	6.5	$107,687	27.9	$451,200
49.3	4.8	$105,260	52.8	$473,900
50.5	2.6	$94,803	52.9	$426,400
65.3	6.8	$126,402	60.0	$324,000
52.6	5.8	$100,997	73.0	$181,600
52.9	6.6	$105,994	82.8	$318,600
52.4	5.6	$107,314	65.9	$311,700
51.3	5.9	$91,806	37.7	$215,900
49.1	3.4	$86,422	35.7	$413,400
40.5	3.4	$76,082	64.1	$155,900
50.2	5.8	$99,953	51.4	$201,700

Bibliography

Aboud, John M., and Richard B. Freeman. "The Internationalization of the U.S. Labor Market." NBER working paper no. 332, April 1990. http://www.nber.org/papers/w3321 (payment required).

Altshuler, Alan, William Morrill, Harold Wolman, and Faith Mitchell, eds. "Spatial Segregation within U.S. Metropolitan Areas." *Metropolitan Governance and Urban Problems.* Washington, D.C.: National Academy Press, 1999.

Arthur, Michael B., and Denise M. Rousseau, eds. *The Boundaryless Career: A New Employment Principle for a New Organizational Era.* New York: Oxford University Press, 1996.

Atlas Worldwide Group. "Results 2007: Corporate Relocation Survey." Evansville, Ind.: Atlas Worldwide Group, 2007. http://www.atlasworldgroup.com/survey/results.aspx?id=c2007. Survey of 390 respondents with relocation responsibilities for a company that either has relocated employees within the past two years or plans to relocate employees this year.

Baldridge, David C., Kimberly A. Eddleston, and John F. Veiga. "Saying 'No' to Being Uprooted: The Impact of Family and Gender on Willingness to Relocate." *Journal of Occupational and Organizational Psychology,* March 2006.

Banai, Moshe, and Harry Wes. "Boundaryless Global Careers: The International Itinerants." *International Studies of Management and Organization*, Fall 2004.

Barone, Michael, *Our Country: Shaping of America from Roosevelt to Reagan.* New York: Free Press, 1990.

Beuka, Robert A. *SuburbiaNation: Reading Suburban Landscape in Twentieth-Century American Fiction and Film.* New York: Palgrave Macmillan, 2004.

Black, Susan. "Searching for Stability." *American School Board Journal*, September 2006.

Brett, Jeanne M. "Job Transfer and Well-Being." *Journal of Applied Psychology*, August 1982.

Brett, Jeanne M., Linda K. Smith, and Anne H. Reilly. "Pulling Up Roots in the 1990s: Who's Willing to Relocate?" *Journal of Organizational Behavior*, January 1993.

Brett, Jeanne M., and Linda K. Stroh. "Jumping Ship: Who Benefits from an External Labor Market Strategy?" *Journal of Applied Psychology*, June 1997.

Brooks, David. *Bobos in Paradise: The New Upper Class and How They Got There.* New York: Simon & Schuster, 2000.

———. *On Paradise Drive: How We Live Now (And Always Have) in the Future Tense.* New York: Simon & Schuster, 2005.

Bruegmann, Robert. *Sprawl: A Compact History.* Chicago: University of Chicago Press, 2005.

Carr, Stuart C., Kerr Inkson, and Kaye Thorn. "From Global Careers to Talent Flow: Reinterpreting the 'Brain Drain.'" *Journal of World Business*, November 2005.

Cohany, Sharon R., and Emy Sok. "Trends in Labor Force Participation of Married Mothers of Infants." *Monthly Labor Review*, Bureau of Labor Statistics, February 2007.

Coles-James, Kay. "Memorandum for Heads of Executive Departments and Agencies." Washington, D.C.: U.S. Office of Personnel Management, Nov. 1, 2004.

Coontz, Stephanie. *The Way We Never Were: American Families and the Nostalgia Trap.* New York: Basic Books, 2000.

Couto, Vinay, Mahadeva Mani, Arte Y. Lewin, and Carine Peeters. "The Globalization of White-Collar Work: The Facts and Fallout of Next-

Generation Offshoring." Chicago: Booz Allen Hamilton, Oct. 31, 2006. http://www.booz.com/media/uploads/The_Globalization_of_White-Collar _Work.pdf.

Csikszentmihaly, Mihaly. *Flow: The Psychology of Optimal Experience.* New York: Harper & Row, 1990.

Dau-Schmidt, Kenneth G., and Carmen Brun. "Protecting Families in a Global Economy." *Indiana Journal of Global Legal Studies,* January 2006.

De Jung, G. F., J. M. Wilmoth, J. L. Angel, and G. T. Cornwell. "Motive and Geographic Mobility of Very Old Americans." *Journals of Gerontology B,* November 1995.

Della Cava, Maria A. "New Home in Old Age: Seniors Start Over in Different Cities to Be Near Families." *USA Today,* Apr. 12, 2007.

Downs, Anthony. *Opening Up the Suburbs: An Urban Strategy for America.* New Haven, Conn.: Yale University Press, 1975.

Duany, Andres, Elizabeth Plater-Zyberk, and Jeff Speck. *Suburban Nation: The Rise of Sprawl and the Decline of the American Dream.* New York: North Point Press, 2000.

Dunham-Jones, Ellen. "Temporary Contracts, on the Economy of the Post-Industrial Landscape." *Harvard Design Magazine,* Fall 1997.

Ehrenhalt, Alan. *The Lost City: The Forgotten Virtues of Community in America.* New York: Basic Books, 1995.

Employee Relocation Council/Worldwide ERC and Prudential Financial, Inc. "Relocating Women in the U.S.: Trends and Comparisons." ERC, 2005. http://www.erc.org/pdf/pru-erc_wirsurvey.pdf.

Engel, Rozlyn C., Luke B. Gallagher, and David S. Lyle. "Military Deploy-ments and Children's Academic Achievement: Evidence from Department of Defense Education Activity Schools." American Economic Association, working draft, Dec. 20, 2006. http://www.aeaweb.org/annual_mtg_papers/ 2007/0105_1430_1602.pdf.

Federal Interagency Forum on Age-Related Statistics. "Older Americans Update 2006: Key Indicators of Well-Being." Washington, D.C.: U.S. Govern-ment Printing Office, May 2006. http://digitalcommons.ilr.cornell.edu/ key_workplace/283/.

Finkel, Lisa B., Michelle L. Kelley, and Jayne Ashby. "Geographic Mobility, Family, and Maternal Variables as Related to the Psychosocial Adjustment of Military Children." *Military Medicine,* December 2003.

Fischel, William A. *The Homevoter Hypothesis: How Home Values Influence Local Government Taxation, School Finance, and Land-Use Policies.* Cambridge, Mass.: Harvard University Press, 2001.

Fishman, Robert. *Bourgeois Utopias: The Rise and Fall of Suburbia.* New York: Basic Books, 1989.

Florida, Richard. *The Flight of the Creative Class: The New Global Competition for Talent.* New York: HarperCollins, 2005.

Forbes, J. Benjamin, and James E. Piercy. *Corporate Paths to the Top: Studies for Human Resource Management Development Specialists.* New York: Quantum Books, 1991.

Friese, Barbara H. *Family Routines and Rituals.* New Haven, Conn.: Yale University Press, 2006.

Fullilove, Mindy Thompson. *The House of Joshua: Meditations on Family and Place.* Lincoln, Neb.: University of Nebraska Press, 1999.

Galbraith, John Kenneth. *The New Industrial State.* Boston: Houghton Mifflin, 1967.

Gans, Herbert J. *The Levittowners: Life and Politics in a New Suburban Community.* New York: Alfred A. Knopf, 1967.

Garreau, Joel. *Edge City: Life on the New Frontier.* New York: Doubleday Anchor, 1991.

Gerner, Michael, Fred Perry, Mark A. Moselle, and Mike Archbold. "Characteristics of Internationally Mobile Students." *Journal of School Psychology,* Summer 1992.

Gillis, John R. "Our Imagined Families: The Myths and Rituals We Live By." Working paper for the Emory Center for Myth and Ritual in American Life, Emory University, Atlanta, Ga., February 2002.

———. *A World of Their Own Making: Myth, Ritual, and the Quest for Family Values.* New York: Basic Books, 1996.

Goss, Ernst P., and Chris Paul. "Age and Work Experience in the Decision to Migrate." *Journal of Human Resources,* Summer 1986.

Haas, William H., III, Don E. Bradley, et al. "In Retirement Migration, Who Counts? A Methodological Question with Economic Policy Implications." *The Gerontologist,* December 2006.

Handlin, David P. *American Architecture.* New York: Thames and Hudson, 1985.

Hango, Darcy W. "The Long-Term Effect of Childhood Residential Mobility on Educational Attaiment." *Sociological Quarterly,* November 2006.

Haour-Knipe, Mary. *Moving Families: Expatriation, Stress and Coping.* New York: Routledge, 2001.

Hayden, Dolores. *Redesigning the American Dream: The Future of Housing, Work, and Family Life.* New York: W. W. Norton, 1984.

Haynie, Dana L., and Scott J. South. "Residential Mobility and Adolescent Violence." *Social Forces, International Journal of Social Research,* September 2005.

Haynie, Dana L., Scott J. South, and Sunita Bose. "Residential Mobility and Attempted Suicide among Adolescents." *Sociological Quarterly* (journal of the Midwest Sociological Society), October 2006.

Hobbs, Frank, and Nicole Stoops. *Demographic Trends in the 20th Century.* Census 2000 Special Reports, Series CENSR-4. Washington, D.C.: U.S. Census Bureau, 2000.

Hudnut, William H., III. *Cities on the Rebound: A Vision for Urban America.* Washington, D.C.: Urban Land Institute, 1998.

———. *Halfway to Everywhere: A Portrait of America's First-Tier Suburbs.* Washington, D.C.: Urban Land Institute, 2003.

———. *Changing Metropolitan America: Planning for a Sustainable Future.* Washington, D.C.: Urban Land Institute. 2008.

Jackson, Kenneth. *Crabgrass Frontier: The Suburbanization of the United States.* New York: Oxford University Press, 1985.

Jacobs, Jane. *The Death and Life of Great American Cities.* New York: Vintage Books, 1961.

Jasper, James M. *Restless Nation: Starting Over in America.* Chicago: University of Chicago Press, 2000.

Kaplan, Robert D. *An Empire Wilderness: Travels into America's Future.* New York: Random House, 1998.

Keats, John. *The Crack in the Picture Window.* Boston: Houghton Mifflin, 1956.

Kirp, David L., John P. Dwyer, and Larry A. Rosenthal. *Our Town: Race, Housing and the Soul of Suburbia.* New Brunswick, N.J.: Rutgers University Press, 1997.

Konopaske, Robert, Chet Robiw, and John Ivancevich. "A Preliminary Model of Spouse Influence on Managerial Global Assignment Willingness." *Journal of Human Resource Management,* March 2005.

KPMG. "Survey 2006: Global Assignment Policies and Practices." New York: KPMG, September 2006. http://www.kpmgtaxwatch.com/Pub/Intl/2006GAAP_survey_final.pdf. Survey of 350 multinational organizations.

Kunstler, James Howard. *The City in Mind: Notes on the Urban Condition.* New York: Free Press, 2001.

————. *Geography of Nowhere: The Rise and Decline of America's Man-Made Landscape.* New York: Simon & Schuster, 1993.

————. *Home from Nowhere: Remaking Our Everyday World for the 21st Century.* New York: Simon & Schuster, 1996.

Kuttner, Robert, and Sharland Trotter. *Family Re-Union: Reconnecting Parents and Children in Adulthood.* New York: Simon & Schuster, 2002.

Lambert, Bruce. " 'First' Suburbs Growing Older and Poorer, Report Warns." *New York Times,* Feb. 16, 2006.

Lang, Robert E., and Jennifer LeFurgy. *Boomburbs: The Rise of America's Accidental Cities.* Washington, D.C.: Brookings Institution Press, 2007.

————. *Edgeless Cities: Examining the Noncentered Metropolis.* Washington, D.C.: Fannie Mae Foundation, 2003.

Lang, Robert E. "Valuing the Suburbs: Why Some 'Improvements' Lower Home Prices." *Opolis, International Journal of Suburban and Metropolitan Studies,* October 2004.

Leinberger, Christopher B., and Charles Lockwood. "How Business Is Reshaping America." *Atlantic Monthly,* October 1986.

Lewis, Charles E., Judith M. Siegel, and Mary Ann Lewis. "Feeling Bad: Exploring Sources of Distress among Pre-Adolescent Children." *American Journal of Public Health,* February 1984.

Long, Larry. "International Perspectives on the Residential Mobility of America's Children." *Journal of Marriage and the Family,* November 1992.

Longino, Charles F., Jr. "From Sunbelt to Sunspots." *American Demographics,* November 1994.

————. *Retirement Migration in America: An Analysis of the Size, Trends and Economic Impact of the Country's Newest Growth Industry.* Houston: Vacation Publications, 1995.

Lynd, Helen M., and Robert S. Lynd. *Middletown: A Study in Modern American Culture.* New York: Harcourt, Brace & World, 1929.

Malamud, Ofer, and Abigail Wozniak. "The Impact of College Education on Geographic Mobility: Evidence from the Vietnam Generation." Working paper, seminar, Department of Economics, University of Illinois at Urbana-Champaign, November 2007. http://www.economics.uiuc.edu/docs/seminars/the-impact-of-college-education-on-geographic-mobility.pdf.

McKenzie, Evan. *Privatopia: Homeowner Associations and the Rise of Residential Private Government.* New Haven, Conn.: Yale University Press, 1996.

Miller, Arthur. *Death of a Salesman.* New York: Penguin Group, 1949.

Mintz, Steven, and Susan Kellogg. *Domestic Revolutions: A Social History of American Family Life.* New York: Free Press, 1987.

Muller, Peter O. "The Suburban Transformation of the Globalizing American City." *Annals of the American Academy of Political and Social Science,* 1997.

Mullich, Joe. "On the Move." *Workforce Management,* 2005. http:// www .workforce.com (registration required).

———. "Where Relocation Is Headed Now." *Workforce Management,* May 24, 2004. http://www.workforce.com (registration required).

Mumford, Lewis. *The City in History.* New York: Harcourt, Brace & World, 1961.

Myers, Scott M. "Childhood and Adolescent Mobility and Adult Relations with Parents." *Journal of Family Issues,* April 2005.

Noe, Raymond A., and Alison E. Barber. "Willingness to Accept Mobility Opportunities: Destination Makes a Difference." *Journal of Organizational Behavior,* March 1993.

Oldenburg, Ray. *The Great Good Place: Cafes, Coffee Shops, Bookstores, Heart of a Community.* New York: Marlowe & Co., 1989.

Orthner, D., M. Giddings, and W. Quinn. "Youth in Transition: A Study of Adolescents from Military and Civilian Families." Washington, D.C.: Government Printing Office, 1987.

Packard, Vance. *A Nation of Strangers.* New York: David McKay Co., 1972.

Pinder, Craig C. "The Dark Side of Executive Relocation." *Organizational Dynamics,* Spring 1989.

Plucker, Jonathan A., and Cheri P. Yecke. "The Effect of Relocation on Gifted Students." *Gifted Child Quarterly,* April 1999.

Putnam, Robert D. *Bowling Alone: The Collapse and Revival of American Community.* New York: Simon & Schuster, 2000.

Rogerson, Peter A., and Daejong Kim. "Population Distribution and Redistribution of the Baby-boom Cohort in the United States: Recent Trends and Implications." *Proceedings of the National Academy of Sciences,* 2005. http:// www.pnas.org/content/102/43/15319.full.pdf+html.

Rossi, Peter H. *Why Families Move: A Study in the Social Psychology of Urban Residential Mobility.* Glencoe, Ill.: Free Press, 1955.

Runnion, Timm. "Have International Assignments Lost Their Luster?" *Relo-Journal*, May 15, 2007.

Rybczynski, Witold. *City Life and the Most Beautiful House in the World.* New York: Viking, 1989.

Sandefur, Gary D., and Wilbur J. Scott. "A Dynamic Analysis of Migration: An Assessment of the Effects of Age, Family and Career Variables." *Demography*, August 1981.

Schachter, Jason P., Rachel S. Franklin, and Marc J. Perry. "Migration and Geographic Mobility in Metropolitan and Nonmetropolitan America." Census 2000 Special Reports. Washington, D.C.: U.S. Bureau of the Census, 2003. http://www.census.gov/prod/2003pubs/censr-9.pdf.

Schaetti, Barbara F. "Attachment Theory: A View into the Global Nomad Experience." In Morten G. Ender, ed. *Military Brats and Other Global Nomads Growing Up in Organization Families.* Westport, Conn.: Praeger, 2002.

———, and Sheila J. Ramsey. "The Expatriate Family: Practicing Practical Leadership." *Mobility,* May 1999.

Shihadeh, Edward H. "The Prevalence of Husband-Centered Migration: Employment Consequences for Married Mothers." *Journal of Marriage and the Family*, May 1991.

Shklovski, Irina. "The Effects of Geographic Mobility on Social Ties and Psychological Well Being in the Age of the Internet." Paper presented at 2004 Annual Meeting of the American Psychological Association, Aug. 17, 2004.

Simpson, Gloria A., and Mary Glenn Fowler. "Geographic Mobility and Children's Emotional/Behavioral Adjustment and School Functioning." *Pediatrics,* February 1994.

Stacey, Judith. *Brave New Families: Stories of Domestic Upheaval in Late-Twentieth-Century America.* New York: Basic Books, 1990.

Stroh, Linda K., and Jeanne M. Brett. "Corporate Mobility: Effects on Children." Paper presented at the Annual Meeting of the American Educational Research Association, Mar. 27–Apr. 1, 1989. http://eric.ed.gov/ERICDocs/data/ericdocs2sql/content_storage_01/0000019b/80/1e/b0/6c.pdf.

Suarez, Ray. *The Old Neighborhood: What We Lost in the Great Suburban Migration, 1966–1999.* New York: Free Press, 1999.

Taeuber, Karl E. "Cohort Migration." *Demography,* November 1966.

Tiebout, Charles. "A Pure Theory of Local Expenditures." *Journal of Political Economy,* October 1956.

Tucker, C. Jack, Jonathan Marx, and Larry Long. "'Moving On': Residential

Mobility and Children's School Lives." *Sociology of Education,* vol. 71, no. 2, 1998.

United Nations Conference on Trade and Development. "World Investment Report 2006." New York: United Nations Publications, Oct. 16, 2006. http://www.unctad.org/Templates/webflyer.asp?docid=7431&intItemID=1397&lang=1.

Walters, William H. "Types and Patterns of Later-Life Migration." *Human Geography,* October 2000.

Warner, Sam Bass, Jr. *Streetcar Suburbs: The Process of Growth in Boston, 1870–1900.* Cambridge, Mass.: Harvard University Press, 1962.

Wayman, Peter H. "Global Mobility: Show Me the Money." *Mobility,* April 2007.

Wellner, Alison Stein. "The Mobility Myth." *Reason Magazine,* April 2006.

Whyte, William H., Jr. *The Organization Man.* New York: Doubleday, 1956.

———. "The Transients." A series in *Fortune,* May, June, July, and August 1953.

Wolfe, Tom. *From Bauhaus to Our House.* New York: Farrar Straus Giroux, 1981.

Wood, David, Neal Halfon et al. "Impact of Family Relocation on Children's Growth, Development, School Function, and Behavior." *Journal of the American Medical Association*, September 1993.

Yankow, Jeffrey J. "Migration, Job Change, and Wage Growth: A New Perspective on the Pecuniary Return to Geographic Mobility." *Journal of Regional Science*, August 2003.

Acknowledgments

What inspired this book was the curiosity and unbounded patience of a friend of many years and a senior editor of the *New York Times*, Soma Golden Behr, who set me loose for a year to explore matters of class in America. As I reported and wrote an article about vagabond families who called themselves Relos, another *Times* editor, Chip McGrath, worked marvels steering me past potholes and ditches, and, like Soma, encouraged me to move on to a book. The Alfred P. Sloan Foundation provided vital funding, and the Center for Myth and Ritual in American Life at Emory University in Atlanta, and in particular, Bradd Shore, the anthropologist who directs it, gave me guidance, expertise, and brilliant insights throughout the nearly four years that the book consumed. Early on, Elise Proulx of the Frederick Hill Bonnie Nadell Literary Agency in San Francisco, urged me to tackle the book, saw me through the grueling process of preparing the proposal, and found the publisher, Times Books/Henry Holt and Company. Paul Golob at Holt and Alex Ward at the *Times* put me into the gentle hands of editor Robin Dennis, who performed magic organizing and smoothing the manuscript. Bill Kirtz at Northeastern University read the entire early manuscript and suggested essential changes. Catherine Manegold, then at Emory, and friends Sarah Williams, Tom Dupree, Jim Reston, and Bill Kovach were generous editors and sounding boards. Without the introductions and insights of Bill and Gina Holman, I would never have discovered their subdivision of Medlock Bridge. I am also grateful to hundreds of Relos not cited in the book who welcomed me in to share their stories. I am most indebted to my patient and forgiving wife, Susan, who scrutinized each chapter when I brought it down from my attic aerie and otherwise just let me be.

Index

Frito-Lay, 135
Fullilove, Mindy Thompson, 216

Gaithersburg, Md., 232–33
Garner, Jeffrey C., 182–83
Garreau, Joel, 38
Gates, Lisle, 181–82
gender and employment equality,
    165–66
General Motors
  assembly plant in Atlanta, 64
  foreign-born top officers in, 92
  purchase of EDS, 136
George, Gary, 180
Georgia 400 highway, 35, 51
German Linde Group, 79
Gerner, Michael, 187
Gerstner, Louis V., Jr., 109
Glenlake Office Park, 60
globalization, 91–93
GMAC Global Relocation Services,
    116
Goizueta, Roberto, 92
Google, 61
Graebel Relocation Services, 116
Green, Jody, 199–201, 203–6, 207
Green, Kendall, 200, 203, 206, 207
Green, Larry, 199–203, 204–7
Green, Mitchell, 200, 202, 204, 206–7

Hahn, Julianne, 17
Halfon, Neal, 179
Harvard Business School, 165
Haynie, Dana L., 179
headhunters, 107, 108–9
Heidrick & Struggles, 108, 109
Herbert, Doug, 69, 192
Herbert, Heidi, 69, 192
Herman Miller furniture company, 43
heroin, 182
Hewlett-Packard, 136
Highlands Ranch, Colo., 232–33
Homevoter Hypothesis (Fischel), 41–42
Hooton, Don, 182
Hooton, Taylor, 182

house cleaners, 126
House of Joshua, The (Fullilove), 216
housing
  as an investment, 40–41, 48, 122
  economic downturn and, 48–50,
    119–20
  prestige and, 47–48
  Relos' selection of, 39–40, 122,
    141–42
  temporary, 125–26
Howard, Amber, 66, 67, 68, 69, 70,
    183
Howard, Courtney, 66, 67, 68, 69, 70
Howard, Kathy, 65–68, 69, 70–71
Howard, Ray, 65–71
Hudson Bay's Company, 7
Huntersville, N.C., 232–33

infidelity, 167
inventory management, 99–100
Isdell, Neville, 92
Ivester, M. Douglas, 92

Jargowsky, Paul A., 42–43
Jasper, James, 174
job-hopping, 107–8
Johnson, Erik, 207
Johnson, Melissa, 207
Johnson Controls, 195

Kane, Russ, 144–45, 147–48
Kent, Muhtar, 92
Kilborn, Peter T., 6–7
Kincannon, Diana, 106
Kincannon, Kelly, 106, 107, 109,
    110
Kincannon & Reed, 106–7
Klosterman, Mary Ann, 79, 81, 83,
    85, 86
Klosterman, Mike, 81, 85
Koblitz, Ariana, 184–86
Koblitz, Avril, 185
Koblitz, Becky, 184, 185
Koblitz, Donald, 184, 185
Kooistra, Carla, 121–22, 123–24

home values in, 41–42
vandalism in, 23–24, 178–80, 181
working class and, 43
Remson, Brian, 93, 94, 95, 97, 186
Remson, Kerry, 93, 94, 98, 186
Remson, Laura, 93, 94, 95–96, 97,
186, 187–88
Remson, Mark, 93, 94–95, 96–97, 98
Remson, Sandi, 93, 94, 96–97, 98,
156
Restless Nation (Jasper), 173–75
retirement communities, 189, 191
Richardson, Tex., 140
Ridler, Pam, 146
Robinson, George "Robbie," 137, 138
Roden, Kim, 154, 160–61
Rolader, Donald, 43
Roswell, Ga., 155–56, 232–33
Round Rock, Tex., 232–33
Rousseau, Denise, 92
Russell Reynolds Associates, 108
rustlers, 107, 108–9
Ryland, Kimberly, 218–21

salary discrimination, 166
Sampson, Anthony, 115
Sandy Springs, Ga., 232–33
Saunders, John F., 62, 65
Schaetti, Barbara F., 187
Schenker AG, 75
Schering-Plough, 92–93
Schultz, Jennifer, 221–23
Scott, Barbara, 56–58
Scott, Roger, 56–58
Scott County, Minn., 39
scrapbooking, 156
Seasons at Laurel Canyon, 189, 191
Selby, Chris, 195, 197, 198
Selby, Darlene, 194–96, 197
Selby, Ed, 194–96, 197
Selby, Mark, 195, 197–98
self-storage businesses, 126–28
Shore, Bradd, 14, 87
Silva, Carly, 73, 74
Silva, Kevin, 71–77

Silva, Patti, 71, 72–73, 74, 75–77
Silva, Roxanne, 74
Simpson, Gloria A., 175
Sirva, 116, 118, 120, 121
Smith, Richard, 120
Souly Business, 207
South, Scott J., 179
Southland Life Insurance Company,
135
Spencer Stuart
on recruitment, 99
recruitment efforts of, 104–5, 106,
109, 111–12
as a top recruiting firm, 108
spouses, trailing
careers of, 14, 151
friendships between, 22, 152,
156–57, 167
role of, 164, 166–67, 220
Spurlock, Tony G., 180–81
St. Edward, Nebr., 223, 224–25
stateless careerists, 92–93
steroids, 182
STMicroelectronics, 93, 94–95
stress, 13
Stroh, Linda L., 166
Strout, Jeanne
background of, 211
career of, 211–12, 214, 215
divorce, 213
marriage to second husband, 214–15
in Northampton Falls subdivision,
209, 210
picture of, 208
Strout, Jessica, 209, 211, 212, 213,
214
Strout, Steve, 209, 210–11, 213–14
Stryker Corporation, 220
substance abuse, 167, 182

tax breaks, 63
Taylor, David S., 89–90
telecommuting, 170–71
temporary housing, 125–26
The Woodlands, Tex., 232–33

About the Author

PETER T. KILBORN was a reporter and editor for the *New York Times* for thirty years. As a foreign and national correspondent, he covered business, economics, social issues, the workplace, and the changing American scene. He is a contributor to the *Times*'s award-winning series and book *Class Matters*. Kilborn is a graduate of Trinity College in Hartford, Connecticut, holds a master's degree in journalism from Columbia University, and was a professional journalism fellow at Stanford University. He and his wife, Susan, live outside Washington, D.C.